Towards Commemoration
Ireland in War and Revolution, 1912–1923

D1392979

TOWARDS COMMEMORATION
Ireland in War and Revolution, 1912–1923

John Horne and Edward Madigan (eds)

Towards Commemoration: Ireland in war and revolution, 1912–1923

First published 2013

by Royal Irish Academy
19 Dawson St
Dublin 2

www.ria.ie

Copyright © 2013 Royal Irish Academy

ISBN 978-1-908996-17-6

British Library Cataloguing in Publication Data. A CIP catalogue record for this book is available from the British Library.

Typeset by Dominic Carroll, Ardfield, Co. Cork.
Printed in Ireland by Sprint Print Ltd.

10 9 8 7 6 5 4 3 2 1

Contents

continued over

SECTION 3: **COMMEMORATIONS**

Acknowledgements

Most of the essays contained in this volume are based on papers given at a conference entitled 'Ireland in the Decade of the Great War, 1912–1923: Towards Commemoration', which was held in Monaco in October 2011. The event was staged under the auspices of the TCD Centre for War Studies and the Princess Grace Irish Library in Monaco, and was funded by means of a generous benefaction received through the Trinity Foundation. The same benefaction helped with the production of this book. It was a fruitful gathering of historians and people professionally concerned with commemoration from across Ireland, Britain, continental Europe and the US, and the chapters of the book benefited from two days of intense discussions. The editors extend particular thanks to Mary Apied and Ellen Hanley of the Trinity Foundation, and to Judith Gantley of the Princess Grace Irish Library for their assistance in organising the conference. The event simply could not have taken place without their local knowledge, energy and organisational skill. We are also very grateful to Mrs Paul Gallico and to the board of trustees of the Princess Grace Irish Library for their support. We would particularly like to acknowledge the hospitality of His Serene Highness, Prince Albert II of Monaco, and the practical help extended by Mme Anne-Marie Boisbouvier of the Prince's Cabinet. We would also like to express our sincerest gratitude to all those who attended the conference and contributed to the book. Finally, we would like to acknowledge the dedication and professionalism of the editorial team at the Royal Irish Academy, with whom it has been a pleasure to work.

John Horne and Edward Madigan
August 2012

Notes on Contributors

Ian Adamson, OBE, is a retired community paediatrician and well known in Northern Ireland for his political, civic and cultural work. He is founder chair of the Ulster-Scots Language Society, a leading figure in the modern revival of Ulster-Scots, and has published widely on Ulster history, language and culture. A member of Belfast City Council from 1989 until 2011, he was lord mayor from 1996 to 1997, and served as high sheriff of Belfast in 2011. He is active in a wide variety of community groups and associations, and was a founding figure of the Somme Association. He is presently the senior adviser on history and culture to Lord Bannside, the former First Minister of Northern Ireland, Dr Ian Paisley.

Paul Bew received his doctorate at the University of Cambridge, and has been professor of politics at Queen's University, Belfast, since 1991. He is a cross-bench peer serving on the London Local Authority Bill Select Committee, and acts as secretary to the All-Party Group on Archives. He is also an honorary Fellow of Pembroke College, Cambridge, and a Member of the Royal Irish Academy. He has written articles for *The Times* and the *Guardian*, and has appeared on BBC Radio 4's *Today* programme. He is the author of two Thomas Davis Lectures, which were broadcast on RTÉ and subsequently published. His monograph *Enigma: a new life of Charles Stewart Parnell* was published in 2012 by Gill & Macmillan, Dublin. He is the editor of *A Yankee in de Valera's Ireland* (Dublin, 2012), the memoir of David Gray, US minister to Ireland during the Second World War.

Tom Burke, MBE, is a founding member of the Royal Dublin Fusiliers Association, a history society that researches, presents and preserves the history of the Royal Dublin Fusiliers in the First World War. He was a member of the Journey of Reconciliation Trust, the volunteer group responsible for the Island of Ireland Peace Park at Messines in Belgium. In August 2004 he was awarded an honorary MBE for his contribution to the British-Irish peace process. He has acted as a guide/adviser to former Irish president Mary McAleese on her visits to Wytschaete, Belgium, in June 2007 and Gallipoli in March 2010. His publications include *The 16th (Irish) and 36th (Ulster) Divisions at the Battle of Wijtschate-Messines Ridge, 7 June 1917* (Dublin, Royal Dublin Fusiliers Association, 2007), along with several articles on military history in *History Ireland*, *Stand To!* (journal of the Western Front Association) and *The Irish Sword*. He is currently pursuing an M.Litt. degree in military history at University College, Dublin.

Paul Clark presents the news programmes *UTV Live* and *UTV Live Tonight* in Northern Ireland. He has made a number of programmes about Ireland and the Great War, most of which have been broadcast during Remembrance Week, in November. In the documentaries, he has examined the legacy of the Great War in Northern Ireland and the Irish Republic.

Anne Dolan lectures in modern Irish history at Trinity College, Dublin. Her publications include *Commemorating the Irish Civil War: history and memory,*

1922–2000 (Cambridge, 2003) and (with Cormac O'Malley) *'No surrender here!'*
The Civil War papers of Ernie O'Malley, 1922–1924 (Dublin, 2007). She is currently
working on a study of violence and killing in Ireland in the decade of the Great
War.

David Fitzpatrick is professor of modern history at Trinity College, Dublin.
Among other topics he has written various articles on Irish participation in the
Great War and Irish military history, and has edited a volume of essays, *Ireland and*
the First World War, published by Trinity History Workshop in 1986. He edited the
Workshop's fifth volume, *Terror in Ireland, 1916–1923* (Dublin, 2012), published
by Lilliput Press. His biography of Louis MacNeice's father, *'Solitary and wild':*
Frederick MacNeice and the salvation of Ireland (Dublin, 2011), was also published
by Lilliput Press.

Brian Hanley lectures in history at University College, Dublin. He is the author of
The IRA, 1926–1936 (Dublin, 2002), (with Scott Millar) *The lost revolution: the story*
of the Official IRA and the Workers' Party (Dublin, 2009) and *The IRA: a documentary*
history, 1916–2005 (Dublin, 2010).

Tom Hartley has been active in politics for forty-two years, and was first elected
to represent the Lower Falls on Belfast City Council in May 1993. In 2008 he
became the second Sinn Féin lord mayor of Belfast. Since 1998 he has combined
his love of history and interest in the environment by organising historical walks
through Belfast City Cemetery as part of the West Belfast Festival. Now recognised as an authority on the cemetery, he continues to highlight the importance
of this burial site as a repository of the political, social and economic history of
Belfast. He is the author of *Written in stone: the history of Belfast City Cemetery*
(Belfast, 2006).

John Horne is professor of modern European history at Trinity College, Dublin,
and a Member of the Royal Irish Academy. He is an executive member of the
Research Centre of the Historial de la Grande Guerre, Péronne, and has published widely on twentieth-century France and the comparative history of the
First World War. Recent books are (ed.) *A companion to World War One* (Oxford,
2010); (ed.) *Vers la guerre totale: le tournant de 1914–1915* (Paris, 2010); and (with
Robert Gerwarth (eds)) *War in peace: paramilitary violence in Europe after the Great*
War, 1917–1923 (Oxford, 2012). He organised the 2008 Thomas Davis Lectures
broadcast on RTÉ and published as *Our war: Ireland and the Great War* (Dublin,
2008; 2nd edn 2012). He is a member of the French government's Mission for the
Centenary of the First World War

Keith Jeffery is professor of British history at Queen's University, Belfast, and a
Member of the Royal Irish Academy. He is author or editor of fourteen books,
including *Ireland and the Great War* (Cambridge, 2000, new edn 2011), *The GPO*
and the Easter Rising (Dublin, 2006), and a prize-winning biography, *Field Marshal*
Sir Henry Wilson: a political soldier (Oxford, 2006). His ground-breaking official

history, *MI6: the history of the Secret Intelligence Service, 1909–1949*, was published in London in 2010.

Pierre Joannon is a writer, historian and Franco-Irish diplomat. He is a former member of the board of trustees of the Princess Grace Irish Library in Monaco, and since 1973 has been honorary consul general of Ireland in the south of France. In November 2012 he was awarded a Presidential Distinguished Service Award for the Irish Abroad by the president of Ireland. His recent publications include *Un poète dans la tourmente: W.B. Yeats et la révolution irlandaise* (Rennes, 2010), *Histoire de l'Irlande et des Irlandais* (Paris, 2005), and *Michael Collins: une biographie* (Paris, 1997).

Heather Jones is lecturer in international history at the London School of Economics and Political Science. She is a graduate of Trinity College, Dublin— where she was a foundation scholar—and of St John's College, Cambridge. A former Government of Ireland Research Scholar in the humanities and social sciences, she completed her Ph.D. at Trinity College, Dublin, on wartime violence against prisoners of war during the Great War. Dr Jones is a former Irish Research Council for the Humanities and Social Sciences (IRCHSS) lecturer in European history at Trinity College, Dublin, and has held a Max Weber Fellowship at the European University Institute, Florence. She is a member of the board of directors of the Historial de la Grande Guerre, Péronne. Her monograph *Violence against prisoners of war in the First World War: Britain, France and Germany, 1914–1920* was published by Cambridge University Press in 2011.

Edward Madigan is the resident historian at the Commonwealth War Graves Commission and a visiting fellow to the Changing Character of War Programme at the University of Oxford. His work combines military, cultural and religious history, and his main research interests are British faith and identity in wartime, and the British and Irish experience and memory of the Great War. He is a former IRCHSS and Princess Grace fellow, and associate director at the TCD Centre for War Studies. As a historian of the Great War and the Irish Revolution, he has appeared on British, Irish, US and Australian television. His first book, *Faith under fire: Anglican chaplains and the Great War* (London), was published in 2011.

Fearghal McGarry is senior lecturer in history at Queen's University, Belfast, and joint editor of *Irish Historical Studies*. His recent research has focused on grass-roots participation in the Irish Revolution. He is the author of *The Rising: Ireland: Easter 1916* (Oxford, 2010) and *Rebels: voices from the Easter Rising* (Dublin, 2011).

William Mulligan is a lecturer in modern European history at University College, Dublin. He has published *The creation of the modern German army* (New York and Oxford, 2004) and *The origins of the First World War* (Cambridge, 2010).

Fintan O'Toole is a columnist with, and literary editor of the *Irish Times*. He is adjunct professor at the school of Language, Culture and Communication at the

University of Limerick, and Leonard Milberg lecturer in Irish studies at Princeton. He has been drama critic for the *Sunday Tribune*, the *Irish Times* and the New York *Daily News*. His work on political and cultural issues has appeared in the *New Yorker*, the *New York Review of Books*, the *New York Times* and the *Guardian*. He was presenter of the BBC cultural-magazine programme *The Late Show*, and literary adviser to the Abbey Theatre. His many books include *The ex-isle of Erin*; *Shakespeare is hard but so is life* (London, 2002); *A traitor's kiss: the life of Richard Brinsley Sheridan* (London, 1997); *White savage: Sir William Johnson and the invention of America* (New York, 2005); *The* Irish Times *book of the 1916 Rising* (Dublin, 2006); and *Ship of fools: how stupidity and corruption sank the Celtic Tiger* (London, 2009).

Catriona Pennell graduated from Trinity College, Dublin, in 2008 with a Ph.D. in modern British and Irish history. During her research she was awarded two major scholarships: the R.B. McDowell-Ussher Fellowship from Trinity College, Dublin (2003–06) and the RHS Centenary Fellowship from the Institute of Historical Research (2006–07). Since 2009 she has been a lecturer at the University of Exeter's Cornwall Campus. Her first monograph, *A kingdom united: British and Irish responses to the outbreak of the First World War*, was published by Oxford University Press in 2012. She is currently working on various aspects of Ireland's experiences in the First World War, including a reassessment of the 1918 conscription crisis.

Stuart Ward is professor of imperial and global history at the University of Copenhagen. He was educated at the Universities of Queensland and Sydney, and has held previous positions at the European University Institute and King's College, London. He was recently Keith Cameron Chair of Australian History at University College, Dublin (2008–09). His major publications are *Australia and the British embrace* (Melbourne, 2001); (ed) *British culture and the end of empire* (Manchester, 2001); (with James Curran) *The unknown nation: Australia after empire* (Melbourne, 2010); and (eds with Deryck M. Schreuder) the Australian volume for the Oxford History of the British Empire series, *Australia's empire* (Oxford, 2008). His most recent book is a volume of essays on the uses of history in waging public controversy in Ireland and Australia: (eds with Katie Holmes) *Exhuming passions: the pressure of the past in Ireland and Australia* (Dublin, 2011).

Jay Winter teaches history at Yale University. He is the author of *Sites of memory, sites of mourning: the Great War in European cultural history* (Cambridge University Press, 1995); *Remembering war* (New Haven, Yale University Press, 2006), and *Dreams of peace and freedom* (New Haven, Yale University Press, 2006). His biography, *René Cassin and human rights: from the Great War to the Universal Declaration*, co-authored with Antoine Prost, was published in French in 2011 and in English by Cambridge University Press in 2013. He is editor-in-chief of the three-volume *Cambridge history of the First World War*, to be published by Cambridge University Press in 2014.

Introduction

Edward Madigan

The years between 1912 and 1923 were arguably the most transformative in modern Irish history. Beginning with the mass signing of the Ulster Covenant and ending with a bloody civil conflict in the nascent Free State, this long decade of war, revolution and rapid social change gave birth to contemporary Ireland, North and South. Many of us hold different, even conflicting, views on the real significance of this violent but fascinating period, and we are unlikely to reach a consensus on episodes as contentious as the Easter Rising, the Battle of the Somme or the War of Independence. We can all hopefully agree, however, that the centenaries of these momentous events provide a valuable opportunity to engage with our past openly and creatively, and to emerge with a much richer understanding not only of the decade itself but also of the remainder of the twentieth century. What that process might mean, and where its pitfalls and potential lie, is the subject of this book.

We should remind ourselves at the outset that historians, academic or otherwise, hold no monopoly on the interpretation of the past, and that there are many ways in which we can learn about and confront the events our ancestors lived through. How this book is organised reflects three of them: history, memory and commemoration. The first section, 'Histories', looks at some of the key issues raised in recent writing on the period. In particular, it attempts to challenge the notion that events in Ireland were—for all their distinctiveness—unique, and instead seeks to understand them by comparison with what happened elsewhere and by situating them within a broader set of transformations affecting Britain, Europe and the wider world. The last section is concerned with commemoration as an activity—one that has its own history, to be sure, but which addresses the needs of the present and the hopes and fears for the future as much as the past for its own sake. Memory, the most intimate and subjective of our windows into the past, has consciously been placed between the sections on history and commemoration. Here, the emphasis is on the way the public mingles with the private and the present with the past in the individual memories and family stories that, for all of us, have the potential to be more immediate than history and less choreographed than commemoration. Nonetheless, the borders between the three sections are anything but sealed. The preoccupations of each stray into the territory of the others, while the diversity of views contained within all of them is signalled by the use of the plural in the title for each section: histories, memories and commemorations.

An underlying theme of the book is that while each of these approaches to the past serves a different purpose, none is the sole preserve of any one group of scholars, professionals or members of the general public. Each also has its own validity. Crucially, although history and commemoration can conflict with each other, there is no reason why historians and those involved in commemoration (whether as civic activists, media professionals or policy-makers) should not communicate with one another, and even collaborate, during the course of the centenaries. After all, 'commemorators' are by definition interested in history, and may well be in the business of producing it for a particular or a general public, while historians and other academics are also citizens, and have the citizen's interest in what is emphasised in the past and the moral and political values assigned to it. And family history connects everyone to the past whether they are aware of it (as seems increasingly to be the case) or not. Here, too, the distinctions are not hard and fast. The authors invited to contribute to the volume are an eclectic mix of professional historians, public-memory activists and commentators who communicate with the public via journalism, popular history and the broadcast media, but there is no presumption that they will wear only one of these hats.

Yet while there should ideally be as much interaction as possible between history and commemoration, we should recognise that they are emphatically not the same thing. The objectives of the historian are usually quite different to those of the commemorator, and in both cases the motives may be less than impartial. Remembrance of the past in the public sphere tends to be highly politicised. This is very evidently the case with Ireland in the decade of the First World War, the Irish Revolution and partition. For understandable reasons, moreover, the sort of history that informs commemoration tends to be simplified, if not simplistic. And while, in Ireland and elsewhere, there is often a stated desire for a pluralistic, inclusive version of the history of the entire decade of 1912 to 1923, in reality historical actors tend to be pushed into categories that deny their complexity. The frequent overlap between various communities and interest groups is overlooked, as the men and women of the period are assumed to be unionist, nationalist or republican, moderate or extreme, British army or IRA, and so forth.

The tendency to simplify the historical narrative when commemorating makes sense because commemoration tends to be at its most powerful when analysis—the business of the historian—is kept to a minimum, and the emphasis is placed on gestures. This approach to remembrance has a long tradition in continental Europe, but the peace process has brought about a climate in Ireland in which the grand gesture has allowed governments and politicians to circumvent some of the messiness of history in the name of progress and reconciliation. The various commemorative ceremonies that were incorporated into Queen Elizabeth II's visit to Ireland in 2011 illustrate the point.

For many, the most memorable moments of the intensely and, it must be said, beautifully choreographed royal visit were the wreath-laying ceremonies that took place at the Garden of Remembrance in Parnell Square and at the Irish National War Memorial at Islandbridge. That the monarch of the United Kingdom was prepared to bow her head in front of Oisín Kelly's memorial sculpture to the men and women who fought and died to end British rule in Ireland with the same reverence that she shows at the Cenotaph in London each November made for a truly meaningful gesture of conciliation. When President McAleese and Queen Elizabeth performed a similar act of homage at Islandbridge the following day, the atmosphere was just as dignified and moving. The point being made was that the Irishmen and women who fought against the British forces and those who volunteered to fight in the First World War deserved equal respect and commemoration. The equality of treatment accorded to each memorial seemed to challenge the traditional territorialism of popular understandings of Irish history, and was very much in keeping with the 'parity of esteem' that has been integral to the peace process in Northern Ireland.

Yet there was definitely a suggestion in the media commentary that Islandbridge acted as a counter to Parnell Square, and that those commemorated at each site were motivated by very different, even mutually exclusive, impulses. Simply put, the implication was that one group of combatants fought for the British Empire while the other group fought against it. Few commentators questioned this at the time, and the wreath-laying ceremonies were quite rightly received in the manifestly positive spirit in which they were intended. While historians, journalists and other commentators thus made much of the historic nature of the ceremonies, relatively little was said about the complex history that lay behind them, and to which the memorials themselves (and others like them) bear witness. In such circumstances there is a danger that the voice of the professional historian will sound shrill and pedantic, and have a divisive, alienating effect. Yet perhaps it need not be so. The polarisations of the past, and the messiness of the allegiances and experiences resulting from them, might actually deepen the meaning of the commemorations without destabilising them—a point made by the very geography of commemorative monuments in Dublin.

The war memorial gardens at Islandbridge—designed by the great imperial architect Sir Edwin Lutyens, and completed in 1939—were originally destined for Merrion Square. But the political leadership of the 1920s clearly felt that while the Irishmen who died in British uniforms during the Great War were not necessarily unpatriotic and had clearly made sacrifices, they could not be remembered in the heart of the city.[1] Islandbridge was ultimately chosen because it was suitable for a park, and, more importantly, because it was remote from the city and from the consciousness of its people. Yet given the gardens' close proximity to other iconic sites of memory, Islandbridge arguably turned out to be a highly appropriate choice of location.

Just a short walk northwards from the gardens, across the River Liffey in the Phoenix Park, stands the Wellington Monument.[2] At over two hundred feet of hard Wicklow granite, this edifice is deliberately imposing as it was erected to celebrate the towering achievements of that proverbially reluctant Irishman Arthur Wellesley, 1st Duke of Wellington.[3] The idea that a monument to Wellington should be established in Dublin was conceived of in the aftermath of the duke's momentous victory at the Battle of Vitoria in 1813. When the foundation stone was laid two years later, Wellington had gone on to attain immortality by defeating Napoleon at Waterloo. Funding for the memorial came mostly from the Anglo-Irish aristocracy and from British soldiers—many of them Irishmen—stationed in Ireland. The former group wanted the world to know that one of their own had vanquished the mighty tyrant; many of the latter simply revered their leader and felt that he should be fittingly remembered. The project ran into financial trouble, and the obelisk was only unveiled in 1861, almost a decade after the death of the Iron Duke. Today, it is one of the last of the so-called imperial monuments in the city. It can be seen for miles around and is clearly visible from Islandbridge.[4]

If you were to walk south from the Memorial Gardens you would soon arrive at Kilmainham Gaol. There can be few buildings in Ireland more loaded with the weight of history than this eighteenth-century prison. Among its first inmates were republicans incarcerated for espousing the same revolutionary ideology against which the British army of Wellington's period had originally gone to war. Henry Joy McCracken, a Belfast Presbyterian and co-founder of the United Irishmen, was imprisoned in the gaol shortly after it opened in 1796. Over the course of the next 120 years some of the most iconic figures in nationalist history found themselves within its walls. Yet the inmates who would really ensure Kilmainham's status as an unrivalled monument to republican idealism and martyrdom were the leaders of the Easter Rising, who were executed there in the weeks after they surrendered to the British forces in 1916. Éamon de Valera and Michael Collins were also imprisoned at Kilmainham in the aftermath of the Rising, but both, of course, escaped execution. The gaol was subsequently used to house republican prisoners during both the War of Independence and the Civil War, before being closed in 1924. It is now rightly seen as encapsulating the story of armed resistance to British rule in Ireland. Importantly, however, as the list of the gaol's residents includes constitutional nationalists of the calibre of Charles Stewart Parnell and John Dillon, both imprisoned there in 1882, it is also associated with the more moderate but no less passionate brand of Irish nationalism.

Within the same square mile, then, the cityscape of west Dublin contains a colossal monument to a legendary Irish imperialist in the Phoenix Park and a shrine to Irish republicanism at Kilmainham, while, between the two, the Irish dead of the Great War are commemorated at Islandbridge. And it is apt that the Memorial Gardens lie between the other structures, because in the context of the First World War the two opposing, often bitterly antagonistic traditions in Irish history—nationalism and unionism—overlap to a remarkable extent. The Irish war dead honoured at Islandbridge include men who were deeply committed to the two traditions that were on the brink of civil war in 1914, and we should not overlook the fact that many of these men had diametrically opposed visions of Ireland's future, and often regarded each other with contempt. Yet although they usually served in different units, the nationalists and unionists who fought on the Western Front and elsewhere endured the same deprivation and horror, and in one major action, the Battle of Messines in June 1917, they fought and died together. Since the 1990s, this shared experience of war has been used as a means of finding common ground between members of the unionist and nationalist communities in both Northern Ireland and Ireland as a whole. What has thus emerged in the last twenty years is an ironic but positive situation in which popular interest in a war that was unprecedented in its violence and destruction has allowed people from both sides of the northern divide and from the Republic to focus on a shared history, and to slowly move beyond the violence of a more recent past.

The Memorial Gardens at Islandbridge have clearly played, and will continue to play, an important role in this process. In July 2012 the unionist lord mayor of Belfast, Gavin Robinson, joined his Dublin counterpart, Naoise Ó Muirí, at the gardens to pay tribute to the common sacrifice of Ireland's First World War dead. On that occasion, Robinson, a member of the DUP, emphasised the value of shared remembrance and mutual esteem: 'It is important', he said, 'that along with the Lord Mayor of Dublin I lay a wreath that acknowledges people from the Republic of Ireland and people from the north. They collectively spilt blood together and sacrificed themselves for us and it is important that we acknowledge that.'[5] One has only to remember the IRA bombing of the Remembrance Sunday service at Enniskillen in 1987 to realise just how significant the lord mayor's words were.

Yet if we reduce the history of the Irish experience of the First World War to a simple tale of unionists and nationalists fighting side by side against a common foe, we risk missing much of the fascinating but unsettling complexity of the period. Ascribing motives to our ancestors is always a tricky business, and if over two hundred thousand Irishmen served in the British armed forces between 1914 and 1918, they had at least that many reasons for doing so. Many were, of course, committed to one or other of the two main political traditions, but many others resist easy categorisation. Consider, for example, the two best-known Irish war poets, Francis Ledwidge and Tom Kettle. They came from very different social backgrounds, but both were Catholic nationalists staunchly loyal to the Irish Volunteer movement. Yet not long after war broke out, each joined the British army and both were later killed on the Western Front. What exactly motivated men like Kettle and Ledwidge to volunteer? Both men appear to have genuinely viewed the conflict as a war against tyranny in which Ireland was morally obliged to participate, but neither had any sense of loyalty to Britain, and both felt deeply ambivalent about their status as British soldiers by the time they were killed. The same could be said of Willie Redmond, MP and brother of the leader of the Irish Party. Redmond was imprisoned at Kilmainham with Parnell as a young man, and by 1914 had been a vocal advocate of home rule for over thirty years. Yet despite his nationalism and his age, it seemed obvious to him that he should go to war as a British officer. During his time on the Western Front with the 16th (Irish) Division he began to hope that the shared experience of the trenches might reconcile unionists and nationalists. He was killed in 1917 going forward with his men during the Battle of Messines.

Ledwidge, Kettle and Redmond all appear to have been sincerely patriotic. They fought in British uniforms but were 'good' Irishmen who believed they were fighting for their country, and can thus be easily embraced by nationalists of the twenty-first century from both North and South. But what do we do with men commemorated at Islandbridge whose details of service are perhaps more difficult to romanticise? Men like Cornelius Duggan, a young private from Donegal serving in the Royal Irish Regiment when he was mortally wounded fighting the rebels during the Easter Rising. Duggan is buried just up the road from Islandbridge in the grounds of the Royal Hospital at Kilmainham. He died in the hospital and was laid to rest there, along with seven other soldiers from English and Irish regiments who met their deaths during Easter Week. Duggan, who was just twenty-three when he died, is an obscure, forgotten figure, and we know nothing of his reasons for enlisting or his views on the national question. But do we have the right to doubt his patriotism simply because he died fighting on the 'wrong' side of the Rising? What place will there be for men like Duggan in the centenary commemorations?

The picture becomes even more complex and intriguing if we consider those who survived active service in the First World War and went on to fight in the republican forces during the War of Independence. The fact that Tom Barry, probably the most successful republican commander in the south, had served with the 10th (Irish) Division for over three years reminds us that service in the British army did not rule out membership of the IRA. Indeed, while many in the republican movement clearly regarded Irish veterans with suspicion, weapons training and experience of active service must have been attractive assets in a poorly trained guerrilla army. And service in the British forces by no means reflected pro-British sentiment. Indeed, in his polemical memoir, *Guerrilla days in Ireland*, Barry famously claimed that his decision to join up had nothing to do with politics:

> I cannot plead I went on the advice of John Redmond or any other politician, that if we fought for the British we would secure Home Rule for Ireland, nor can I say I understood what Home Rule meant. I was not influenced by the lurid appeal to fight to save Belgium or small nations. I knew nothing about nations, large or small. I went to the war for no other reason than that I wanted to see what war was like, to get a gun, to see new countries and to feel a grown man.[6]

How many Irish soldiers who we now refer to as nationalists or unionists were driven to enlist by the simple promise of a 'manly' experience in a foreign land? Barry's case illustrates not only that service in the British and republican forces were not mutually exclusive but also that the views of our ancestors often changed and matured over time. And Barry was certainly not the only veteran of the war who exchanged a European battlefield for an Irish one in the years after the armistice. Emmet Dalton, a former Irish Volunteer from Dublin, served with distinction as an officer in the 16th (Irish) Division on the Western Front. Indeed, he was awarded the Military Cross for gallant conduct during the capture of Ginchy in September 1916, the action in which his close friend Tom Kettle was killed. When he returned to Ireland in 1919, Dalton joined the Dublin Brigade of the IRA, and during the War of Independence became a close associate of Michael Collins and played a key role in the republican campaign in the capital. He went on to serve as a major general in the Free State Army during the Civil War.

Both Barry and Dalton came from Catholic backgrounds, and Barry, at least, was devoutly religious. One of the encouraging features of the popular and academic discourse on Irish involvement in the First World War over the past decade or so is the degree to which the Catholic Irish soldier has been written back into the history of the conflict. A good deal less has been said about the admittedly much smaller number of Protestants who were active in the republican movement. This much-overlooked group includes men like Erskine Childers, who served in the Royal Navy during the war, and his cousin Robert Barton. Barton gained a commission as an officer in the Royal Dublin Fusiliers not long after the outbreak of war, and was stationed in Dublin during Easter 1916. He resigned his commission in protest at the British response to the Rising, and joined Sinn Féin just as it was beginning to establish itself as a major political force. He stood as a candidate for Wicklow West in the 1918 general election, and became a member of the first Dáil in 1919. He later acted as secretary to the Irish delegation that negotiated the Anglo-Irish Treaty, and was the only member of the delegation to vote against the Treaty in the subsequent Dáil debates.

The activity of women from non-Catholic or mixed backgrounds during the Irish Revolution further emphasises the point about the diversity of those who were committed to Irish independence, and reminds us that it was not just men who made sacrifices a century ago. The stories of Constance Markievicz, Maude Gonne and Grace Gifford (who married Joseph Plunkett in Kilmainham Gaol the night before he was executed) are well known. But tens of thousands of Irish women, from every conceivable social and religious background, played a very active role either in supporting the First World War or in the nationalist struggle for independence. Many Irishwomen served as nurses or auxiliaries in the British forces between 1914 and 1918, either on the home front or in one of the various theatres of war. Indeed, among the war dead commemorated at Islandbridge are women such as Margaret Cameron Young from Belfast and Nellie O'Neill from Cork, both of whom died while serving as nurses in France.[7] Irishwomen also worked in munitions factories across the United Kingdom, and busied themselves with various types of 'war work'. Other women were militantly opposed to the war from the outset, and became actively involved in the republican movement. This more radical group includes suffragettes such as Hanna Sheehy-Skeffington, Helena Moloney and Winifred Carney. Both Moloney and Carney were prominent members of Cumann na mBan, and both were imprisoned for taking part in the Easter Rising. With the exception of colourful figures such as Countess Markievicz, however, women have often been overlooked in popular and academic commentary on Ireland in the decade of the First World War. This is partly a result of the tendency to see war as a primarily male endeavour, but also reflects the social and cultural marginalisation of women in Ireland, North and South, in the decades after partition and independence. The centenaries present both a challenge and an opportunity to properly incorporate women into the story of the foundation of modern Ireland.[8]

The personal stories of the men and women associated with Islandbridge and Kilmainham, and hundreds of other sites of memory around Ireland and on the former battlefields of the First World War, paint a remarkably complex picture of a nation in war and revolution. Whether we feel we owe these people a debt or are simply curious about the world they lived in, the centenaries provide us with an unprecedented moment in which to learn about and remember them. If this volume contributes to the discussion of how this process of re-evaluation, re-imagination and remembrance might occur, and what it might achieve, it will have served its purpose.

Notes

1   When the issue of the location of the national war memorial was debated in the Dáil in 1927, Kevin O'Higgins, whose brother had been killed on the Western Front, summed up the government position as follows: 'No one denies the sacrifice and no one denies the patriotic motives which induced the vast majority of those men to join the British Army to take part in the Great War, and yet it is not on *their* sacrifice that this State is based, and I have no desire to see it suggested that it is.' See Keith Jeffery, *Ireland and the Great War* (Cambridge, 2000), 114.

2   As it was originally intended as a tribute to a living man, the 'monument' is also occasionally referred to as the 'Wellington Testimonial'.

3   Although the remark 'If a gentleman happens to be born in a stable it does not follow that he should be called a horse', or some variation thereof, is often attributed to Wellington and cited as proof of his disdain for his Irish background, there is no evidence that he ever made such a statement.

4   Nelson's Pillar and the equestrian statues of William III on College Green and General Hubert Gough in the Phoenix Park were all destroyed by republican elements over the course of the twentieth century. The enormous statue of Queen Victoria in front of Leinster House was removed in 1947. The statue of her husband, Prince Albert, which stands at the back of Leinster House, was allowed to remain.

5   *Irish Times*, 7 July 2012.

6   Tom Barry, *Guerilla days in Ireland* (Tralee, 1993), 38.

7   Margaret Cameron Young died while serving as a Voluntary Aid Detachment nurse near Boulogne in the summer of 1918. Nellie O'Neill, who was originally from Cloyne and served with Queen Mary's Army Auxiliary Corps, is buried in Abbeville.

8   The involvement of Irishwomen in the Rising and in the British war effort has been referenced in varying degrees of detail in most of the major histories of the period published within the last ten years, including Keith Jeffery's *Ireland and the Great War* and Charles Townshend's and Fearghal McGarry's books on the Easter Rising. Popular books by Sinéad McCoole, Cal McCarthy and Ann Matthews have also done a great deal to enrich our understanding of the role played by women during the revolutionary decade. To date, however, no attempt has been made to provide a detailed scholarly analysis of the political and social aspirations and activity of Irishwomen during the decade of the First World War, or to evaluate the real legacy of the Irish Revolution for women during the remainder of the twentieth century.

SECTION ONE

Histories

1

Violence and War in Europe and Ireland, 1911–14

William Mulligan

Both Irish and European politics were riven with conflict between 1911 and 1914. For all the difference of scale between them, they were connected both by the nature of the tensions involved and also by the potential impact of the Irish crisis on the United Kingdom as one of the leading great powers. At the international level there were wars between Italy and the Ottoman Empire in 1911 and 1912, and two wars in the Balkans in 1912 and 1913. In addition, the great powers consolidated their alliances, gave increasing weight to narrowly defined conceptions of military security, and embarked on an arms race. At the level of domestic politics there was severe labour unrest—particularly in Russia and Italy—constitutional conflicts over the role of Parliament became increasingly bitter in Germany and the United Kingdom, and the politics of nationalism threatened political stability in the United Kingdom and Austria-Hungary. With the benefit of hindsight it is possible to view the years between 1911 and 1914 as a prelude to the violent remaking of Europe that would take place between 1914 and the mid-1920s. The number and intensity of domestic and international crises suggest that a relatively peaceful transition from the great-power system of the nineteenth century to a system based on sover-eign (and notionally equal) nation states was impossible, and that a general European war was inevitable, a war that would become interwoven with civil wars and ethnic conflicts from Russia and the lands of the Ottoman Empire in Eastern Europe to the much less violent upheavals in Ireland and Spain.

Yet contemporary opinion was divided about the inevitability of European war. In January 1914, following the Italian–Ottoman and Balkan Wars, Arthur Nicolson, under-secretary of state at the British Foreign Office and married into a unionist family, argued that the worst crises of international politics had been overcome and that peace was assured for the foreseeable future; indeed, he was more concerned that domestic political crises could undermine a fragile international equilibrium. Increasing tensions over the home rule crisis could lead to civil war in the United Kingdom, rendering it ineffective as a European great power. Several months later, on the eve of the declarations of war in the summer of 1914, European socialists gathered in Brussels in a failed attempt to coordinate a common anti-war strategy. After the meeting broke up, Émile Vandervelde, leader of the Belgian Workers' Party, walked to the train station with Jean Jaurès, the French socialist leader. Before boarding the train to Paris, Jaurès assured his Belgian colleague that the July crisis would be resolved. The following day Jaurès was assassinated, and within three days Germany declared war on Russia and France.

Almost three years earlier, on the eve of the Italian invasion of the Ottoman Empire's provinces of Tripolitania and Cyrenaica in present-day Libya—an invasion that triggered a chain reaction of wars that marked the end of the great-power system and peace of the nineteenth century—European commentators discussed the likely scenarios for international relations in the coming years. The French newspaper *Le Matin*, a nationalist organ, placed two photos on the front page of its issue of 25 September 1911: one showed the port of Tripoli, a shabby, crumbling site, ruined, according to the caption, by Turkish civilisation; the other showed the port of Algeria, a thriving commercial hub, which owed its success to French civilisation. The associated article argued that an Italian conquest of Tripoli was part of a broader European civilising mission in Africa. Italy was a fellow Latin country, and would rescue Tripolitania from its Ottoman-induced torpor. On this reading, Italy's war against the Ottoman Empire was justified by the standards of civilisation and progress. This optimism—hypocritical and misplaced as it was—can be best understood when contrasted with a series of articles in the leading Viennese paper, *Neue Freie Presse*. On 25 September its editorial predicted that the conflict would spread to Europe, as the Ottoman Empire would respond to military attack by boycotting Italian goods and expelling Italian citizens from the empire. The racial and religious hatred between Muslims and Christians would resonate in the Balkans, leading to conflict there. National hatred and the use of military power unfettered by moral and legal restraints would change the international system. The restrained international system of the nineteenth century, on this reading, was about to give way to one characterised by uncontrollable violence.

The summer of 1911 marked an intensification and qualitative change in the militarisation of European politics. The most obvious sign of this militarisation was the land arms race between Germany and, to a lesser extent, its alliance partner Austria-Hungary on the one hand, and the members of the Dual Alliance, France and Russia, on the other. The arms race sharpened international tensions, and is often considered a primary cause of the First World War. Yet conflict and crises in a political system do not necessarily imply that system's imminent collapse; indeed, conflict is an essential part of politics, as it results from different interests. The elimination of conflict would require the elimination of difference. The important question, therefore, about the crises in Europe before 1914 is whether governments, especially the great powers, could manage these conflicts within the existing framework of international politics or whether they marked the failure of that system. This article will suggest that the great powers could manage the arms race because it operated within the logic of great-power politics.

Two other processes of militarisation presented a radical challenge to the international system because they could not be accommodated within the logic of great-power politics. The home rule crisis in Ireland is an excellent example of these processes of militarisation that threatened not just civil peace in the United Kingdom but the international order sustained by the great powers throughout the nineteenth century. First, the emergence of civilian militarism challenged the state's monopoly of legitimate violence. Civilian militarism was evident in groups as diverse as the Army League in Germany, the Conscription League in Britain, and the Combat Organisation of the Polish Socialist Party, not to mention the Ulster Volunteers and Irish Volunteers. Second, the independent military action of small nations and states contravened perhaps the primary norm of nineteenth-century politics—that no new political order could emerge without the approval of the great powers. The wars fought by the Balkan states in 1912 and 1913 are the primary example of this new mode of international politics, while the threat of political violence in Ireland was also directed against a great power, Britain.

Many of the conflicts between the great powers could be accommodated within the international system as it had developed from the late nineteenth century—after all, the great powers had maintained peace with each other for four decades since the end of the Franco-Prussian War. They had also contained violence and wars between the small states within Europe. Nicolson had good grounds for his optimistic view of international politics in January 1914: the great powers had no territorial claims on each other, while the lost provinces of Alsace and Lorraine and the *terra irredenta* claimed from the Habsburg Empire by Italian nationalists were largely irrelevant to international relations—French nationalists loudly mourned the lost provinces but rarely thought systematically about launching a war against Germany to win them back. Imperial rivalries did lead to serious clashes between the great powers, such as the Second Moroccan Crisis in the summer of 1911, which fuelled a war scare between Germany on the one hand and France and Britain on the other, but by 1914 these three powers were busy cooperating for mutual benefit in the Ottoman Empire, and had plans for what they called 'furthering civilisation' in Africa. Great powers regularly invoked honour, prestige and vital interests as justification for belligerent posturing during crises, but, fortunately, concepts of honour, prestige and vital interests were sufficiently malleable to enable each side to save face. The Anglo-German antagonism that had led to naval races, press wars and commercial conflict had been overcome by 1912; indeed, contemporaries spoke of an Anglo-German détente. That one of the most intense great-power rivalries could be overcome without triggering a major European war suggests that the international system remained flexible and viable.

Yet there were also more troubling developments. The most significant of these, after the Second Moroccan Crisis in 1911, was the increasing militarisation of international politics. This was reflected first and foremost in the land arms race between Germany and Austria-Hungary on the one hand and France and Russia on the other. In 1912 and 1913 the German government passed bills, including the 1913 Army Bill, increasing the size of their army by sixty-three thousand soldiers. In 1913 the French government responded by increasing the time a conscript served from two years to three, while in 1914 Tsar Nicholas II finally signed off on the 'big programme', which proposed an armaments programme that would be complete in 1917.

Although the arms race was the most concrete manifestation of the militarisation of international politics, the ways in which political and military leaders thought about international politics also changed. Governments judged their alliances with other powers increasingly by calculating military power and security: great-power politics was sometimes reduced to a simple military calculus of railway timetables and the numbers of soldiers. Generals in Berlin and Vienna urged political leaders to take advantage of what became known as the 'window of opportunity'—the moment when one side was militarily stronger than the other—to launch a preventative war. They feared that, as early as 1917, the growth of Russian and French military power would squeeze the Austro-German Alliance, remove their diplomatic freedom, and relegate them to second-class powers.

Historians have argued that this militarisation of international politics was a, if not *the*, decisive cause of the erosion of peace and the coming war. Two words of caution should be entered. First, the militarisation of international politics had taken place on previous occasions, most notably between 1887 and 1894. Bills to increase army strength, the influence of the military on foreign policy, and the demands for preventative war had placed enormous pressure on the international system, but Europe remained at peace. The militarisation of international politics was not an irreversible process, and it remained under the control of men who had the power to make fundamental choices over war and peace. Second, the militarisation process could be accommodated within the logic of great-power politics. Political leaders considered the arms bills as defensive measures, not precursors to a war of aggression. When the French Three Year Military Service Bill was proposed in spring 1913, the influential French journalist André Tardieu wrote: 'We hope that Germany will greet with *sang froid* the armaments, which France judges necessary'.[1] He argued that neither France nor Germany had any intention of attacking the other, but that the arms bills passed on both sides of the Rhine in 1912 and 1913 were justified as acts of self-defence and as measures for maintaining the balance between the two alliance blocs in Europe. Raymond Poincaré, French president, and Theobald von Bethmann Hollweg, German chancellor, both justified armaments increases by pointing to their deterrent effect. The former, at a speech in Nantes, claimed that 'the peoples most faithful to the ideal of peace are obliged to remain prepared for any eventuality'.[2] Others were more sceptical about the merits of the Roman adage 'Si vis pacem, para bellum' (if you want peace, prepare for war). The British pacifist MP Wilfrid Lawson ridiculed the idea, likening it to telling a drunk 'If you want sobriety, live in a public house'.[3] Political leaders also retained control of the military, rejecting calls for preventative war. Leopold von Berchtold, foreign minister of Austria-Hungary, ridiculed the idea of a window of opportunity as a hopelessly inflexible military solution to a political problem.

However, the other two processes of militarisation could not be accommodated within the logic of the great-power system. The most significant development in the militarisation of European politics was also its most explicit—the Balkan Wars waged in 1912 and 1913. In south-east Europe, the emerging nation states of Serbia, Bulgaria, Greece and Montenegro had formed the Balkan League in 1912, and sought to expel the Ottoman Empire—'bag and baggage', as Gladstone had put it almost forty years previously—from Europe. However, the great-power sponsor of the Balkan League,

Russia, considered the alliance an obstacle to Austro-Hungarian expansion in the Balkans rather than a threat to the Ottoman Empire. In 1910 the German foreign secretary, Alfred von Kiderlen-Wächter, had commented that 'the Balkan dogs will not bite as long as the great white Papa in St Petersburg does not want them to; they will only yelp'.[4] His analogy, disparaging as it was, reflected a key assumption of the international system, namely that the great powers controlled the smaller states, often viewing them as clients. Instead, the Balkan states refused to behave in accordance with the norms of the great-power system. The outbreak of war in October 1912 between the Balkan League and the Ottoman Empire was not simply a challenge to the latter, it was a challenge to the great-power system. On previous occasions when small states had stepped out of line, the great powers acted to cow them back to their carefully prescribed paths. This time, however, the great powers dithered for two months before calling a conference in London. The Treaty of London (1913) was imposed on the protagonists, but in July 1913 Bulgaria and its erstwhile allies fell out over the sharing of the territory captured from Turkey; Bulgaria, dissatisfied with its meagre gains, attacked its erstwhile allies. The Second Balkan War lasted just a month, and this time was ended by the Peace of Bucharest. The Balkan states, including the Ottoman Empire, had altered the regional and therefore European balance of power without the sanction of the great powers.

The conduct of the Balkan Wars also challenged the logic of great-power violence. Since the Franco-Prussian War and the Paris Commune in 1871, generals had feared that a future European war would be a people's war rather than a cabinet war. The quintessential cabinet wars were the short conflicts of the mid-nineteenth century, such as the Austro-Prussian War of 1866, which culminated in a politically decisive major battle. Wars were limited to fighting between armies, peace was a compromise. In people's wars generals and politicians could no longer control violence. Regular armies were liable to attack by irregular forces, soldiers carried out atrocities against civilians, and the complex politics of the war defied compromise and an early peace. Revolution might ensue. Generals hoped to avoid this catastrophic form of warfare by conducting decisive campaigns. However, the Balkan Wars demonstrated that even relatively short wars could have catastrophic human, social and political consequences. In short, what was at issue was not whether a war would be short or long but what its consequences might be.

The Balkan Wars of 1912 and 1913 saw over four hundred thousand Muslims expelled from the Balkans as a result of ethnic cleansing, rape, forced conversions and atrocities committed on grounds of nationality and ethnicity. There was also violence against other religious and ethnic groups, as well as sieges, such as the siege of Edirne (then named Adrianople). An imam at the mosque in Edirne, Hafiz Rakim Ertür, noted that 'Being besieged within a fortress is an experience that resembles none other on this earth—neither prison, nor exile…It is impossible to leave the confines of the fort. All one can see, night and day, is the face of the sky.'[5] The relevance of the Balkan Wars to visions of future warfare throughout Europe was disputed at the time, particularly by those who considered the region to be culturally and socially apart from Europe. Others viewed the wars as a warning of what would befall the Continent in a general European war. Jean Jaurès, writing in December 1912, argued that the war in the Balkans gave an idea of what modern war was like. He noted the high casualty rate, the spread of disease, the atrocities against civilians. 'It is the reproduction, in a civilised era, of the great destruction of barbaric times, when entire armies, entire peoples disappeared.'[6] He regarded the wars not as reflecting the wild character of the Balkans or European periphery but as signalling the essence of modern European war: barbarism enhanced by scientific and technological progress.

These wars aroused considerable interest in Ireland. The Irish Parliamentary Party MP John Dillon highlighted the humanitarian catastrophe. In addition to these humanitarian concerns, issues underpinning the Balkan Wars corresponded to the major questions in Irish politics regarding the relationship between empires and nations, constitutional and violent means of pursuing political change, and the international system and domestic politics. The emergence of small independent nation states in the Balkans ran counter to the classic unionist argument that the twentieth century would belong to major empires. The Balkan Wars suggested that there was space in the international system for small nations, be they autonomous units within a larger empire or fully independent sovereign states. Irish nationalists of all stripes noted the success of the Balkan states. The *Freeman's Journal* praised Montenegro, 'with a population much less than that of the single county of Cork and very little larger in area', as a 'glorious and inspiring example'.[7] However, Irish nationalists disagreed on whether change should be pursued through constitutional or violent means. At one level the militarisation of Irish politics after 1912 suggests that unionists and nationalists were willing to use violence to accomplish their political goals. Yet if we view the home rule crisis through the lens of nation-state-making elsewhere, the comparative absence of violence is a striking feature of Irish politics. Guns were shipped in, men drilled and marched in formation, and threats were uttered, yet violent acts remained isolated incidents.

It is perhaps true that Ireland and Britain were saved from a bloody civil war by the First World War. Nonetheless, the failure of even the most radical nationalists to use violence and embark on terrorist campaigns before the outbreak of the war reveals the tight restraints on using military force for political ends within Ireland. In the Balkans, particularly in the contested Ottoman province of Macedonia, there were several terrorist organisations, notably the Internal Macedonian Revolutionary Organisation, supported by the Bulgarian government. Gavrilo Princip, the assassin of Archduke Franz Ferdinand, was a member of Young Bosnia, which had links to the Serbian terrorist organisation the Black Hand. The containment of the militarisation of Irish politics requires explanation when set against the backdrop of European history between 1912 and 1914—indeed, between 1912 and 1923. Moreover, contemporaries offered their own answer to this question. Irish nationalists bemoaned that while there was an 'Eastern question', there was no 'Western question'. In other words, the

Balkan states had been able to draw on outside sponsors in their struggle for national status since the 1870s. Yet no great power planned to intervene in the domestic affairs of the United Kingdom to support Irish nationalists of any kind. This changed after the outbreak of war in August 1914, when Germany began to hatch plans to support separatist nationalists in Ireland and elsewhere in the British, French and Russian empires.

Discussing Anglo-German relations in the summer of 1913, the *Irish Times* referred to the 'all-pervading' German Navy League.[8] This final aspect of the militarisation of European politics—the growth of civilian militarist associations—was epitomised in Ireland between 1912 and 1914. The arming of Ulster, with the establishment of the Ulster Volunteer Force in January 1913, led nationalists to follow suit with the founding of the Irish Volunteer Force that September. The presence of large groups of illegally armed men was an obvious challenge to the state's monopoly of violence. This process of civilian militarisation reached its zenith in Europe with the Curragh Mutiny of March 1914. The British system of government—admired by many for its parliamentary regime and strict civilian control of the military—seemed as though it would be unable to implement a law passed through Parliament because sections of its army were unwilling to obey government orders. Moreover, it is striking that Ulster unionists and mutinying officers could justify their actions on the grounds of patriotism. Even the hyper-patriot Heinrich Class, author of *If I were the Kaiser*, might have blushed had he thought of using military force to overthrow his monarch's government.

At first glance the relationship between civilian militarism and international instability seems remote. The impact, however, can be sketched in two ways. First, as Nicolson noted, civil war in Ireland and Britain would render Britain powerless as a European great power. In a revealing remark, he declared that the Russian government would find it difficult to respect a great power that treated its national minorities as gently as London did.[9] There is some evidence that during the July crisis, German decision-makers hoped that the home rule crisis would prevent Britain from participating in a European war; even the *prospect* of civil war had seeped into the calculations of the great powers. Second, civilian militarists posed the most extreme challenge of popular opinion to professional diplomats' management of foreign policy. These groups pressed their governments to follow more aggressive foreign policies and to expand their military and naval forces. Diplomats were often at a loss as to whether a politician's belligerent remark, a military or naval manoeuvre, or a press war reflected the policy of a great power or was a meaningless sop to noisy militarists. Civilian militarists' criticisms of foreign policy challenged the role of diplomats as the operators of great-power politics in the same way as they challenged the army's control of military policy. They made international politics less calculable, more uncertain, and tugged at the threads of the great-power system.

In conclusion, let us examine the interaction between these different processes of militarisation. The key point of intersection was Austria-Hungary. As had been predicted in the *Neue Freie Presse* in September 1911, the nationalising character of the Balkan Wars posed a political and military challenge to Austria-Hungary. The increase of Serbian power made it a focal point for Slavic separatism in the Habsburg Empire. It also raised the question of whether the Habsburg Empire still had a 'European mission' in an international system dominated by the principle of the nation state. In late 1912 Berchtold made one last, rather abject, attempt to contain the Serbian challenge: he offered Belgrade a customs union, which would have tied the Serbian economy so closely to the Austro-Hungarian one that Serbia would effectively lose its independence. After the Serbian prime minister, Nicolai Pašić, duly rejected it, Berchtold accepted that war between Austria-Hungary and Serbia was inevitable.

Austro-Hungarian statesmen believed that they had to wage war against Serbia in order to sustain the empire; indeed, some even believed that nothing could preserve the empire, and that war would at least offer a glorious downfall (*Untergang*). For leaders in Berlin the disintegration of Austria-Hungary made the growth of French and Russian military power, supported by British naval power, an even more terrifying prospect. German leaders worried that even if governments in St Petersburg and Paris wanted peace, they would be pushed towards war by increasingly vocal and influential pan-Slavic and French nationalist associations. The assassination of Archduke Franz Ferdinand, heir to the Habsburg throne, was at the confluence of three processes of militarisation: one between the great powers, which destabilised the existing international system; one encompassing small states and nations and focused on the Balkans, which revolutionised the international system; and one at the level of popular politics, which undermined the domestic political basis of the international system. In many respects the latter two were more important because their logic of violence questioned the dominance of great powers, the legitimacy of multinational empires, and the restraints on violence against civilians. These were questions that also spoke to nationalists and unionists in Ireland, and would only be answered in the mid-1920s.

Notes

1 Quoted in William Mulligan, *The origins of the First World War* (Cambridge, 2010), 125.
2 Quoted in Klaus Wilsberg, '*Terrible ami—aimable ennemi': kooperation und konflikte in den deutsch-französischen Beziehungen 1911–1914* (Bonn, 1998), 88–90.
3 Quoted in Paul Laity, *The British Peace Movement, 1870–1914* (Oxford, 2001), 2.
4 William Mulligan, *The origins of the First World War* (Cambridge, 2010), 78.
5 Quoted in Syed Tanvir Wasti, 'The 1912–13 Balkan Wars and the siege of Edirne', *Middle Eastern Studies* 40 (4), 59–78: 62.
6 'L'odeur de ce charnier', *La Dépêche de Toulouse* [25 Nov. 1912] in Jean Pierre Rioux (ed.), *Jean Jaurès: rallumer tous les soleils* (Paris, 2006), 878.
7 Cited in Florian Keisinger, *Unzivilisierte kriege im zivilisierten Europa. Die Balkankriege und die öffentliche meinung in Deutschland, England und Irland 1876–1913* (Paderborn, 2008), 169.
8 'Men around the Kaiser', *Irish Times*, 25 July 1913.
9 Nicolson to Bunsen, Nicolson papers, TNA FO 800/373, ff. 80–3, 30 Mar. 1914.

2

The Strange Death of Liberal Ireland: William Flavelle Monypenny's *The Two Irish Nations*[1]

Paul Bew

> The tragic world is a world of action and action is the translation of thought into reality. We see men and women confidently attempting it. They strike into the existing order of things in pursuance of their ideas. But what they achieve is not what they intended; it is terribly unlike it. They understand nothing, we say to ourselves, of the world in which they operate. They fight blindly in the dark, and the power that works through them makes them the instrument of a design that is not theirs. They act freely, and yet, their action binds them hand and foot. And it makes no difference whether they meant well or ill.
>
> A.C. Bradley, *Shakespearean tragedy*[2]

George Dangerfield's *The strange death of Liberal England* (1935) is a conundrum. All the senior historians of either Labour or Liberalism—scholars like Henry Pelling, Ross McKibben or Roy Douglas—refute his thesis that the Liberal Party received a decisive destructive blow before 1914. If we shift the argument and say that Dangerfield was merely talking about a liberal *mentalité*, this hardly helps. The liberal *mentalité* is still strong in England, and is to be found in all the major parties, which, of course, includes the Liberal Democrats.

Yet, in one respect, Dangerfield has received wide historiographical support. This lies in the widespread respect for the thesis that the Tories and the Ulster Unionists hypocritically broke through the lines of British constitutionalism during the home rule crisis of 1912–14. To put it bluntly, the party of law and order became the party of rampant illegality conniving at gun-running and counter-revolution. The Tories thus aborted a benign historic compromise between Ireland and Britain, and paved the way for the violence of the Irish Revolution of 1916–23. The mainstream of the modern conservative intelligentsia—senior scholars like Robert Blake, John Ramsden and Ferdinand Mount—all accept the indictment. Perhaps only Winston Churchill, briefly in *The world crisis*, published in 1923, and the careful scholar Patricia Jalland, in *The Liberals and Ireland* (1980), have raised the issue of Liberal responsibility for the crisis—in particular, the self-serving strategy of delaying a compromise on Ulster, which the Cabinet knew to be inevitable as early as 1909. Conservative lamentation and Liberal indignation in general drowns out the scepticism about the working of Liberal policy. Yet the remarkable contemporary work by W.F. Monypenny, *The two Irish nations: an essay on home rule* (London, 1913), made just this critique of the fundamentally illiberal and coercive nature of contemporary Liberalism in its policies towards Ireland, although Monypenny's work has remained largely unread by historians and others.

In a way, this is surprising. Since 1998, two major developments may have been expected to have had an effect on the historical debate on the home rule crisis. The first is the acceptance by all factions in nationalist Ireland of the doctrine of consent. The second is the rise of Scottish nationalism. It is now accepted that a majority in Northern Ireland has a right to refuse its consent to an independent Irish Republic. Does this not have any implication for the consideration of the unionist case against home rule in 1912?[3] It will be said that the home rule bill contained a commitment to the supremacy of the Westminster Parliament and that, therefore, the two cases are not the same. They are not. But nor are they so very different.

The unionist leader Sir Edward Carson insisted that once a Dublin parliament was established, it would be extremely difficult for Westminster to interfere with its decisions, still less stop a drift towards independence—and Monypenny, in *The two Irish nations*, explicitly agreed with him. In recent years, Scotland has provided a classic proof of this thesis. It is worth noting also that Scottish nationalism historically has been a far weaker force than Irish nationalism. Scotland may or may not achieve independence; what is not in doubt is that the optimistic assumptions so prevalent in 1998 about the stability of a devolution compromise have been shattered. Neither of these major developments would surprise a reader of Monypenny—but they would surprise a reader of Dangerfield.

George Dangerfield's bibliography is impressive; it draws heavily on the Liberal polemics of the period, texts such as George Peel's *The reign of Sir Edward Carson*. But in a striking omission, it fails to include Monypenny's book. William Flavelle Monypenny, born in Dungannon, Co. Tyrone, in 1866, was a senior writer with the London *Times*, and his *The two Irish nations* was by far the most impressive unionist polemic of the period.[4] *The Times* may, indeed, have been the organ of a racist, cultural imperialism, but Monypenny's arguments in this do not fit that mould in any obvious sense. A biographer of Disraeli, Monypenny had the two-nations phrase knocking about in his head. But he was very careful in the way that he applied it to the conflict between the 'two Irish nations'. 'Irish history', he said, 'is a constant tragedy, a tragedy in the deeper sense, not as the clash of right and wrong, but [...] the clash of two rights.'[5] This is an idea that had its roots in A.C. Bradley's recent work on tragedy in Shakespeare, which ultimately drew its source from Hegel.[6]

Monypenny described the Irish question in sombre and bleak but, he felt, realistic terms:

> I have shown how deep is the feud between the two nations, how it has contrived to draw its bitterness from all the various animosities of race and class and religion, and maintains itself on the memories of centuries of struggles. We may regret that there is such a cleavage in Irish society; we may look forward to the day when it will have ceased to exist; but at present it is as much an ultimate fact of the situation as the Irish Sea itself.

He looked forward to an ultimate reconciliation:

> To bridge the gulf that separates these two sectarian nations and combine them into one, to unite the strength and practical ability of the North to the sensibility and imagination and enthusiasm of the South, is a noble ideal for statesmanship; its fulfilment would heal a sore which has long poisoned British politics. It is, moreover, an ideal which is by no means unattainable from the nature of the case; for both nations, as has been said, are essentially Irish, and between Irishmen every of creed and class and province there is at bottom a common ground of sympathy and intelligence. In the very depths of their antagonism there is something essentially Irish. But to the realization of such ideals there is no royal road; time alone can do the work, and the problem for the statesman is how best to co-operate with time in its healing efficacy.[7]

Dangerfield and Monypenny are, however, united by one striking feature of their contrasting books—both give very considerable, even disproportionate, weight to the interventions of Winston Churchill. Let us not forget that both books were written long before Churchill achieved his pre-eminence as a wartime prime minister. Yet both Dangerfield and Monypenny assume that his role is actually more worthy of comment than that of, say, H.H. Asquith, the prime minister.

Churchill's conversion from Conservatism to Liberalism owed everything to domestic social pressures in Britain and nothing to the Irish question. At the moment of conversion in April 1904, he signalled to the Liberals of Manchester North West that he was not impressed by the great Gladstonian theme of home rule: 'I remain of the opinion that a separate parliament for Ireland would be dangerous and impractical.'[8] His support for the home rule bill in 1912 was qualified by a view that a substantial partitionist concession should be made to Ulster unionism. This sympathy for their case was combined with exasperation when he felt they rejected reasonable offers of compromise— exasperation that led him to agree to speak to a Belfast nationalist meeting at the Ulster Hall on 8 February 1912. The Ulster Unionists regarded this as an act of gross provocation. At this venue, Winston's father Randolph had declared in 1886 his passionate identification with their cause. In the end, the meeting was shifted to Celtic Park in Belfast. Nevertheless, an angry Belfast loyalist crowd waited for Churchill and his wife Clemmie outside their hotel in Berry Street. 'The roar that greeted the attempt to start the motor car was as angry as had been heard in Belfast for many a day.'[9] In the narrow confines of the tiny and enclosed Berry Street, the car was jolted by beefy shipyard workers including, ironically, one William Grant, who was to be minister of public security in the Ulster Unionist government during the Second World War. The *Northern Whig*, a local Liberal Unionist paper, wished to downplay the level of threat, and argued that the crowd merely wished to send a strong political message. But 'it was as rough a five minutes as anybody could desire until at last, with a final rush, the police got the car around the corner and all danger was at an end'.[10] Perhaps not all dangers, however; in March, Clementine Churchill had a miscarriage, and one can only imagine Churchill's anger when, at a 1917 dinner, Lloyd George twitted him that he fully deserved his Belfast reception.[11]

Churchill's speech in Belfast has been rather neglected by historians. Unlike 1904, he now defended the creation of a Dublin parliament: 'History and poetry, justice and good sense, alike demand that this race, gifted, virtuous and brave, which has lived so long and endured so much, should not, in view of her passionate desire, be shut out of the family of nations, and should not be lost forever among indiscriminate multitudes of men'. He saw the new relationship of Great Britain and Ireland as fostering 'the federation of English-speaking peoples all over the world'.[12]

Churchill assumed that the growing Westminster subvention of Ireland undermined the case for significant economic powers for a Dublin parliament. Monypenny seized on these words of Churchill:

> The separation of Ireland from Great Britain is absolutely impossible. The interests and affairs of the two islands are eternally interwoven…the whole tendency of things, the whole inevitable drift of things is towards a more intimate connection. The economic dependence of Ireland on England is so absolute and quite apart from moral, military and constitutional arguments… the two nations are bound together till the end of time by the national force of circumstances.[13]

For Monypenny, such a statement had a more obviously unionist than nationalist implication, but Churchill argued that the new loyal Ireland would constitute a strategic security asset for Britain. But for Monypenny, the key aspect of Churchill's speech lay in his treatment of the two-nations issue. Monypenny, who covered the meeting, had seen the violence directed against Churchill's car: 'the vehicle was, for a second, poised on the nearside wheel. I am convinced that the crowd had no intention of overturning the car, but this is what might have happened if the police had not driven off the people immediately'.[14] He described Churchill's passage onto the Lower Falls Road as passing the boundary between the 'two nations'. As for the two-nations theme in the speech itself:

> Mr Churchill was compelled almost against his will to give it recognition. He devoted the greater part of his speech to what he called the 'Irish argument', and the time so spent was divided between an enumeration of the fetters that are to be placed on one of the Irish nations to save the other from oppression, varying in tones of entreaty to expostulation to sink its own identity.[15]

As for an imperial veto, *The Times* reported that in Toronto it was being pointed out that the Canadian government had found it impossible to operate this veto. It is hard not to deny, a century later, that Monypenny's analysis had a certain purchase on reality.

Dangerfield is, however, right about one very important aspect of the story: he detects a self-satisfied intimidatory aspect in Ulster unionist culture. It worried English supporters such as Dicey, who vigorously argued that Churchill should be given a fair hearing in Belfast. Monypenny himself describes Belfast crowds rushing around even after Churchill's departure, looking for someone to attack. It helps to explain the tone of Churchill's final words on his Ulster trip: 'It was a splendid meeting. The wicked dug the pit into which they have tumbled themselves'.[16]

The Act of Union was based on the concept that it was possible to create one people, one imagined community, across two islands. The key developments of the nineteenth century—the delay in Catholic emancipation, the Famine and mass nationalist mobilisation—destroyed this conception. Only one group that was disaffected in the late eighteenth century bought into the union concept: the Ulster Presbyterians. Unionism became an argument not for creating one people across two islands but, rather, that there were two peoples on one island, Ireland. W.F. Monypenny is the great chronicler of this development. But to put it like that evades a rather important issue. What are we to say about the often repeated charge that the Tory–Ulster Unionist alliance bears a direct responsibility for the rising of 1916 and the violence of 1916–23—violence that often had a distinctly sectarian tinge? There is a robust unionist reply: Ronald McNeill dismissed the idea that Irish republicans needed to learn about physical force from unionists when they had a perfectly good physical-force tradition of their own going back to 1798. There is a good point here, but it hardly settles the matter. Sir Edward Carson admitted this: 'I am not sorry for the armed drilling of those opposed to me. I certainly have no right to complain of it. I started that with my friends.'[17]

In his recent Ford Lectures at Oxford University, Professor Roy Foster has demonstrated beyond all doubt—in particular, through his study of the diaries of the revolutionary generation—that the Ulster unionist mobilisation radicalised nationalist Ireland in a significant way. The intimidatory aspect of the unionist campaign—while it is important to note that it fell short of murderous violence—so evident in Churchill's visit to Belfast, was of critical significance. It is not true to say, however, that there is a straight line between the Carson mobilisation and the Rising of 1916. In the first place, John Redmond retained the loyalty of a majority of Irish nationalists, despite all the provocations of 'Ulsteria', until Easter 1916. A study of popular politics leaves us in no doubt on this score. The Irish Parliamentary Party's (IPP) electoral performances in the period between the outbreak of the First World War and the Easter Rising requires some analysis. There were five contested seats, each possessing considerable political interest; in addition, two seats—Wicklow West, in August 1914, and Galway East, in December of that year—fell vacant and were uncontested, and Sir James Browne Dougherty, the former under-secretary, took Londonderry City as a Liberal pro-home ruler. But what do the five contested seats reveal about the evolution of nationalist opinion? The conclusion of any analysis of wartime by-elections in nationalist Ireland is unambiguous. The Irish Party won all five of the contested seats, as well, of course, as retaining the non-contested ones. The *Weekly Freeman's Journal* was quite correct to criticise the separatists for their failure to put up candidates: 'There were vacancies in the south, in the west, in the east and in the north. They could have tested their views in Tipperary, in Galway, King's County or Derry, but they did not budge'.[18] The two seats where separatists stood—College Green and North Louth—were won by the Irish Parliamentary Party. Nevertheless, there is clear evidence of the weakness of the IPP's structures. As a decisive study of regional grass-roots sentiment concludes: 'Redmond's political leadership had for years been placed rather uncomfortably at the head of the less compromising Nationalism of the mass of his followers'.[19] In general, the rural results were better than the urban: in Tipperary, given a choice of three parliamentarians, the electors selected the candidate closest to Redmond's personal philosophy; in Dublin Harbour, in the same situation, they did not. But even in rural areas there was evidence of a correspondingly low level of involvement in the Irish Party's apparatus. This was due in significant measure to the fading resonance of the land question.

These are not spectacular results for 'Redmondism', but they are solid enough and confer a certain democratic legitimacy on it. John Redmond viewed with contempt the activities of the revolutionaries on his left flank. Redmond looked upon this as play-acting by nobodies—a manifestation of the histrionic side of the Irish character by persons of no consequence. He was without fear for his position in Ireland—had not his influence over the coalition saved Ireland from the threatened disruption of its civil life by conscription, and had not the south and west voluntarily joined the colours to the number of forty-five thousand? That, indeed, was a remarkable response, everything considered. Looking to the future, Redmond saw the reconciliation of North and South, and home rule established by general consent at the victorious conclusion of a terrible war, out of which all came softened by suffering.[20] These are important words. They reveal the challenge the Redmondites were offering to a more traditional radical-nationalist view.

The truth is that the radicals felt compelled to act in 1916 because they feared they would be marginalised for ever if they did not. The words of one of the revolutionaries, Desmond FitzGerald, are very revealing:

> Home Rule was in the air. The overwhelming majority of the people supported Redmond. Insofar as that support had waned, it was due to a growing cynicism among the people. Home Rule had been promised so long and had not materialised. If it failed again, there was no evidence to lead one to expect that the people would do more than shrug their shoulders and say they expected as much.
>
> On the other hand, it did really look as though some Bill would become law. Those of us who thought of Home Rule as something utterly inadequate were a very small minority, without influence, impotent... In the circumstances of the time, in the cold light of reason, one could really have foreseen only the success of the Home Rule movement with a subordinate government established, whose restricted powers would be

acclaimed as fulfilling all aspirations, or the failure of Home Rule, which would have been acceptable to the majority of the people as a proof that it was too much to hope for.

[…] On the very declaration of war, Mr Redmond made a statement assuring the English people that the Irish Volunteers would protect Ireland…But more disturbing than that mere statement was the fact immediately it became apparent that it really represented the views of the majority of the Irish people…There were reports of the success of recruiting, of Volunteer bands marching to the station to see off their comrades who had volunteered for service in the British army.

The movement on which all our dreams had centred seemed merely to have canalised the martial spirit of the Irish people for the defence of England. Our dream castles toppled about us with a crash. It was brought home to us that the very fever that had possessed us was due to a subconscious awareness that the final end of the Irish nation was at hand. For centuries, England had held Ireland materially. But now it seemed she held her in a new and utterly complete way.

Our national identity was obliterated not only politically, but also in our minds. The Irish people had recognised themselves as part of England.[21]

Of particular importance here is the changing economic relationship between Ireland and England. From the epoch of Gladstone's budgets of the early 1850s—which increased the weight of indirect taxation on the poor—until the end of the century, it could be reasonably argued, and was so argued, that Ireland was overtaxed. With the implementation of the 'new Liberal reforms' after 1906—particularly, in the field of national insurance and the old-age pension—it became impossible to make such an argument. This is why Churchill made so much of old-age pensions in his Belfast speech: he assumed that the deepening economic dependence of Ireland upon Britain reduced the possibility of separation. He also knew that his host, Joe Devlin, the west Belfast MP, agreed, and was hardly worried by the prospect. Monypenny and *The Times* noted the point but wondered if London would end up subsidising Dublin while losing control of the money—as some would argue has happened in the recent case of Scotland.

Liberal Ireland was destroyed in the 1912–16 period. Political leaders such as Carson and Redmond had considerable personal respect for each other, and both could plausibly lay claim to a shared inheritance from the nineteenth-century Liberal tradition. Carson began his career as a Liberal Unionist, while one of Redmond's closest intellectual associates, R. Barry O'Brien, devoted much of his career to arguing that Gladstonian home rule formed the logical culmination of nineteenth-century Liberal reform measures for Ireland, and that only a measure endowed with the symbolic power that Gladstone offered could reconcile Irish nationalism to wider British allegiance in a 'union of hearts'. Yet both men were in the end unable to prevent the destruction of Liberal Ireland. For those who wish to understand why leaders who shared so many aspirations and terms of reference, who puzzled their British allies at times by agreeing that they quite saw each other's point of view yet were unable to compromise on apparently miniscule differences, who tragically failed to reach a mutually satisfying settlement, and why two solitudes and the politics of militarism displaced the aspiration to a shared political community, W.F. Monypenny's *The two Irish nations* is an indispensable resource.

Notes

1   I wish to thank Dr Patrick Maume for reading an earlier version of this paper and enriching it with his suggestions.
2   A.C. Bradley, *Shakespearean tragedy* [1904] (New York, 1968), 28–9.
3   This is discussed at some length, as is the nationalist counter-argument, in Paul Bew, *Ideology and the Irish question: Ulster unionism and Irish nationalism 1912–1916* (Oxford, 1994).
4   Jacqueline Beaumont, 'An Irish perspective on empire: William Flavelle Monypenny' in Simon Potter (ed.), *Newspapers and empire in Ireland and Britain: reporting the British Empire, c. 1857–1921* (Dublin, 2004), 177–94.
5   William Flavelle Monypenny, *Two Irish nations* (London, 1913), 3.
6   I owe this point to Professor James McCormack.
7   Monypenny, *Two Irish nations*, 15–16.
8   *Belfast Newsletter*, 8 Feb. 1912.
9   *Northern Whig*, 9 Feb. 1912.
10 *Northern Whig*, 9 Feb. 1912.
11 Margaret Baguley (ed.), *World War I and the question of Ulster: the correspondence of Lilian and Wilfrid Spender* (Dublin, 2009), 295.
12 *Northern Whig*, 9 Feb. 1912.
13 Monypenny, *Two Irish nations*, 77.
14 *The Times*, 9 Feb. 1912.
15 Monypenny, *Two Irish nations*, 65.
16 *The Times*, 9 Feb. 1912.
17 Bew, *Ideology and the Irish question*, 95.
18 *Freeman's Journal*, 6 Nov. 1915.
19 Michael Wheatley, *Nationalism and the Irish Party: provincial Ireland 1910–1916* (Oxford, 2005), 266.
20 Emily Lawless and Michael MacDonagh, *Ireland* (3rd edn, London, 1923), 446.
21 Quoted in Garrett FitzGerald, '1916 and Irish independence: I—the motivation of 1916' (headlined 'The final end of the Irish nation'), *Irish Times*, 13 July 1991 (one of a series of five articles by Dr FitzGerald on the meaning of the Rising: *Irish Times*, 13, 15, 16, 17, 18 July 1991).

3

Parallel Lives, Poles Apart: Commemorating Gallipoli in Ireland and Australia

Stuart Ward

At a key moment in Sebastian Barry's award-winning *The secret scripture* (2008), the ageing Roseanne McNulty casts her mind back to Ireland's turbulent Twenties and Thirties, reflecting:

> I wonder is that the difficulty, that my memories and my imaginings are lying deeply in the same place? Or one on top of the other like layers of shells and sand in a piece of limestone, so that they both have the same element, and I cannot distinguish one from the other with any ease, unless it is from close, close looking?[1]

As for individuals, so, too, for whole communities the business of remembering is never as straightforward as it appears, never merely the simple recall and rendering of bygone events. An imaginative 'element' is fundamental to any narrative tradition, and is all the more pervasive in the realm of 'collective memory'. The field is vast, unwieldy and marked by a conceptual looseness about the range of social phenomena that might fall within its ambit. Yet most would accept the basic proposition that communities possess ways of storing narratives about their past and deploy them in myriad ways for a variety of social and cultural purposes. More specifically, collective memories of the past are sorted, segmented and made sense of with reference to group-belonging. This was the major insight of Maurice Halbwachs, generally regarded as the founder of modern memory studies in the 1920s and 1930s. He set out to demonstrate how the durability of social memories was inevitably linked to the survival of the social groups that sustained them. Conversely, the nurturing of collective memory was fundamentally about group durability—about securing the cohesion and viability of communities into the future,[2] or in Jeffrey Olick's reformulation: 'It is not just that we remember as members of groups but that we also constitute those groups and their members simultaneously in the act, thus "re-member-ing".'[3]

One way of illustrating this is to compare the imaginative response of two distinct communities to a single, self-contained historical event. In the coming decade of First World War centenary commemorations, one particular episode that will undoubtedly achieve prominence is the centenary of the Gallipoli campaign of 1915. Here, Irish and Australian divisions fought alongside one another in an ultimately futile bid to force the Dardanelles, with the aim of eliminating the Ottoman Empire from the war. But whereas the events of 25 April 1915 would provide the foundation for a rich commemorative tradition in Australia (amounting to a veritable cult as the centenary draws near), in Ireland the same battlefield would soon be lost to a commemorative calendar crowded with memories of Easter 1916 and the Anglo-Irish War—this despite the fact that Australia and Ireland suffered roughly equal casualty figures at Gallipoli as a proportion of their total losses in the Great War.[4]

This was to have profound consequences for the politics of memory, setting Australia and the Irish Free State on widely divergent paths. As Anzac Day became established in the 1920s as Australia's principal national holiday, and plans unfolded in the 1930s to build an imposing national war memorial and museum in the new federal capital, Ireland's key dates and sites of war memory became the source of enduring controversy. This was clearly apparent in the decade-long delays over the erection of the Irish National War Memorial at Islandbridge, deliberately tucked away on the western edge of the city. Although completed in 1938, its formal dedication was delayed a further fifty years. The contrast with the Australian War Memorial in Canberra (completed within three years of its Irish counterpart yet dedicated a full forty-seven years earlier) could not be starker. Situated at the foot of Mount Ainslie, dominating the surrounding landscape at the northern reach of the parliamentary axis, the building is occasionally mistaken by overseas visitors for Parliament itself.

Here, then, is a central irony: a military encounter that engulfed Irishmen and Australians in unprecedented numbers came to occupy markedly different places in the national imaginary. By the 1980s, the Irish National War Memorial had fallen into disrepair, a derelict open site for the caravans and animals of the Irish Traveller community. Meanwhile, in Turkey, at the site of the original landing at 'Anzac Cove', the first Australian travellers were setting up their own camp for a makeshift Anzac Day dawn service in what would become a mass backpacker pilgrimage in the decades ahead. One simple explanation for this would be the vastly different composition and character of the two communities in question—the loyal Australian dominion proving its worth in an imperial cause and relishing the moment for posterity on the one hand, and the rebellious, republican Irish duped into defending Britain's great-power pretensions on the other. Yet anyone who knows the first thing about either country would recognise the reductive clichés at work here.

On closer examination, Irish and Australian responses to the outbreak of the Great War were not so far apart. In 1914 the fledgling Australian federation was widely regarded as a nation-in-waiting, ripe for the proving ground of war. In Ireland, John Redmond's appeal to the Irish Volunteers to enlist drew on a similar logic. In both cases a sense of expectant nationhood became a rallying cry in the early stages of the war. This gave rise to a number of interesting parallels in Irish and Australian popular renderings—and rememberings—parallels that would be obscured by the stark divergence in Irish and Australian commemorative cultures in the post-war era.

Of particular relevance is the 10th (Irish) Division of Kitchener's New Army, which was first deployed at Gallipoli at Suvla Bay in August 1915. The 10th was the first Irish division to be formed in the immediate aftermath of the outbreak of war in 1914. It would also be the first Irish formation of volunteer recruits to be thrown into the heat of battle in the Great War. Although detachments of Irish regulars serving under British divisional command had seen action in Flanders in 1914, and in the initial, calamitous, raid on Cape Helles at Gallipoli in April 1915, it was the landing of the 10th at Suvla on 7 August 1915 that saw the first major engagement of an all-Irish volunteer division in the Great War.[5] They were also the first of their kind to be completely decimated. Within a month of the landing at Suvla Bay, nearly half of their seventeen-thousand strength were either dead, wounded, sick or missing. Unlike the later exploits of the better-known 16th or the Ulster 36th, the recruitment of the Irish 10th was not directly implicated in the home rule crisis, and comprised a genuine intermixture of Catholics and Protestants volunteering to fight alongside one another (or, at least, voicing no audible qualms at the prospect).[6]

It is not widely recognised that the initial deployment of the 10th (Irish) Division at Suvla Bay generated a public fanfare that bore remarkable similarities to Australia's 'Anzac legend'. Like the war correspondence of Charles Bean and Ellis Ashmead-Bartlett, who first chronicled Australia's remarkable feat of arms at Anzac Cove, early reports of Ireland's baptism of fire at Gallipoli were greeted with expectant jubilation. In contemporary newspaper reportage and published accounts, such as Michael MacDonagh's *The Irish at the front* (1916), Stuart Parnell Kerr's *What the Irish regiments have done* (1916), and Bryan Cooper's *The Tenth (Irish) Division in Gallipoli* (1918), the inclination was to herald Ireland's achievement as the mark of the coming nation. Indeed, a number of recurring themes can be identified in early Irish war writing that bear an undeniable family resemblance to their generic counterparts in Australia.

In both the Australian and Irish experience, much was made of the fact that this was the first time that 'national' divisional formations had been deployed in the field. While Irish and Australian soldiers had fought in many a British regiment in previous wars, only with the Gallipoli campaign did they enter a major military encounter as Irishmen and Australians with their own divisional integrity and chain of command. John Redmond's boast that the Irish had 'for the first time in their history—a memorable fact—put a national army into the field, a glorious army!' was widely echoed in Australian accounts of the first Anzacs.[7] The key distinction made in both Ireland and Australia was between regulars and volunteers: the former were easily subsumed within a longer history of British military endeavour, whereas the latter signified a new national departure. The *Irish Times* made the distinction clear:

> The fighting in the Dardanelles will be a landmark in the history of the Irish people. Our men have fought grandly in Flanders…but there has been a more striking concentration of Irish effort in Gallipoli; more than once it has been possible to regard the Army of Gallipoli as an Irish Army…But there is another, and entirely new, element in our Irish interest in the Gallipoli campaign—an element that gives a poignant intensity to our pride, our hopes, and our anxieties. The professional Army, as it was before the war, embraced certain classes of the Irish people; the new Army embraces all.[8]

The volunteer status of the 10th Division was fundamental to the idea of a 'concentration' of nationhood. But it also brought nagging doubts about an untried force with something to prove. When Ashmead-Bartlett concluded that the Australians 'were happy because they knew they had been tried for the first time, and had not been found wanting', he was responding to the same question posed by the *Irish Times*: 'How would they fare—these lads equipped only with the hasty training of a few months; these officers, fresh from the desk, on whose young shoulders such a heavy burden of responsibility is now imposed? Would they uphold the credit of the great names that they carried on their shoulder straps?'[9] Parnell Kerr described this as the question that 'trembled on the lips of Irishmen and Irishwomen when they heard that the 10th Division had been ordered to the Dardanelles'.[10]

Early reports of the Irish landings in the August offensive provided only the haziest indications of the success or otherwise of the Suvla Bay campaign. But much as Bean and Ashmead-Bartlett issued optimistic assessments of the initial landings at Anzac Cove in April 1915, so the accounts that began to appear of the Irish at Suvla were similarly exaggerated. One officer's report on the deeds of the 5th Battalion, Connaught Rangers, published in September, suggested that the Irish had surpassed the achievements of their Antipodean brothers in arms:

> To Australia and New Zealand belong the first honour of the Anzac landing, the maintenance of the foothold then gained…Against unparalleled difficulties, in the teeth of fierce and sustained resistance, the present British [10th (Irish) Division] line has been established. Theirs was the lion's share of the work, theirs justly will be the greater fame.[11]

Rather than recount the details of specific feats in arms, an array of unique characteristics was commonly ascribed to the Irish regiments in Gallipoli and Flanders. They were rough and ready recruits who made up for their deficiencies in drill and discipline on the parade ground with a fierce independence and tenacity under fire. Indeed, for the likes of Redmond, their rough manners and devil-may-care attitude was the key to their status as 'the cream of the Army…a *corps d'elite*'.[12] The superior martial qualities of the Irish were consistently depicted as the product of inherently national characteristics: their dash, initiative, impatience and instinctive aggression (often presaged by 'a wild Irish yell') were widely deemed the product of local conditioning.[13] Yet these self-same characteristics—so familiar to Australians—had also been depicted by Bean and others as the consequence of habitual exposure to the harsh Australian outback. All the 'fighting with men and with nature', he observed, 'has made of the Australian as fine a fighting man as exists'.[14] In both cases, these were characteristics that could only be ascribed to *volunteer* recruits, rough-hewn from the national fibre after only the briefest brush with formal training and discipline.

This made for fine copy and was eagerly devoured, but the logic was not easily reconciled with the abject failure of the campaign to secure any major strategic objective. This was circumvented by the emphasis on the timeless human qualities displayed for posterity rather than on the grim reality of defeat. Chroniclers in both countries were at pains to point out that it was no moral or martial failure on the part of the citizen soldiers but a failure in military high command (combined with 'the perhaps not very trustworthy genius of Mr Winston Churchill') that had doomed the campaign.[15] Much as Australian accounts made great play of the landing of the Anzacs at 'the wrong beach'—far more treacherous in topography than the intended site—so, too, Ireland's misfortunes were ascribed to 'the natural difficulties of the country' and the absence of a ready water supply on Suvla's vast salt pan.[16]

It was not so much the outcome as the timing of the Gallipoli campaign that was instrumental to the overriding theme of emergent nationhood. For a newly federated assemblage of Australian colonies, barely fifteen years old and with little in the way of a binding federal story, the Anzac legend provided a subtle but potent means of forging a single national idea from the sum of its disparate parts. This provided the formative context for Bean's celebrated verdict—solemnly reiterated at every Anzac ceremony since—that 'a consciousness of Australian nationhood was born' at Gallipoli.

Similarly in Ireland, at a time of deep community divisions over the home rule bill of 1912, the recruitment, deployment and sacrifice of Irish lives in a shared struggle against a foreign menace held out the promise of burying the hatchet at home. As Redmond declared in November 1915, 'I need not point out the moral to you'.[17] And for those who needed it spelled out, the *Irish Times* obliged:

[The soldier's] death is a message of hope to his country. Mr Ashmead Bartlett relates that on the height of Sari Bair he saw lying dead, side by side, a Colonial, an Englishman, a Maori, and a Gurkha—surely a solemn and wonderful illustration of imperial unity. Is the spectacle of Irish Unionists and Nationalists fighting side by side in Flanders and Gallipoli…any less inspiring? A little more than a year ago they were preparing to kill one another. Today many of them have died for one another. When this war is ended we shall resume our political controversies in a new Ireland. The Unionists and Nationalists who fought at Ypres and stormed the hill at Suvla have sealed a new bond of patriotism. The spirits of our dead Irish soldiers will cry trumpet-tongued against the deep damnation of internecine strife in Ireland'.[18]

Bean readily assumed that the deeds of the Australians at Gallipoli would be retold for generations to come. And he was to devote the rest of his life to fulfilling his own prophecy, editing the multivolume official history of Australians in the Great War, and playing an instrumental role in the establishment and completion of the Australian War Memorial in Canberra. Also in Ireland, there was no shortage of voices ready to proclaim the 'indelible' memory of the 10th (Irish) Division at Gallipoli. Bryan Cooper's misplaced confidence that 'Ireland will not easily forget the deeds of the 10th Division' seems remarkable in retrospect.[19] On the eve of the evacuation of the peninsula,

London's *Daily Express* also predicted that Gallipoli 'will forever be associated with the gallantry of the Australians and New Zealanders…and of the 10th Irish Division'.[20] The *Irish Times* concurred:

> The name of Gallipoli will be uttered with tears in hundreds of Irish homes for many years to come. Some of our bravest and best lie there. From University, shop, and plough, our gallant lads went straight into the jaws of battle, and proved themselves faithful and dauntless heirs of the traditions of their race. The story of the Munsters and Dublins at Seddul Bahr and of the Irish Division at Suvla Bay is imperishable…We must leave posterity to realise what we cannot realise today—that in Gallipoli Australians and Irishmen were fighting not only to beat the Turk, but to consolidate a mighty Empire and to create a united Ireland.[21]

Even more unequivocal was Michael MacDonagh's 1916 verdict on the Suvla landing: 'Because of those dead Gallipoli will ever be to the Irish race a place of glorious pride and sorrow'[22]—'The date, August 7th, 1915, should be ever memorable in the history of Ireland'.[23]

That 7 August failed to live up to these expectations is clear enough. Even before the evacuation of January 1916, it was becoming apparent that Ireland's name had not been accorded the kind of laurels bestowed on the Australians and New Zealanders. John Redmond suspected a unionist plot in the War Office to play down any suggestion of Irish singularity or distinction. He demanded to know the reason for 'the obstinate refusal to allow the Irish people to learn officially of the achievements of the Irish regiments, and the total absence of official recognition of their gallantry'.[24] The *Irish Times* ran an equally bitter series of editorials against the official censors for having 'drugged the national spirit' and for attempting to 'suppress the whole story of Suvla Bay'.[25] Dublin barrister Henry Hanna railed publicly against the failure to send Irish war correspondents to accompany the 10th Division. Here he clearly seems to have had the remarkable relationship between Bean and the Anzac Corps in mind. He saw in Bean's *Anzac* book—a collection of memoirs, poetry, tales and sketches from the men in the trenches—the chance to reach beyond the scanty official war reports, and compile a 'fitting literary record' of Suvla Bay. 'It has been done by the Australians for themselves', he declared—'why not do it for ourselves?'[26] The *Irish Times* echoed and amplified Hanna's plea: 'there is no reason except red tape why every national division on every one of our fronts should not have its national chronicler…If the War Office knew anything about Ireland…it would surely perceive that an Irish chronicler with every one of these Divisions would be worth a battalion in himself'.[27] Hanna would later to go on to publish his own account, in 1917, entitled *The pals of Suvla Bay*.

But by then the memory of the 10th (Irish) Division at Gallipoli was already fading, the reasons for which are not difficult to discern. Within a year of the Suvla landings, the Easter Rising of 1916 set processes in train that would profoundly reconfigure nationalist perceptions of the war and the memory of Ireland's role in it—tentatively at first but with growing conviction as the war progressed. With the conscription crisis of 1918 and the collapse of the Redmondite project, Ireland's war was rapidly superseded by the more immediate concerns of the Anglo-Irish War and its corrosive denouement. By the close of the Irish Civil War and the shoring up of the Irish Free State, any talk of official war commemoration (of any war) was inevitably shot through with ambivalence and internal division.[28] But one memory that was particularly ill-placed for public endorsement or official promotion was that of the thirty thousand-plus Irish dead at Gallipoli and the Western Front.[29]

Perhaps the most vivid illustration of the divergent paths of Ireland's and Australia's Gallipoli myth is the subtle change in nomenclature at the railway end of Dublin's Croke Park. Initially christened 'Hill 60' after a major Irish objective successfully obtained in the Suvla Bay offensive (also known as 'Chocolate Hill'), it was later altered to 'Hill 16' in honour of the men of the Easter Rising. Today, virtually no one attending GAA events would associate this sacred cauldron of Irish nationalism with the lost legend of Gallipoli. The republican verdict on Suvla Bay was encapsulated in the song 'The foggy dew', written immediately after the war and popularised in the 1920s:

> Right proudly high over Dublin Town they hung out the flag of war
> 'Twas better to die 'neath an Irish sky than at Suvla or Sud-El-Bar[30]
> ...
> 'Twas England bade our wild geese go, that 'small nations might be free';
> Their lonely graves are by Suvla's waves or the fringe of the great North Sea.[31]

All of this suggests that the stark divergence in commemorative traditions in the Irish and Australian 'collective memory' of Gallipoli is more than a case of deep and inherent cultural differences between the two communities. Clearly, there was considerable scope for a plausible Irish variant of Australia's 'birth of nationhood' myth, with several prominent figures eagerly willing to promote it. What the comparison reveals is that the contours of collective memory are constantly subject to changes in group dynamics—socially and especially politically—and that it is subsequent upheavals in the Irish body politic that cast the two narratives in such divergent moulds. Sebastian Barry terms this 'the damage [that] came after independence, when a new narrative had to be established in order to assist the birth of a country'.[32] The word 'damage' implies a prior state of balance, of harmony, from which 'purer' memories can be struck. Yet communities are constantly in flux and thus forever moulding and reshaping the vision of their past. The Australian myth of Gallipoli has also passed through several iterations over the last hundred years, despite the outward appearance of timeless observance and ritual.

In recent decades we have seen a further illustration of this in the subtle but undeniable process of rehabilitation of Ireland's Great War, with the Gallipoli story playing an increasingly prominent part. In March 2010 President Mary McAleese attended a wreath-laying ceremony at Suvla Bay as a means of symbolically redressing the balance. Recent books by Philip Orr and Jeff Kildea, reissued wartime memoirs such as Bryan Cooper's *The Tenth (Irish) Division in Gallipoli*, and Keith Jeffery's documentary film and other writings have brought a once-obscure slice of Irish military history back into view.[33] Novelists have also chimed in, with two recent offerings from 2010 alone: Alan Monaghan's *The soldier's song* set largely in Gallipoli, and Paul Murray's *Skippy dies* both make pointed references to the redeemed memory of Gallipoli. In Murray's novel, one of the protagonists becomes fascinated by a wartime photograph of his friend's great-grandfather, a veteran of Gallipoli:

> He studies the photograph in the book again. Is he imagining it, or can he see a family resemblance there, between Molloy and his great-grandson? Over the generations the set mouth has grown uncertain, reticent, the blue eyes dazed, as if the genes themselves had never recovered from the disintegration of Suvla Bay and its aftermath, as if some infinitesimal but vital part had got lost in the churn of time.[34]

The subliminal message was given full voice by President McAleese in her wreath-laying speech at Green Hill Cemetery: the Irish at Gallipoli were 'doubly overwhelmed', she declared—first, by tenacious Turkish defence and later by the vagaries of history. In calling for a 'shared commemoration' that might redress the 'deficit of remembrance', she expressed optimism for 'the much-needed healing of memory on our own divided island'.[35] The common assumption in so many of these accounts is the idea of memory loss as a clinical disorder, blighting the Irish body politic and urgently in need of 'recovery' (and, hence, 'healing'). Looking ahead to the centenary celebrations of 2015, there is every indication that the parallel lives of Irish–Australian 'memories and imaginings' of Gallipoli are moving steadily into alignment once more.

Notes

1   Sebastian Barry, *The secret scripture* (London, 2008), 227.
2   Maurice Halbwachs, *The collective memory* (New York, 1980), 22, 27.
3   J.K. Olick, *The politics of regret: on collective memory and historical responsibility* (New York, 2007), 29.
4   Keith Jeffery, 'Gallipoli and Ireland' in Jenny McLeod (ed.), *Gallipoli: making history* (London, 2004), 98.
5   Or not quite. In truth, early recruitment fell slightly short of a full division, and their numbers were augmented by a Hampshire regiment (which itself contained a good number of Irishmen recruited in England). Phillip Orr, *Field of bones: an Irish division at Gallipoli* (Dublin, 2006), 17. See also Jeff Kildea, *Anzacs and Ireland* (Cork, 2007).
6   The former in preponderance in the ranks, the latter making up the bulk of the officers.
7   John Redmond, foreword to Michael MacDonagh, *The Irish at the front* (London, 1916), 6.
8   *Irish Times*, 4 Sept. 1915.
9   *Irish Times*, 4 Sept. 1915.
10 S. Parnell Kerr, *What the Irish regiments have done* (London, 1916), 150–1; Ashmead-Bartlett's despatch, first published on 12 May 1915, can be viewed in full at http://www.anzacsite.gov.au/1landing/bartlett.html (accessed 17 Nov. 2012).
11 *Irish Times*, 16 Oct. 1915.

12 Redmond, foreword to MacDonagh, *The Irish at the front*, 3.
13 See for example Parnell Kerr, *What the Irish regiments have done,* 135: 'Shall we be wrong in thinking that they were so chosen because it has been proved over and over that the Irish soldier, with his high courage and contempt for danger, his dash and initiative, is peculiarly fitted for work of this kind'. See also MacDonagh on the 6th Munsters at Suvla Bay: 'Fixing bayonets they rushed up with a wild Irish yell, and so great was their dash that they actually reached the crest…They were like so many madmen', MacDonagh, *The Irish at the front*, 92.
14 See for example Bean, *The story of ANZAC*, vol. 1 (Sydney, 1933), 46: 'The Australian of the bush is frequently called upon to fight bush-fires…and fighting bush-fires, more than any other human experience, resembles the fighting of a pitched battle'.
15 *Weekly Irish Times*, 30 Oct. 1915.
16 *Irish Times*, 17 Sept. 1915.
17 *Account of a visit to the front by J.E. Redmond, MP in November 1915: with a speech delivered by Mr Redmond on 23 November 1915* (London, 1915).
18 *Irish Times*, 4 Sept. 1915.
19 Bryan Ricco Cooper, *The Tenth (Irish) Division in Gallipoli* (London, 1918), 139; this was echoed by Parnell Kerr's claim that 'these deeds are secure for other days than ours—for "time immemorial"', Parnell Kerr, *What the Irish regiments have done,* 148.
20 Cited in the *Weekly Irish Times*, 25 Dec. 1915.
21 *Weekly Irish Times*, 25 Dec. 1915.
22 MacDonagh, *The Irish at the front*, 102.
23 MacDonagh, *The Irish at the front*, 73.
24 Redmond, speech to the House of Commons, Nov. 1915, reprinted in *Irish Times*, 3 Nov. 1915.
25 *Irish Times*, 5 Nov. 1915.
26 Henry Hanna, 'The Irish at Suvla Bay', *Irish Times*, 7 Dec. 1915.
27 'Valour and the censor', *Irish Times*, 7 Dec. 1915.
28 See Anne Dolan, *Commemorating the Irish Civil War: history and memory, 1923–2000* (Cambridge, 2003), *passim*.
29 The figure itself is open to dispute due to the number of Irishmen who enlisted in British and colonial regiments, and the number of non-Irish who served in the Irish divisions. The Irish National War Memorial at Islandbridge records a figure of 49,400—a figure widely thought to be inflated.
30 More commonly 'Sedd-el-bar': the name of the town and Turkish fortress at the southern-most tip of Gallipoli that visited carnage upon the Dublin and Munster Fusiliers (British 29th Division) at V-beach on the morning of 25 April 1915.
31 See Orr, *Field of bones*, 228.
32 Sebastian Barry interview with Sophie Rochester on being nominated for the 2008 Booker Prize, see http://www.themanbookerprize.com/perspective/articles/1137 (accessed 17 Jan. 2013).
33 Orr, *Field of bones*; Kildea, *Anzacs and Ireland*. See also the 2005 documentary, *Revealing Gallipoli*, with Keith Jeffery, Savas Karakas and Peter Stanley (December Films, 2005).
34 Paul Murray, *Skippy dies* (London, 2010), 542. Thanks to Margaret Ayres for bringing this to my attention.
35 *Irish Times*, 25 Mar. 2010.

4

More than a 'Curious Footnote': Irish Voluntary Participation in the First World War and British Popular Memory

Catriona Pennell

A 'curious footnote'

In 2009 the popular British Radio 1 DJ and television presenter Chris Moyles took part in the much-watched BBC genealogy series, *Who do you think you are?* in order to trace his Irish heritage.[1] His journey ended in western Belgium. Here, on 2 November 1914, his great-grandfather, James 'Jimmy' Moyles, aged forty, was shot dead whilst serving with the Connaught Rangers. A tragically familiar story, he was one of the more than fifty-eight thousand British casualties of the First Battle of Ypres (October–November 1914). However, what came as a surprise to both Moyles junior and the television audience was the fact that Jimmy was an Irish nationalist raised in rural west of Ireland, and had trained Irish Volunteers in the summer of 1914 in preparation for armed conflict with their paramilitary opposites, the Ulster Volunteer Force (UVF), at the height of Anglo-Irish antagonism over the introduction of home rule.

Following the programme's broadcast, a British journalist described this discovery as 'another curious footnote' in British history.[2] In three simple words, the eager readiness with which Irish nationalists signed up to fight in the British army in the First World War was consigned to a long list of minor 'additions' that should not distract from the dominant story of the British Tommy who fought in the trenches of France and Flanders. As a British-born historian of the First World War whose undergraduate and postgraduate education was undertaken in Ireland and whose research interests for the past decade have, therefore, included Irish participation in the conflict, I found this dismissal intriguing if not a little insulting.

In this chapter I take this notion of a 'curious footnote' as my start and end point. First, I will briefly outline the latest historiography relating to Irish military and civilian participation in the First World War in order to demonstrate the level of voluntary self-mobilisation that existed *across* the United Kingdom of Britain and Ireland between 1914 and 1916. I will then return to the 'curious footnote'. Despite significant inroads in the historiography of this topic, why has this idea of Irishmen and women *consenting* to participate in the First World War failed to penetrate British popular understandings of the war? Why, in Britain, does this part of the story remain a 'curious footnote'?

Irish participation in the war, 1914–16

Nowhere is this sense of voluntary participation more acute than in the issue of Irishmen enlisting in the British army. It is well known that, unlike the

Continental armies, Britain had to rely on volunteerism, rather than conscription, to swell the ranks of its armed forces in 1914. This was the case until conscription was introduced in January 1916, a fate that Ireland avoided, albeit narrowly, for the duration of the war. This was due to the fragile political situation in Ireland; for Britain to impose conscription on a nation whose independence it withheld was interpreted by many in Ireland as a step too far. Nonetheless, it is worth emphasising that, unlike Britain, Irish enlistment in the British army during the First World War remained voluntary throughout.

Around 210,000 Irishmen contributed to the British wartime forces, although this figure does not include natives of Ireland who joined units in Britain and elsewhere. Whilst Ireland's response to the call for recruits was always lower than in other parts of the United Kingdom, research by Patrick Callan and David Fitzpatrick, among others, has indicated that Ireland, in the words of Keith Jeffery, 'was not so dramatically out of kilter with other parts of Britain and the empire as has sometimes been assumed'.[3] Patrick Callan has calculated a six-monthly recruiting index for the whole war. Taking the first six-month period as 100, the recruiting response then declines considerably over the next twelve months to 50, then 40. But whilst the numbers of Irishmen enlisting were lower than elsewhere in the UK, the actual rate of decline was very similar. The British index for the first three periods of six months—100, 50 and 39—shows hardly any difference at all. Even after the Easter Rising in 1916, the British were still able to obtain a large number of recruits from Ireland via volunteerism rather than compulsion. Between 15 March and 15 June 1916, six thousand men volunteered from Ireland, fifty-six per cent of them after the Rising. This revival was particularly marked in Dublin and among Catholics.[4]

What was the make-up of these Irish recruits? Not all Irishmen who volunteered were unionists naturally affiliated to the British. The example of Belfast illustrates the limited relationship between political affiliation and recruitment. Based on police records and figures published in the press, just under thirty per cent of the pre-war Belfast UVF had enlisted by December 1914; by the same point, thirty-seven per cent of the city's National Volunteers had also enlisted—hardly any difference between the two. Despite Belfast being the most politically polarised city in Ireland, similar levels of volunteering occurred on both sides. This trend of marginal difference continued: by January 1918, seventeen per cent of Irish recruits were identified as National Volunteers, with nineteen per cent from the UVF. Across Ireland, the evidence attests to the fact that Irish nationalists volunteered at reasonably high levels.

Lower rates of enlistment in nationalist southern Ireland can be best explained by the rural–urban, agricultural–industrial divide rather than any sense of anti-British political antipathy. David Fitzpatrick argues that the difference between Irish and British volunteering rates can largely be accounted for 'by the scarcity of urban adult males who constituted the most likely material for the army'.[5] The family farm remained dominant in the organisation of Irish labour in 1914; evidence suggests that men from farming families were discouraged from enlisting owing to the negative impact this would have on the communal-family income.[6] As in Britain, the bulk of the rural population supported the war but believed their loyalty was better expressed through increased agricultural output than by enlistment in the armed forces. Although statistically Ulster did provide the majority of Irish recruits in 1914, this cannot be explained by religious beliefs and political loyalty; it was more likely due to the influence of Belfast and its urban population, who would have been inclined to join the army regardless of their politics.[7]

It was not only the Irishmen who enlisted in the British army who displayed a marked sense of voluntary self-mobilisation for the British war effort; many Irish non-combatants, particularly women, responded to the new wartime circumstances by offering assistance to soldiers who they believed were 'now fighting for our rights and liberties'.[8] Voluntary work in Ireland drew support from all classes, religious denominations and political affiliations. Soldiers were cared for via fund-raising events, letter-writing and the sending of comforts. Local businesses sponsored this work, such as the Cork Steam Packet Company, which transported Red Cross goods free of charge.[9] Soldiers' dependants were also looked after by the Prince of Wales' National Relief Fund; in Cork alone, by 28 September over £2,600 had been raised via this fund, which was a symbol of the British royal family. The intense feeling for Belgium and sympathy with its sufferings were manifested in a practical way when the refugees began to arrive in Ireland. Associations and organisations sprang up to help these 'victims of the monstrous barbarity of the enemy', and as representatives of a Catholic nation, Irish people felt inclined to answer the call.[10] When Belgian refugees were entertained at the Palace Theatre in Cork, the 'house was specially decorated for the occasion, prominently displayed being the Irish and Belgian flags entwined, and surmounted by the Union Jack'.[11] On 7 December Mabel O'Brien described to her painter husband Dermod how, at the end of a charitable concert in Newcastle, Co. Down, 'God Save the King was sung and the audience all rose to their feet. Think of that now!'[12] As casualty lists and news of the missing trickled to the home front, Irish people also mobilised to support the domestic victims of war, offering comfort and time with grieving and devastated families.

Voluntary self-mobilisation did not always manifest itself in practical, positive support for victims of war. Other less positive emotions such as anger, fear, hatred, grief and loneliness began to be felt as the shock of the outbreak of war dissipated. On the whole, the population in Ireland, just as in Britain, felt that Germany was the enemy and that the cause against it was just. People feared Germany's aggression, her tyrannical rule and, in Catholic Ireland, her Protestantism. On 11 September, Desmond Ryan, a boarder at St Enda's—the bilingual school founded in 1908 in Ranelagh (later transferred to Rathfarnham) by Patrick Pearse—described to his father the anti-German attitude of the staff and priests at the school.[13] Stories of German atrocities in Belgium were so horrific that they cemented the belief that the Germans were in the wrong and needed to be beaten. Reports of German atrocities—later proven to have a strong basis in fact—were believed by many Irish people in 1914, and this sense of anger and fear at the prospect of similar horrors happening on Irish soil galvanised people into violent action. On 15 and 16

August a series of attacks on German pork-butchers' shops occurred across Dublin. Led by a soldier who had recently enlisted and wanted to start fighting the 'barbarians' immediately, the most serious attacks were on the premises of Frederick Lang in Wexford Street and George Reitz at Leonard's Corner on South Circular Road, Portobello; another attack occurred in Thomas Street. According to the *Freeman's Journal*, the crowd were 'principally of youths' and 'completely wrecked the shop—threw all furniture, fixtures and meat stocks out onto the street'; no reason for the attacks could be ascribed 'except that the proprietors of the premises were believed to be German'.[14] Further, smaller, attacks also occurred in Dublin following the destruction of Louvain on 25 August. German atrocities and violations of Catholic landmarks in Belgium had stirred certain people into action.

Irish people also self-mobilised to defend against suspected spies. On 4 August a gentleman of 'foreign appearance' and two women who accompanied him were arrested in Crosshaven, Co. Cork, on charges of espionage; sketches and photos of the harbour were found in the man's possession.[15] Shortly after war broke out, leading Cork chess player F.U. Beamish was arrested for suspicious behaviour after being seen 'studying a position on a pocket chess board' in a local park.[16] Some people even believed that German spies in Ireland had caused the outbreak of the war: they were able to convey to the Kaiser the extent of domestic discontent within the country in July 1914, suggesting to the Germans that it was the optimum moment to start a war on the Continent.

Just as it is a falsification of reality to say that in 1914 Ulster offered complete support to the war whilst nationalist Ireland saw 'England's difficulty as Ireland's opportunity', it would be inaccurate to paint a rosy picture of 1914 Ireland as entirely united and in agreement regarding the justice of Britain's war effort. Dissent amongst a minority of Irish nationalists continued during the first five months of war. John Redmond's September extension of Irish support for the war to foreign battlefields produced the well-known crisis within the Volunteer movement; it split into two sections, the bulk of its membership remaining with Redmond whilst a small minority—retaining the name of the Irish Volunteers—vehemently opposed the war and, above all, campaigned against Irishmen volunteering to fight in it. Although the anti-war faction led by Eoin MacNeill made up only around six per cent of the Volunteers, the split would have serious ramifications. A revolutionary conspiracy began to take shape in which the whole concept of home rule was irrelevant. However, the crucial point is that prior to Easter 1916 their impact was limited. For the state, the major security concerns in Ireland in the first year of the war related to the German enemy rather than to dissident nationalists. By November 1914 the British authorities in Ireland felt that advanced nationalist opinion was of little significance; a memorandum on the publication and circulation of seditious newspapers in Ireland published in early January 1915 stated that for the time being the threat they posed had dissipated.[17]

Bringing the margins into the mainstream

Placing Ireland in an all-UK context rather than projecting back onto 1914 the divergent responses that occurred after the Easter Rising two years later has demonstrated the significant degree of volunteerism and consent that was embodied in the initial Irish response to war. Although the terms of Irish support were not those of Britain, the level of support (in nationalist as well as unionist Ireland) was very high. The immediate outbreak of war caused similar feelings of anxiety, shock and concern, and comparable levels of dislocation and change across the United Kingdom. Irish people, on the whole and regardless of political affiliation, rallied voluntarily in support of charitable-relief efforts. These acts of solidarity allowed room for Irish and British identities to work together. At fund-raising events, Union Jacks were used alongside Irish and Belgian flags. Equally, Irish people felt anger and suspicion towards the German enemy both within and without. The enemy for the majority of Irish people in 1914 was Germany—not unionists or nationalists. Moreover, a large number of Irishmen volunteered for the British army, and the peaks and troughs of recruitment followed a UK-wide pattern.

The major difference between the British and Irish experience in 1914 was the complicated political situation. However, nationalist Ireland did enter the war in 1914, and believed that support for the declared aims of Britain—honour, freedom and the liberty of small nations—would benefit Ireland. Irish nationalists contributed on an almost equal level with unionists in terms of volunteers and charity, and experienced fear, rumour, anticipation and emotion in parallel with that experienced in Britain. British fears of dissident nationalist reactions were vastly exaggerated, although these, too, would contribute to the polarising effect of the 1916 Rising due to the severity of the British response.

Nonetheless, the level of voluntary and self-mobilised support for the war amongst the Irish in the first sixteen months of the conflict makes it abundantly clear that this all added up to a lot more than a 'curious footnote' casually tagged onto British histories of the war. So why has the most recent research not penetrated popular understandings in Britain?

To a large extent, Ireland's absence can be explained by the Anglocentric exclusivity of First World War remembrance in Britain. Certain tropes, stereotypes and clichés combine to create a British national perception of the conflict. The war is seen as a tragic disaster fought mainly in the muddied, rat-filled and lice-ridden trenches of the Western Front by young, innocent 'Tommies' led by imbecile generals who wilfully sacrificed their men for a cause that would, with the outbreak of the Second World War, be proven to be utterly pointless. It is overwhelmingly an *English* story with little room for the reality of a multinational, multi-ethnic, multifaith British army that consisted of soldiers not only from Ireland but also Wales, Scotland, Australia, Canada, India, Newfoundland, New Zealand, South Africa and from areas of Africa and the Middle East. Together, they participated in a global conflict that would eventually, to varying degrees, involve around a hundred countries in Africa, the Americas, Asia, Australasia and Europe.

For over twenty years, academics have challenged the myths and misrepresentations of the war. Revisionist studies have pointed to the wide diversity of experiences of soldiers, the tactical advances made by the British army, and the reasons for the Allies' eventual victory. By their own admissions, however, these attempts have largely failed to undermine the popular memory of the war in Britain. The grip of 'memory' has proved too hard to shift.[18] Academic historians are battling in an 'uphill struggle' to reach a British public brought up on the 'war poets' and informed by newspaper articles and television programmes that, on the whole, continue 'plucking the chords of memory' to remind audiences of what they already remembered about the war, and reinforcing the standard images of horror, slaughter and futility.[19] Focusing on the war poets in the teaching of the war in schools has skewed the memory of the war in Britain, boiling it down to the experiences of a handful of ethnically and socially homogeneous literary 'truth-speakers'. Ian Beckett and Gary Sheffield have written critically about the way in which the First World War is taught in British schools, noting how very little revisionist history has filtered into recommended school textbooks.[20]

When it comes to the way the First World War is taught, there appears to be an implicit assumption that pupils should have a fixed canon of topics; these are both exclusive and ethnocentric. The closest students usually get to any 'global' sense of the First World War in British classrooms is an occasional discussion of the US entry in 1917. An examination of some of the standard texts used at key stages 3 and 4 of the National Curriculum reveal a dominant focus on the Western Front from an English perspective. Ireland—either in terms of an Irish contribution to the Battle of the Somme or the 1916 Easter Rising as a major event of the world war—is almost entirely absent.[21] This is reflective of the Anglocentric nature of the National Curriculum more generally. Despite support arising from policy initiatives such as the Parekh report (2000) and the Ajegbo report (2007) for teaching a national story that includes all of the communities within Britain and Ireland, non-English dimensions are included at key stages 2 and 3 only 'where appropriate'—hardly a compelling endorsement for already overstretched primary and secondary schoolteachers of history in the UK.[22]

The Anglocentric nature of British understandings of the First World War was exemplified in the London-based coverage of the state visit by Queen Elizabeth to Ireland in May 2011. The visit included highly symbolic wreath-laying ceremonies at the Garden of Remembrance in Parnell Square, commemorating the generations of republican Irishmen and women who fought and died to end British rule in Ireland, and the National War Memorial at Islandbridge, where the 49,400 Irish war dead of the First World War are remembered. Whilst the historic occasion was covered with great interest and a sense of prestige and goodwill by all the major British newspapers and television channels, the analysis did not go much further than 'isn't this good for Anglo-Irish relations and the peace process'. Even the usually nuanced *Channel 4 News* reported the memorial visits in terms of 'moving forward' from a troubled past, without any suggestion of what that past actually meant in terms of the crucial period of 1914–21.[23] The point is that, even on this auspicious occasion, Ireland's participation in the First World War was seen as newsworthy in mainstream British media only in terms of current politics and with virtually no understanding of the past.

At the end of Chris Moyles's journey through his family history, the military historian Peter Barton (who had accompanied him to Ypres) hands him a piece of webbing and a brass buckle from a British uniform of the First World War. Moyles responds enthusiastically:

> Chris Moyles: Wow, that belonged to a British soldier?
> Peter Barton: [Yes] We'll never know who he was…Australian or South African or New Zealand or [pause] Irish.[24]

How many British viewers understood the significance of what Barton had said? How many got past Moyles' focus on that buckle belonging to a 'British soldier' and acknowledged the multinational make-up of the British army during the war? Not many at all, I fear.

Ideally, the British public should be made familiar with more complex interpretations of the war. There should be less obsession with British troops, British battles and British casualties, and, at the very least, an awareness that it took many peoples to make a world war. The centenary offers a unique chance to develop a broadly based and inclusive map of the past, allowing space for Irish—and *all* non-English—participation in the war to be remembered in commemorative and educational activities. Relatively simple changes that broaden and complicate understandings of the war could be made to the National Curriculum with immediate effect. Even if teachers of English rather than history still have more influence in the shaping of views on the First World War, as Brian Bond suggests, what is to stop them from examining the work of Francis Ledwidge, the Irish nationalist war poet from Co. Meath who was killed in action at the Battle of Passchendaele in July 1917?[25] In twenty-first century multicultural Britain there is no reason why the history of the First World War, whether taught in schools or broadcast in the media, should be isolationist, parochial or inward-looking.[26] The centenary should be taken as a once-in-a-lifetime opportunity to help British audiences of all ages—whether via museums, the media or education—to break free from national navel-gazing and open their minds to the multiple experiences of 1914–18.

Notes

1   *Who do you think you are?*, ser. 6, first broadcast on BBC, 22 July 2009.

2   Tom Sutcliffe, 'Last night's television: Who do you think you are?, BBC 1; Wildest dreams, BBC 1', *Independent*, 23 July 2009, http://www.independent.co.uk/arts-entertainment/tv/reviews/last-nights-television-who-do-you-think-you-are-bbc1br-wildest-dreams-bbc1-1757398.html (accessed 3 Oct. 2011).

3   Keith Jeffery, *Ireland and the Great War* (Cambridge, 2000), 6.

4   David Fitzpatrick, 'The logic of collective sacrifice: Ireland and the British army, 1914–1918', *Historical Journal* 38 (1995), 1017–30: 1021. It is also worth noting that there was a further upturn in recruiting after August 1917, quite marked in the last three-and-a-half months of the war despite the debacle over imposing conscription in Ireland in the spring of 1918.

5   David Fitzpatrick, '"The overflow of the deluge": Anglo-Irish relationships, 1914–1922' in Oliver MacDonagh and W.F. Mandle (eds), *Ireland and Irish Australia: studies in cultural and political history* (London, 1986), 83.

6   Fitzpatrick, 'The logic of collective sacrifice', 1028.

7   David Fitzpatrick, *Politics and Irish life, 1913–1921: provincial experience of war and revolution* (Dublin, 1977; new edn Cork, 1998), 110–11.

8   *Church of Ireland Gazette,* 21 Aug. 1914.

9   *Cork Constitution,* 23 Sept. 1914.

10 *Cork Examiner,* 28 Sept. 1914; *Cork Examiner,* 25 Sept. 1914.

11 *Cork Constitution,* 10 Oct. 1914.

12 National Library of Ireland, Dermod O'Brien papers, MS 36,702/4, 7 Dec. 1914.

13 UCD Archives, William Patrick Ryan papers, LA11/E/190/29, 11 Sept. 1914.

14 *Freeman's Journal,* 17 Aug. 1914.

15 National Archives, Kew, CO 903/18, Intelligence notes, 1914.

16 *Cork Weekly News,* 22 Aug. 1914.

17 National Library of Ireland, Joseph Brennan papers, MS 26,159, 22 Jan. 1915.

18 Ian Beckett, *The Great War, 1914–1918* (Harlow, 2001), 464.

19 Brian Bond, *The unquiet Western Front: Britain's role in literature and history* (Cambridge, 2002), 100.

20 Ian Beckett, 'The military historian and the popular image of the Western Front' in *The Historian* 53 (1997), 11–14; Gary Sheffield, *Forgotten victory: the First World War, myths and realities* (London, 2001), 17–18.

21 My thanks to Dr Paul Bracey, University of Northampton, for his assistance on this matter of the First World War, Ireland and the National Curriculum.

22 See Bhikhu Parekh, *The future of multi-ethnic Britain: the Parekh report* (London, 2000); Keith Ajegbo, Dina Kuwan and Seema Sharma, *Diversity & citizenship: curriculum review* (Nottingham, 2007). Note also the impressive work of the 'Ireland in Schools' project, a voluntary body that seeks to make Ireland a part of the normal curriculum in Britain—from primary schools to sixth forms—by making it easy for teachers to draw upon Ireland in their teaching; to this end, it has produced a number of student/teacher work packs, including one on the First World War in an Irish context: 'Fighting for whom? 1916: the Easter Rising and the Western Front', www.iisresource.org (accessed 13 Apr. 2012).

23 See 'Queen's visit to Ireland: "We are ready now to move on"', 17 May 2011, www. channel4.com/news/queens-visit-to-ireland-we-are-ready-now-to-move-on (accessed 10 Apr. 2012).

24 *Who do you think you are?,* ser. 6, first broadcast on BBC, 22 July 2009.

25 Bond, *The unquiet Western Front,* 88.

26 Robert Phillips, *History teaching, nationhood and the state: a study in educational politics* (London, 1998), 134.

5

1916 and Irish Republicanism: between Myth and History

Fearghal McGarry

By exploring the question of what republicanism meant to the rebels of 1916, before the Rising became burdened by the weight of its own myth, this chapter seeks to identify some connections between the history of an event and its commemoration. It emphasises how unpredictable the Rising's success in creating popular support for republicanism was, and argues that this contingent outcome was largely a product of its wartime context. Although the Rising is now synonymous with republicanism, its ideological significance was less apparent at the time: many rebels fought for Irish freedom rather than a republic. The implications of this in terms of contemporary remembrance of the Rising are considered in the conclusion.

Shortly after noon on Easter Monday 1916, Patrick Pearse proclaimed the Irish Republic beneath the shadow of the porch of the General Post Office. In doing so, he provided posterity with the iconic moment of a week that changed Irish history. As a revolutionary, Pearse had many shortcomings, but an understanding of the importance of the power of symbolism, myth and imagination was not among them. Modern Irish history is, admittedly, not short on turning points, and the revolutionary decade has more than its fair share, but the Rising remains the pivotal event of the period. Before 1916, Irish nationalism was dominated by the constitutional tradition represented by John Redmond's Irish Parliamentary Party. A 'home rule' parliament—a constitutional settlement that would keep Ireland not merely within the Empire but the United Kingdom—appeared the most likely outcome of the political crisis that had convulsed Ireland since 1912. Along with much of the centre of Dublin, that alternative future went up in flames in Easter 1916.

By killing home rule, the rebels transformed Ireland, reviving a moribund physical-force tradition and establishing republicanism as the dominant ideology of Irish nationalism. The Rising was not just propaganda of the deed. Legitimised by the sacrifice of its signatories, the Proclamation established the Republic not merely as an aspiration but an existing entity, one that was endorsed in the 1918 general election and given institutional form by the Dáil government of 1919. The rebellion hastened the attainment of independence, but at a cost—whether the death of Dublin's civilians (who accounted for over half the 482 fatalities that occurred) or the subsequent violence that accompanied the shortcut to sovereignty the Rising set in train.

The idea of the Rising as the moment of transformation raises tantalising questions: what if—as appeared likely in the chaotic week leading up to it—there had been no rebellion? Violence against Britain may still have occurred—the Irish Party was struggling, and the Irish Volunteer faction that opposed the rebellion had always maintained that violence was justified under certain circumstances. But the nature and objectives of that violence would have been different. Along with creating a new political elite, the most significant outcome of 1916 was the emergence of a popular movement committed to a republic rather than a lesser form of self-government. It is questionable whether this would have occurred without the Rising given both the lack of popular support for republicanism prior to 1916 and the fact that it was the most extreme and least attainable of the competing objectives advocated by advanced nationalists. As W.B. Yeats quickly recognised, one feature of the Rising was its potential to undermine compromise: 'who can talk of give and take…While those dead men are loitering there'.[1] At the Sinn Féin convention of 1917, Éamon de Valera justified the adoption of a commitment to the Republic as 'a monument to the brave dead'.[2] The emotional legacy of the Rising—a unifying force during the War of Independence—would prove divisive after the end of that conflict, contributing to the Irish Civil War and the tradition of political violence that endured long after the Irish Revolution.

In light of its subsequent importance, perhaps the most striking aspect of Pearse's Proclamation was just how little attention it commanded at the time. Few rebels in the GPO noticed it, and the handful of accounts that survive describe an underwhelming ceremony observed by a 'bemused and indifferent crowd of onlookers'.[3] There is even disagreement as to where it occurred. Pearse is often described as proclaiming the Republic from 'the steps of the GPO' although the building has no steps, while some accounts suggest that it occurred near Nelson's Pillar. Were the rank-and-file rebels simply too busy to appreciate its significance, or does this confusion signify something more revealing: a lack of understanding of—and commitment to—republicanism?

This essay draws on evidence from the Bureau of Military History to consider this question. Established by the Irish government in 1947, the Bureau's investigators (mostly military officers) collected 1,773 witness statements from participants in the Irish Revolution over the course of the following ten years. Only released in 2003, the statements raise questions about subjectivity and the reliability of memory and bias (not least because of the Irish Civil War), but also provide the most important source to date for understanding the Irish Revolution. Their greatest strength lies in the insights they allow into the experiences of rank-and-file revolutionaries—men and women from working- or lower-middle-class backgrounds who rarely recorded their thoughts in letters, diaries or memoirs.[4]

What do the statements tell us about the politicisation of the revolutionary generation and the importance of republican ideology for the rebels? A key question about the period between the fall of Parnell in 1890 and the decade of the Great War is whether, due to the demoralisation that followed the Irish Party split and the impact of the nationalist Cultural Revival, it witnessed a gradual but inexorable shift towards militant separatism. The belief that a revolutionary challenge to British rule was not merely a positive but an inevitable development was endorsed by the nationalist history written after independence.

In contrast, the scholarly historiography that began to appear several decades later emphasised the resilience of the Irish Party and the lack of popular support for separatism until the unpredictable derailing of home rule by the impact of the Ulster crisis, the Great War and the Rising. These contrasting interpretations are identified with opposing political positions: was violence unavoidable in the struggle for freedom, or did it represent a tragic, needless deviation from a constitutional path to independence?

The witness statements submitted by members of the Irish Republican Brotherhood (IRB), the secret society committed to achieving a republic through violent means, reinforce the scholarly interpretation of a weak—even dying—republican tradition. Fenianism was in sharp decline—something many separatists attributed to the appeal of the Irish Party. Diarmuid Lynch, a member of the IRB's supreme council, recalled in his statement: 'in those days of denationalisation there may not have been in a whole district a single man imbued with republican ideas'.[5] The experience of Robert Kelly, an IRB organiser in Newry, typified that of many provincial Fenians: he infiltrated the Gaelic League and Gaelic Athletic Association (GAA), established advanced-nationalist organisations, ran the local trades council, promoted endless campaigns against army recruitment, English imports and imperialism, but failed to win popular support for republicanism. Newry, he concluded, 'was from the separatist viewpoint rotten'.[6]

The witness statements also make clear that, as in earlier periods, the attractions of the IRB for many members were not necessarily ideological; in the west, for example, its appeal often lay in its agrarian radicalism. Even sympathetic observers, such as Kevin O'Shiel, regarded republicanism as anachronistic: 'every sizable town possessed a tiny sprinkling of diehard separatists', he recorded, and 'they were respected as idealists, living in a world and an age to which they did not belong'.[7] And while it is true that an older IRB leadership that was judged too complacent about this was purged in 1912 by the Young Turks grouped around the veteran revolutionary Tom Clarke, the significance of this episode was exaggerated by what followed in 1916. On the eve of the Ulster crisis, the IRB was 'little more than a tiny committee struggling to stay alive'.[8] It was pessimism—rather than confidence—about the future that spurred the determination of a radical minority to rise.

Rather than republicanism, it was the flourishing cultural-nationalist movement, exemplified by the GAA and Gaelic League, that generated much of the energy and enthusiasm of this period. Although many Irish Party politicians and—more so—supporters embraced Irish-Ireland ideals, the movement's success in promoting the notion of a distinctive Irish culture, separate to that of Britain, strengthened the position of those who argued that real independence necessitated something more than a limited form of devolution within the United Kingdom.

The most significant, if unsuccessful, political development of the period was the formation of Sinn Féin in 1905. This initiative reflected a politicisation of the cultural-nationalist agenda and a compromise between the attractions of constitutional politics and the impracticability of physical-force republicanism.

But despite winning the tactical support of republicans, Arthur Griffith's Sinn Féin did not aim to achieve a republic, and sought to use passive resistance and (abstentionist) politics rather than violence to win self-government. Many separatists were frank in describing their support for Sinn Féin as a consequence of the weakness of republicanism: 'a republic did not appeal to the masses, as they considered its attainment impossible', Pat McCartan conceded: 'Outside the IRB there were few republicans and Griffith knew it and so did we. We were mere propagandists and we realised it.'[9]

What light do the witness statements shed on those who grew to adulthood between the fall of Parnell and the Great War? Given how many of those who participated in the revolution were born around 1890, it is possible to speak of a revolutionary generation. They formed the first generation to grow to adulthood after the development of a powerful nationalist movement, and the first to view home rule not as a distant aspiration but a reasonable demand that had been unjustly denied throughout their lifetime. A diverse range of factors contributed to the formation of their political identity: family background and childhood influences; local and communal influences; intergenerational tensions; education; popular traditions of Irish history; print culture; and associational activity. But there is little discussion of ideology in the statements: beyond an activist core, few mention the appeal of Griffith's dual monarchy, Connolly's socialism, or republican thought. For many, politicisation stemmed from hostility to British rule, resentment of the everyday grievances attributed to this, devotion to Gaelic culture, and a commitment to Irish freedom. Even the accounts of members of Na Fianna Éireann—one of the few republican organisations of the pre-war era, and one that produced some of the leading rebels of 1916—indicate that cultural nationalism, Catholicism and militarism were more influential than republican ideology.

A similar ethos characterised the Irish Volunteers, established in 1913 in response to the formation of the Ulster Volunteers. Although the Irish Volunteers presented the IRB—which played an important but secret role in forming the paramilitary force—with an opportunity to infiltrate its leadership, volunteering did not popularise republicanism. Although the movement's rhetoric—with its emphasis on the relationship between manliness, armed citizenship and self-government, and the inadequacy of relying solely on parliamentary means as a means to secure freedom—was republican in tone, the Volunteers were formed to counter the unionist threat to home rule rather than fight for Irish independence. Mass support for the Volunteers derived from the Irish-Ireland movement and popular nationalism rather than the IRB, as was demonstrated by the split triggered by the Irish Party's support for the war effort in September 1914 when over ninety per cent of the 150,000-strong Volunteers backed Redmond. Moreover, as the Rising made clear, there remained much opposition to the IRB's insurrectionists within the Volunteers' depleted ranks.

But although republicanism remained a marginal influence on the eve of the Great War, popular support for the Irish Party did not represent an ideological commitment to the strikingly moderate, conciliatory and imperialistic

vision of nationalism advocated by Redmond and some of his Irish Party col-
leagues. On the contrary, the prevailing discourse of the Irish Party at its grass
roots was one of 'Catholicity, sense of victimhood, glorification of struggle,
identification of enemies, and antipathy to England'.[10] Provincial Irish Party
politicians often proclaimed themselves the legitimate heirs to the revolutionary tradition (just as some Fenians laid claim to the cult of Parnell). Drawing
on the shared cultural and historical influences of popular nationalist tradition, constitutional nationalism and republicanism formed opposing ends of a
spectrum of shifting opinion rather than a rigid dichotomy; hence the alacrity
with which many nationalists deserted the Irish Party for Sinn Féin after 1916:
for many Irish people, the journey from constitutional nationalism to republicanism represented a shift in party loyalties rather than political consciousness.

More unexpectedly, the witness statements raise questions about the
importance of republican ideology within the IRB in the period leading up to
the Rising. Volunteers sworn into the movement during this period describe
remarkably perfunctory ceremonies: 'Eamon Ceannt swore me in looking
over the wall of the Liffey', Liam Tannam recalled.[11] Ceannt swore another
Volunteer in on a busy Dublin street: 'You needn't raise your right hand.
Just remove it from the handlebars of your bicycle.'[12] When he joined, John
MacDonagh recalled, Ceannt was unable to remember the oath.[13] The extent
to which such recruits (including Ceannt, a devout Catholic Irish-Irelander
who—like many of the rebellion's organisers—had only recently joined the
IRB) could be considered republicans in any ideological sense is questionable;
the movement had become primarily a means of secretly coordinating the
insurrection.

Many of the Volunteers who participated in the Rising were—until Easter
Monday—unaware not just of the secret role of the IRB's military council in
bringing it about but also its objective of proclaiming a republic. Shortly before
the Rising, Ned Daly, 1st Battalion commandant, startled Jerry Golden by
telling him how 'he was sure I would do my duty as a soldier of the Republic':

> This was the first mention I had heard from anyone about a Republic, and
> when I asked him what he meant by it…he replied that…the Irish Republic
> would be proclaimed by the provisional government of the Republic. Every
> Volunteer in arms would be expected to defend the Republic with his life if
> necessary and some of the leaders would fall in the fight, but the others would
> carry on even in face of overwhelming odds. While he was speaking to me I
> noticed his eyes. They appeared to shine, and I saw that he was in earnest in
> every word he spoke.[14]

Some rebels recorded their surprise when they learned that a republic had
been declared. When Min Ryan cornered Tom Clarke in the kitchen of the
GPO, where most of the women had been consigned, she asked him what it
was all about:

> I asked him: 'Why a republic?' He replied: 'You must have something striking

in order to appeal to the imagination of the world.' He also said that at all periods in the history of Ireland the shedding of blood had always succeeded in raising the spirit and morale of the people. He said that our only chance was to make ourselves felt by an armed rebellion. 'Of course', he added, 'we shall be all wiped out.'[15]

In contrast to the marginal influence of republicanism, the witness statements indicate that the impact of the Great War was more central to the fluctuations of separatist fortunes and militancy. Frustration, humiliation and pessimism about popular nationalist enthusiasm for the war (described by several witnesses as 'sickening') confirmed the belief of militant separatists in the necessity for a spectacular act of violence. 'It was nearly impossible to see a difference between Ireland and England', Joseph O'Connor recalled; 'Something big should happen to awaken the country.'[16] 'The war was on, and Dublin citizens cheered the fellows going away at the North Wall', Dan McCarthy recollected; 'Something must be done to save the soul of the nation'.[17]

For separatist insurrectionists, the war provided the rationale—or pretext— for the Rising. As early as September 1914, its outbreak had allowed a militant faction to persuade a hesitant IRB supreme council to commit itself to rebellion despite the unpropitious circumstances. Their argument was entirely premised on the Great War and how it provided numerous reasons for insurrection: a distracted Britain, a powerful ally, the promise of weapons and support. Even a wartime defeat would be transformed into diplomatic victory when—as the rebels assumed—Germany won the war. The war provided vital ammunition in the all-important debate within separatism as to whether there should even be an insurrection. W.T. Cosgrave, Ernest Blythe and Denis McCullough recorded how Thomas MacDonagh and Seán MacDermott sought to persuade them to support a rebellion on the basis of what each regarded as implausible claims of German military support: 'I can't decide, in my own mind even yet', McCullough reflected on his conversation with MacDermott, 'whether or not he was trying to deceive me or was deceiving himself.'[18]

The emotional aspects of the wartime context may have outweighed the strategic. Ceannt spoke of the disgrace of allowing the war to pass without rising. Clarke argued that a failure to strike (as his generation had failed during the Boer War) would be humiliating. Pearse spoke of the shame and ridicule that would follow. 'If this thing passed off without us making a fight I don't want to live', MacDermott told a leading Fenian, 'And Tom [Clarke] feels the same.'[19] What united the rebellion's disparate organisers was the belief that, in time of war, action was preferable to inaction; that the advantages of an unsuccessful insurrection—the reassertion of separatist credibility, the survival of the physical-force tradition, the possibility of inspiring popular support and sabotaging home rule—outweighed the consequences of probable military defeat. History, of course, proved them correct, as what must have seemed (particularly by Easter Sunday, with the collapse of the plans for a nationwide insurrection) a desperate roll of the dice reaped spectacular propaganda and political returns.

And Pearse's Proclamation was central. With its dramatic revelation that the Rising had been coordinated by a secret body, it united—at least for posterity—the disparate coalition of secular republicans, Catholic intellectuals, Irish-Irelanders and socialists that had brought it about. Over the years that followed, its ritualistic re-enactment created a powerful impression of ideological coherency that the Rising did not embody at the time. It was a testament to the triumph of the Rising as an act of propaganda that the tricolour that commanded little public recognition at the time would soon be taken for granted as the unquestioned symbol of the independence movement, and the republic its natural objective.

Yet how does this interpretation relate to commemoration of 1916? Three points might be emphasised. First, drawing attention to how the Rising as a historical event was infinitely more complex than the historical myth of the Rising is perhaps the most important contribution that historians can make to its commemoration. For those who lived through this period—for whom the future was as unpredictable as our own is to us—the triumph of republicanism was an unexpected outcome rather than a historical inevitability.

Second, although the memory of 1916 is routinely invoked to critique the many shortcomings of the present-day Irish state, the testimony of rank-and-file rebels illustrates tensions between the Proclamation's egalitarian rhetoric and the social conservatism that characterised much of the revolutionary movement. Prior to 1916, few veteran Fenians could have anticipated how quickly republicanism would emerge as the dominant ideology of nationalist Ireland. Equally, many would have been surprised by the extent to which it came to be defined by a narrow commitment to a means (physical force) and an end (a separate thirty-two-county state) rather than the more radical ideals advocated by earlier generations of republicans. The patriarchal, clericalist and conservative state that emerged from Ireland's revolution was perhaps less a betrayal of the Proclamation than a consequence of the fact that its ideals were never deeply rooted within the nationalist movement that won independence.

Third, the centrality of the war reinforces the idea—long advocated by historians but less publicly accepted—that 1916 formed part of the broader historical experience of the Great War rather than an event that occurred parallel to it. It is perhaps impossible to disentangle the triumph of republicanism from its wartime context. The war explains much that is otherwise inexplicable about the British state's response to the rebellion: the army's tactics at Mount Street; the willingness to devastate the city centre by artillery bombardment; the peremptory nature of the executions; and the heavy-handed coercion that followed. The attempt to impose conscription on Ireland—possibly as important as the Rising in ensuring republican success in the 1918 general election—is similarly explicable only in terms of the subordination of Irish policy to British wartime interests.

The road to 1916 illustrates the interdependent nature of the fortunes of unionism, nationalism and republicanism during the revolutionary decade. That there would have been no Proclamation without the Covenant demonstrates the inadequacy of cherry-picking some events to remember while ignoring others, as has been the practice in the past. Although commemoration of the Covenant on the Falls was no more likely (or, perhaps, advisable) than the presence of Orangemen in Casement Park in 2016, the willingness of both states' politicians and countless civic organisations to approach the decade of centenaries in a spirit of respect and inclusiveness suggests that a shared understanding of our divided past can reinforce rather than undermine the remarkable political transformation of recent decades. Commemoration, after all, is shaped by how those in the present choose to remember their history rather than the atavistic passions of the past.[20] As the inclusion of Croke Park and the Garden of Remembrance on the itinerary of Queen Elizabeth II's state visit to Ireland demonstrated, commemoration of even the most divisive events can have a powerful, if symbolic, conciliatory impact.

Notes

1   Quoted in Charles Townsend, *Easter 1916* (London, 2005), 348.
2   Quoted in Fearghal McGarry, *The Rising. Ireland: Easter 1916* (Oxford, 2010).
3   Clair Wills, *Dublin 1916: the siege of the GPO* (London, 2009), 27.
4   Fearghal McGarry, *Rebels: voices from the Easter Rising* (Dublin, 2011).
5   Bureau of Military History (BMH) witness statement (WS) 4 (Diarmuid Lynch).
6   BMH WS 181 (Robert Kelly).
7   BMH WS 1770 (Kevin O'Shiel).
8   Owen McGee, 'Who were the "Fenian dead"? The IRB and the background to the 1916 Rising' in Gabriel Doherty and Dermot Keogh (eds), *1916: the long revolution* (Cork, 2007), 109.
9   BMH WS 99 (Patrick McCartan).
10 Michael Wheatley, *Nationalism and the Irish Party: provincial Ireland 1910–1916* (Oxford, 2005), 266.
11 BMH WS 242 (Liam Tannam).
12 BMH WS 511 (Michael Lynch).
13 BMH WS 219 (John MacDonagh).
14 BMH WS 521 (Jerry Golden).
15 BMH WS 399 (Mrs Richard Mulcahy).
16 BMH WS 157 (Joseph O'Connor).
17 BMH WS 722 (Dan McCarthy).
18 BMH WS 915 (Denis McCullough).
19 Quoted in M.J. Kelly, *The Fenian ideal and Irish nationalism, 1882–1916* (Woodbridge, 2006), 240.
20 Maurice Halbwachs, *On collective memory* (Chicago, 1992).

6

Ireland and the Wars After the War, 1917–23

John Horne

What happens if we enlarge the time frame of the Great War? European and world politics were militarised well before the war. In both Ireland and the Balkans, the violence that fed directly into the war started in 1912–13, as William Mulligan has shown in chapter 1. Continued militarisation of politics and far worse violence prolonged the fighting beyond 1918. In fact, the Great War was the epicentre of a larger cycle of conflict that did not finish until 1923, with the end of the war between Greece and Turkey, the resolution of the crisis over German reparations—which had led to the French occupation of the Ruhr—and the Bolsheviks' acceptance that for the time being there would be 'socialism in one country', not international revolution. Only in 1924, a decade after the assassination at Sarajevo, did the shadow of the Great War finally dissolve. The ending of Ireland's Civil War coincided with this change in mood and tempo, and arguably was part of it.

The idea is not new. Many contemporaries understood that the Great War had unleashed far more than it could resolve. As Churchill remarked dismissively, 'The War of the Giants has ended; the quarrels of the pygmies have begun.'[1] But not until recently have historians begun to integrate the post-war conflicts—Churchill's 'quarrels of the pygmies'—into our understanding of the war itself. This move is particularly important for Ireland, where even the four years of the Great War have long been seen as merely the backdrop to a national story of revolution, unionist resistance and partition.[2] In Ireland, as elsewhere, the 'quarrels of the pygmies' proved far from negligible in terms of their violence and outcomes. However, by reconnecting them to the epicentre of violence in 1914–18, the significance of the entire cycle is transformed. At least, that is what I want to suggest, and in so doing to ask whether taking a transnational approach to this enlarged time scale offers any new insights into the War of Independence, partition and the Civil War in Ireland.

The claim is not that the Great War explains everything. All the divisions and conflicts that contributed to the war had long pre-histories. But the Great War interacted with those prior trajectories, affecting them—and sometimes totally reshaping them—by its own internal dynamics. 'Dynamic' does not seem too strong a term for a war that lasted so long, required unimagined forms of mobilisation, cost ten million military dead, and exposed the societies that fought it to challenges that many could not meet but which changed them all.

Among those dynamics, three stand out as particularly relevant to the wars after the war. The first is nationality. The Great War confirmed the nation state as the key form of political organisation, and also nationality as the overriding form of political 'identity' in contemporary Europe. Before 1914, multinational dynastic empires (Austria, Russia, Turkey) still presided over much of Eastern Europe. Britain, France and Germany possessed colonial empires beyond Europe, but behaved as nation states within Europe even if their colonial assets bolstered their claims to great-power status. However, in the case of Britain the imperial identity that had emerged with particular strength in the late Victorian and Edwardian periods complicated further an already complex relationship with Ireland, just as the failure to integrate Ireland fully into the United Kingdom gave rise to home rule nationalism and unionist counter-mobilisation, especially in Ulster. The dynastic states of Eastern Europe offered one way of thinking about how to reorganise the relationship between Britain and Ireland, as Arthur Griffith showed with his celebrated 1904 pamphlet proposing the partnership of Austria-Hungary as a model. More influential, however, was the idea of colonial nationhood within the imperial relationship. The example of the settler dominions (Australia, Canada, South Africa) appealed particularly to Irish home rulers well before the onset of the Great War.[3]

One reason why the Great War was so violent and intractable was precisely because it exacerbated nationality and nationalist feeling. It was experienced by most Europeans as a struggle for the defence and even survival of the nation state where it existed, or as a means of bringing it into existence where it did not. The multinational empires laboured under a double burden. They could not safely mobilise a sense of nationality but had to oppose the dissident nationalists who could. This contributed to the downfall of Austria-Hungary and Russia, which faced the demand for national self-determination by significant minority groups. With the defeat of those powers, nation states emerged in the wake of the war in Eastern Europe based on the principle of 'national self-determination'. In the case of Ottoman Turkey, the Young Turks who controlled the government carried out a form of national mobilisation during the war that resulted in murderous campaigns against religious and national minorities, who were seen as the enemy within. This led to the genocide of at least a million Ottoman Armenians in 1915–16, triggered in part by the Franco-British landing in the Dardanelles in which (as Stuart Ward points out in chapter 3) the 10th (Irish) Division participated.[4]

National mobilisation during the war also created problems for Britain in Ireland, where two nations (or two versions of the nation) contended with each other, and generated different, incompatible versions of loyalty (nationalist and unionist) before the radical nationalist challenge of the Easter Rising converted nationalist Ireland to a growing, though never complete, disaffection with the British war effort, and led to the demand for independent nationhood at war's end. As the big guns fell silent in France, Italy and the Balkans in October and November 1918, the rattle of fire could be heard in the so-called 'shatter zones' of the former empires of Eastern Europe, where Russia had withdrawn from the conflict a year earlier and where the successor nation states, soon to be sanctioned by the Paris Peace Conference in 1919, fought to secure their borders or to reclaim minorities trapped in foreign territory.[5] The strife spread to defeated Germany, Austria and Hungary, and to Ireland, north and south, as radical nationalists mounted a guerrilla war against those they saw as the occupying British.

A second wartime dynamic subtly redefined the relations of force within the colonial empires. When Woodrow Wilson rebranded the Allied cause a war for democracy and national self-determination upon American entry into the conflict in 1917, he was thinking of how to put the politics of the Old World onto a new footing. Yet their colonial empires had played a notable role in how Britain and France fought the war, and the 'Wilsonian moment' struck a chord in the nascent nationalist movements of colonies across the world. From Korea and China to India, Egypt and Algeria, intellectuals and nationalist leaders whose aspirations had been spurred on by the ideological rhetoric of the war, and also in some cases by the role their country had played in the imperial war effort, demanded a place at the Peace Conference. Few made it to Paris, and when disappointment turned to disaffection it was met with repression, as occurred with the massacre at Amritsar in the Punjab in April 1919 and the suppression of the nationalist revolt in Egypt the same year.[6] The British and French Empires reached their height in 1919 as they absorbed Germany's colonies and the Ottoman Middle East. But the seeds of post-1945 decolonisation were sown by this second dynamic of the Great War.

The third dynamic was that of class. Class conflict was polarised by the unanticipated need to harness the economy to a war effort that lasted longer than had been anticipated. The Great War ultimately turned on the capacity of each camp to apply the factors of production—food, capital, manufacturing and labour—to its own destructive effort in greater volume than its opponent could. The resultant pressure on living standards and acute labour shortages gave workers considerable leverage, resulting in strikes and protest movements in the last part of the war that fed into revolution in the countries faced with defeat. But it was the success of the Bolshevik revolution that defined class as a new pole of international relations by making it the key preoccupation of one of the great powers, Russia. Both the reality of the revolution and the fantasy of a vast Bolshevik conspiracy to undermine 'civilization' by means of proletarian revolution prompted an ideological counter-revolution in defence of an idealised 'old order' in Central Europe. This overlapped with ethnic and border wars so that in Germany, Hungary and elsewhere, *Freikorps* paramilitaries fought both class and national enemies, as did the fascists in Italy.[7]

The first and second dynamics, those of nationality and colonial empire, seem particularly relevant to the case of Ireland. If true, this suggests that for all its particularity, the Irish Revolution—which by 1923 had given violent birth to two new states embodying sharply opposed senses of nationality, each with an internal minority—can also be studied in relation to how the same two dynamics operated more broadly. Here, I can only suggest how the argument might work.

First, in relation to nationality, the Irish Free State (and the republican tradition of the IRA) was not alone by 1923 in drawing on armed resistance against the prior imperial power as a source of legitimacy for a new or aspirant nation state. Czech and Polish Legionaries who fought with the Allies provided potent myths of military opposition to the old empires and of sacrifice for the new nation states of Czechoslovakia and Poland after 1918, even though most Czech and Polish soldiers had fought as conscripts for those empires. True, military revolt did not take the form of direct insurrection, as in Ireland in 1916, but rather of volunteering for combat with the enemy. But Roger Casement had attempted to raise an Irish brigade in Germany, and the Proclamation famously referred to 'our gallant allies in Europe', both invoking this same logic. It is no accident that the 1916 insurgents modelled their organisation and conduct on conventional armed forces—as befitted the claim to incarnate the Irish nation—rather than seeking to fight a guerrilla campaign. The point is that military action by a volunteer minority was held to embody the will to national sovereignty not just in Ireland but also in several emergent nations.

This became even more important as the 'quarrels of the pygmies' succeeded the 'war of the giants'. In diverse conflicts starting after Russia withdrew from the war at the end of 1917, a mixture of self-constituted militias and paramilitary forces interacted with regular armies as they established or contested the frontiers of new or reconfigured nation states. Irregulars helped to assert the new borders of Poland against Germany, Lithuania and Ukraine before opposing Soviet Russia in 1920 as the latter invaded Poland. In Latvia and Lithuania, military volunteers fought to claim territory but also to express a national project against both the Bolsheviks and the *Freikorps*, who backed the German landed elite. A briefly independent Ukraine was defined through competing paramilitary forces. There were similar events in the Caucasus as Armenians clashed with Azeris and Turks before control was finally reimposed by Bolshevik Russia and the new Republic of Turkey under Kemal Atatürk.

The differences in military and political conditions between these various cases, as well as between all of them and Ireland, are substantial. Prior imperial power had disintegrated more completely in Eastern Europe than had British rule in Ireland. The twin track of insurrection/repression and negotiation was far more characteristic of the Anglo-Irish War than of the conflicts in Eastern Europe because British state power remained operational and able to suspend military repression in order to make political concessions. For all the violence, dialogue was stitched into the process. As Curzon told the Cabinet in July 1920, 'you must negotiate with Sinn Fein. We shall be driven to dominion Home Rule [for the south] sooner or later.'[8] In the case of Silesia, bitterly fought over by German and Polish paramilitaries, it was the League of Nations that had to substitute for state authority, negotiating and policing a settlement.

A further difference lies in the relative importance of inter-communitarian violence in Ireland compared to Central and Eastern Europe and the Caucasus. Forging the nation was a question not just of defending it against the prior imperial power or rival nation states but also of defining its content in ethnic, religious and national terms. The mixture of ethnicities east of the Elbe and on the Caucasian frontier between Russia and Turkey produced some of the most violent episodes in the extended Great War, with the large Jewish population of the former Russian 'pale' (now Lithuania, eastern Poland, Belorussia and

Ukraine) acting as a lightning conductor for ethnic hostilities in the worst pogroms so far seen in the region.[9] Ireland was not exempt from this kind of sectarian violence, especially against the Protestant minority in southern Ireland and where Catholics and Protestants overlapped in working-class areas in the North.[10] For those experiencing it, the sectarian strife in Belfast in 1920–22, recalling the Western Front for some, was truly frightening.[11]

But it is important to keep a sense of proportion. Tim Wilson has shown in his comparative study that communitarian hostility was worse in Upper Silesia than Ulster because in the former case it was a question of forging separate national identities through violence in what had been a very mixed area, whereas in Ulster it was a matter of redrawing the boundaries between long-polarised communities, though admittedly in a climate of heightened political insecurity.[12] Ireland experienced at certain moments and in particular localities something of the logic of national purification—of expelling the ethnic enemy within—that marked much of the post-war violence in Eastern Europe, Turkey and the Caucasus. Had pro- and anti-Treaty forces patched up their quarrel and engaged in a serious war to take Northern Ireland in 1922, the violence against the minorities on both sides might have been far worse. As it was, ethnic strife remained episodic and localised even as it was institutionalised in Northern Ireland. Levels of violence and death bore no comparison to the conflicts further east.

The strongest comparison between the wars in Ireland and Eastern Europe lies in how military action legitimated the national project and even actively forged it. The sophistication with which a parallel-state structure was established in Ireland during the War of Independence (with the underground Dáil administration and law courts) had no counterpart in Eastern Europe, although the Poles did create precisely such a shadow state under infinitely harsher conditions in the Second World War. But, as in Ireland, the military and paramilitary effort in many Eastern European wars helped construct the sense of the nation. Targeting the enemy (the Crown forces and sometimes the Protestant minority in Ireland, Ukrainians and Lithuanians in the case of Poland) forged a sense of loyalty to the national community. Enrolling civil society behind that effort (including women, the young and cultural bodies) replicated something of the national mobilisation for the Great War by the main belligerent societies in 1914–18.

Thus, the Lithuanian Riflemen's Union, which defended Kaunas against the Poles in August 1919, forged one version of the nation and remained a source of national legitimacy in interwar Lithuania, just as Sinn Féin and the IRA saw themselves as the embodiment of the republican nation in the Civil War, and continued to do so long afterwards.[13] The 'unknown soldier' who to this day lies in the Polish national war memorial came not from any of the Great War battles in which Poles fought on opposing sides (in the Austrian, German and Russian armies)—though these are inscribed on the monument— but from the extended struggle with Ukrainian forces at Lwów (Ukrainian: Lviv) from November 1918 to May 1919. The armed volunteer already had a rich past in European national traditions, but he (and occasionally she) operated on an entirely new scale in the creation or confirmation of nation states by military and paramilitary action in the wars after the Great War. In this regard, Ireland fits a much wider European experience.

The impact of the Great War on the colonial empires also places Ireland in a broader context. David Fitzpatrick argues in chapter 14 of this volume that it is historically false and too easy for the purposes of commemoration to present the decade of 1912–23 as one of decolonisation. That is certainly correct insofar as the attempt to create a Greater British nation state in the course of the nineteenth century (including Ireland's representation on an equal footing at Westminster) was politically the opposite of colonisation, while the overlapping connections between such closely related countries might in many cases be better explained in terms of regions. Yet in a more distant past, early modern forms of colonial settlement had left a powerful legacy in Ireland (not least the dense Protestant settlement of Ulster), while in the present, the multifaceted nature of the British Empire offered different ways to think about reordering the relationship of Ireland to Britain. Hence, the image and languages of empire and the reality of a wider imperial context were central to how contemporaries saw, contested and negotiated the break-up of the United Kingdom.

The best-known expression of this process is the relationship between home rule and dominion status within which, in an ironic reversal, unionist Ulster inherited home rule in a partitioned Ireland while the republican South split over accepting (or rejecting) something closer to dominion status, with the possibility of exceeding it but still within a partitioned Ireland. Ultimately, one trajectory of British colonial evolution—that which led the settler dominions to self-government and independence—did provide the framework for ending the Anglo-Irish War and achieving qualified sovereignty, just as it had supplied a justification for Irish nationalists supporting the British war effort in Europe in 1914. Yet that same conflict had witnessed a 'dirty' war between guerrillas and irregular Crown forces whose violence intensified over time, with the occupying forces obliged to use terror in the battle for crucial military intelligence in the face of a resistant population. In the end, the British confronted the stark alternatives of massive military reinforcement in the face of hostile opinion at home or a negotiated withdrawal of the kind that occurred.

This was a logic that would be repeated in colonial settings in Asia, Africa and the Middle East over the following forty years (the French had their own variants in both Indo-China and Algeria). I am not suggesting that the characteristic vicious spiral of terror and irregular warfare on one side and few-holds-barred counter-insurgency on the other were unknown in the wars of Central and Eastern Europe from 1917 to 1923. But it was built into the trajectory of the British wars to maintain the Empire, and this helps explain why the Irish republican warfare of 1919–21 (and its political heritage) exerted such a strong influence on anti-colonial movements in India and elsewhere, to which it served as a model. Not for nothing did Yitzhak Shamir, fighting the British in Palestine with the Irgun movement, take as his *nom de guerre* 'Michael Collins'. Likewise, the British experience of counter-insurgency in Ireland was immediately applied to colonial hot spots destabilised by the war

(Palestine, Egypt), as Charles Townshend has shown us, and these in turn laid the foundations of British resistance to decolonisation after the Second World War.[14]

The third dynamic, class and class conflict, seems the least evident in Ireland. I do not mean to suggest that it had no importance. A buoyant wartime labour market favoured trade unionism, including that of the long-marginalised agricultural labourers, while a vein of 'syndicalism' saw the ITGWU (Irish Transport and General Workers' Union) swell in size and produced episodes such as the 'Limerick soviet'.[15] But, by and large, class was subordinate to nation and nationality as a source of division and conflict. Where there was a significant working class—in the north-east—it was divided by religion and ethnicity. Most of the workers expelled in 1920 from the Belfast shipyards were Catholics (though some were left-wing Protestants). Most Protestant workers were integrated into the unionist structures of the new Northern Ireland state. In the South, the kind of factory and mining working class that drove wartime militancy in other countries barely existed—little munitions production had come to Ireland.

Class thus seems a minor thread. The country escaped the supercharged ideological conflicts based on class that afflicted parts of Central and Eastern Europe. Finland, for example, had a similar-size population to Ireland but a strong working class and socialist party. Class, not nationality, fuelled a violent civil war in 1918, in which internal tensions were polarised by the proximity of Bolshevik Russia (from which Finland was establishing its independence) and counter-revolutionary *Freikorps*. In what remained a purely Finnish affair, over one per cent of the population died in six months (36,000 people).[16] This contrasts with a death toll in the Irish Revolution of 2,141 from 1917 to 1921.[17]

Elsewhere in Russia, Eastern Europe and also Italy, the demand for land was stoked by the war. It was promised to Italian peasant conscripts, leading to major land seizures in Central Italy in 1919–20 and provoking a reaction that laid one of the foundations for fascism. Rural nationalism championed land expropriation and redistribution in Poland, Bulgaria and elsewhere, and seizures of the landed estates provided one of the dominant threads of the Russian Revolution—something the Bolsheviks were powerless to control until Stalin carried out collectivisation in the early 1930s. In Ireland, forty years of land reform by the British since the agitation of the 1880s seems to have reduced the rural class system to a relatively minor source of division, notwithstanding a vein of small-farmer radicalism in the west. The proof lay in the solidly conservative foundations of the agrarian order in the Irish Free State.

Where does this leave commemoration? I imagine that the hardest phase of the commemorative cycle in both parts of Ireland will be that relating to the wars after the war, because by definition these were the source of division, incomplete or failed projects and continuing differences. Seeing those events in an all-Ireland pattern would be a first step, and historians of Ireland (North and South) are far more qualified than I am to suggest how to do this. But Ireland's history is also part of a wider European and global story. An earlier, equally sensitive turning point in Irish history, 1690, benefited from being reinterpreted as part both of the Wars of the Three Kingdoms of England, Scotland and Ireland and of a larger European turning point that resolved the wars of religion and their relationship to the early modern state. The Irish events of the 1790s only assume their fullest sense in the context of a second European (and this time global) turning point, that of the American and French Revolutions, which unleashed the secular notions of popular and national sovereignty that still lie at the root of our politics.

It is surely no accident if a third fundamental turning point of modern Irish history, the one that created the two Irelands of the present day, should have been so closely connected to a further transformative episode in European and global history, that of the Great War and its associated cycle of conflict, which made nationality and the nation state the foundation of political and cultural organisation in Europe and, later, across the decolonised world. And if it is not an accident, then we can only gain by seeing this seminal period in contemporary Irish history as an integral part of that wider crisis. This may help us understand all sides in the bitter domestic conflicts of the time as part of a broader set of transformations in which Ireland's place, though particular, was not unique. For commemoration, that seems a good place to start.

Notes

1 Quoted in Norman Davies, *White eagle, red star: the Polish-Soviet War, 1919–1920 and 'the miracle of the Vistula'* (1972; new edn London, 2003), 21.

2 For a recent research project funded by the Irish Research Council for the Humanities and the Social Sciences that sought to extend the chronological framework of the war to 1923, and included Ireland in a transnational European approach, see Robert Gerwarth and John Horne (eds), *War in peace: paramilitary violence in Europe after the Great War* (Oxford, 2012); for the Irish case, see Enda Delaney, 'Directions in historiography. Our island story? Towards a transnational history of late modern Ireland' in *Irish Historical Studies* 148 (2011), 599–621. On Ireland and the Great War, see John Horne (ed.), *Our war: Ireland and the Great War* (Dublin, 2008; new edn 2012).

3 Arthur Griffith, *The resurrection of Hungary* (Dublin, 1904); F.S.L. Lyons, *Ireland since the Famine* (London, 1971), 251–3; John Darwin, *The Empire project: the rise and fall of the British world system, 1830–1970* (Cambridge, 2009), 297–301.

4 Ryan Gingeras, *Sorrowful shores: violence, ethnicity and the end of the Ottoman Empire, 1912–1923* (Oxford, 2009); Donald Bloxham, *The great game of genocide: imperialism, nationalism and the destruction of the Ottoman Armenians* (Oxford, 2005).

5 Aviel Roshwald, *Ethnic nationalism and the fall of empire: Central Europe, Russia and the Middle East, 1914–1923* (London, 2001); for the term 'shatter zone', see Donald Bloxham, *The final solution: a genocide* (Oxford, 2009), 81.

6 Erez Manela, *The Wilsonian moment: self-determination and the international origins of anticolonial nationalism* (Cambridge, MA, 2007).

7 Robert Gerwarth, 'The Central European counter-revolution: paramilitary violence in Germany, Austria and Hungary after the Great War', *Past and Present* 200 (2008), 175–209; Emilio Gentile, *The origins of fascist ideology, 1918–1925* (New York, 2005).

8 Quoted in Paul Bew, *Ireland: the politics of enmity, 1789–2006* (Oxford, 2007), 401.

9 Mark Levene, 'Frontiers of genocide: Jews in the eastern war zones, 1914–1920 and 1941' in Panos Panayi (ed.), *Minorities in wartime: national and racial groupings in Europe, North America and Australia in the two world wars* (Oxford, 1992), 83–117.

10 Peter Hart, *The I.R.A. at war, 1916–1923* (Oxford, 2003), 223–58; Tim Wilson, *Frontiers*

of violence: conflict and identity in Ulster and Upper Silesia* (Oxford, 2010).

11   Wilson, *Frontiers of violence*, 179.

12   Wilson, *Frontiers of violence*, 159–211.

13   Tomas Balkelis, 'Turning citizens into soldiers: Baltic paramilitary movements after the Great War' in Gerwarth and Horne (eds), *War in peace*, 124–42; Brian Hanley, *The IRA, 1926–1936* (Dublin, 2002), 93–112.

14   Charles Townshend, *Britain's civil wars: counterinsurgency in the twentieth century* (London, 1986).

15   Emmet O'Connor, *A labour history of Ireland, 1824–2000* (Dublin, 1992; 2nd edn 2011), 102–27.

16   Pertti Haapala and Marko Tikka, 'Revolution, civil war and terror in Finland in 1918' in Gerwarth and Horne, *War in peace*, 72.

17   Eunan O'Halpin, 'Counting terror: Bloody Sunday and the dead of the Irish Revolution' in David Fitzpatrick (ed.), *Terror in Ireland, 1916–1923* (Dublin, 2012), 152–3. Though not known with certainty, death in the Irish Civil War was less than in the War of Independence.

Memories

7

Two Traditions and the Places Between

Paul Clark

When I was growing up in Northern Ireland in the 1960s, your religion defined your identity and there was one common question: 'Are you one of us or one of them?' This was shorthand for 'Are you a Catholic or a Protestant?' In truth, I belonged neither to 'us' nor 'them'. My father, an Ulster Presbyterian, had met my mother, a Leinster Catholic, when she nursed in Belfast in the early 1950s. Such is the power of love that, much to the dismay and anger of his parents, my father turned his back on the religion of his birth. He converted, and lost his inheritance in the process. So it was that Ida and Thompson Clark were married at Holy Cross Church, Ardoyne, in north Belfast, in October 1952. It was not a lavish spread. Apart from the priest and my parents, only two other people were present—both friends who acted as witnesses.

In those days, the rules of the Catholic Church in Ireland were adhered to almost without question, and *Ne Temere* was a central tenet. My father therefore agreed that we, the children, would be brought up Catholics. I grew up in a lower-middle-class—and largely Protestant—housing estate on the outskirts of the city, balancing quite comfortably on the fault lines between cultures. It helped that my name was neutral and betrayed neither one side nor the other. Although a Catholic, I helped my Protestant friends build the bonfire that was burned on the night before the Glorious Twelfth of July. As the effigy of the Pope went up in smoke, my pals used to joke, 'Next year, Clarkie, we're going to put you up there.'

However, once I went to grammar school, I discovered that 'the times, they [were] a changing'. The nearest Catholic school was that of the Christian Brothers on the Falls Road. They educated me, but culturally the school was a world away from my home. From my first day there, my views were challenged and I discovered a history of separation that was quite at odds with the socially mixed part of town from which I came. We were told that there were no connections between the communities in Northern Ireland. One of the mantras was 'Éire Ghaelach—Éire shaor' (Ireland Gaelic, Ireland free!) When I questioned this received wisdom, my fellow pupils accused me of being an apologist for the 'Brits'; this view was occasionally reinforced by some of the teachers. I was forgiven, however, because I had the same surname (albeit with a slight difference in spelling) as one of the signatories of the Proclamation of the Irish Republic, Thomas Clarke. How I envied the certainties of my classmates.

My own views, formed by my family history, were different. For a start, my paternal grandfather, Jack Clark, was an Ulster-Scot whose own father had come from Scotland in the late nineteenth century. On the day the Ulster Covenant was signed, Saturday 28 September 1912, Jack was at the family church, May Street Presbyterian, just behind Belfast City Hall. While many thousands gathered on the streets outside, eager to sign the Covenant, the Clark family attended a special 'Ulster Day' service conducted by Revd William Patterson. The subject of his sermon, 'The Romish yoke', articulated the fears of the Protestant people at that time. The Covenant was ultimately signed by almost a quarter of a million men, while the Declaration—a sister document to be signed only by women—attracted a similar number. The public response was so overwhelming that my grandfather had to wait until Monday 30 September for his turn to sign. He did so in Victoria Hall, just across the road from his church. That Covenant is a piece of family history in our home in Belfast.

My grandfather's brother, great-uncle Donald Clark, was a member of the Young Citizen Volunteers, the youth corps of the (old) Ulster Volunteer Force (UVF). At the outbreak of war in 1914, Edward Carson pledged that the UVF would fight for king and country, and the force's officers and men went on to form the core of the 36th (Ulster) Division. So Donald Clark, an ardent unionist, became a soldier in the 14th Battalion, Royal Irish Rifles, and fought at the Battle of the Somme on 1 July 1916. He survived the bloodiest day in British military history, and when the war ended he was serving as an officer in the Royal Munster Fusiliers. I sometimes wonder what he made of the political and religious complexion of that particular regiment. Donald Clark died in 1980, living long enough to have known that the conflict he fought in had not been the 'war to end all wars'. I regret never asking him about his experiences, though, on reflection, I suspect he would not have talked about them.

My maternal grandfather, Peter Reilly, from Ardee, Co. Louth, came from the 'other tradition'. He could talk to me about the excesses of the Black and Tans during the War of Independence. Many were former soldiers who had learned their trade in the trenches of Flanders during the Great War. Though the fighting was worse in other parts of the country, Grandpa Reilly told me the 'Tans' had a fearsome reputation and that it was their job to make Ireland hell for the rebels. They terrorised communities at will, but all they succeeded in doing was uniting the people against them. I recall a conversation in which he told me the Black and Tans made an example of one young lad by putting a bucket over his head and shooting him. Those who used guerrilla tactics in areas policed by the Black and Tans paid the price.

As a secondary-school student, my interest in history was influenced not so much by my family but by a number of outside events. The first was the broadcast of the BBC's seminal 1964 series, *The Great War*, which captivated me. The second was the death of Sir Winston Churchill in 1965, which was followed by his state funeral and numerous television documentaries about his life. The third was the weekly magazine series *Purnell's History of the Second World War*, followed by *Purnell's History of the First World War*. I read them avidly. This caught the attention of my history teacher, Dan Cashman, who was originally from Cork and was said to have been interned in Northern Ireland during the Second World War. He was aware of my passion for the period, so when we studied the Great War—as part of European history—'Wee Dan', as he was affectionately known, suggested that I take the class. I regret to say that this arrogant teenager rose to the challenge. The record does not reveal how effective I was as a teacher, but I will always be thankful to Mr Cashman for his encouragement.

My recollection of the 1960s is that commemoration was exclusive and nobody really challenged their neighbours' shibboleths. Unionist and nationalist may have lived side by side, but they inhabited parallel worlds, and Catholics were almost a state within a state. I recall the fiftieth anniversary of the Easter Rebellion while at school in 1966. In classroom discussions, the leaders were virtually deified. I remember a popular image of a young boy, about my own age, kneeling and praying with a thought bubble featuring Patrick Pearse above his head; this picture left nothing to the imagination. Yet although I lived in a predominantly Protestant and unionist area, I have no recollection of the fiftieth anniversary of the Battle of the Somme later that same year. This is despite the fact that the Orange Order would have been to the fore at such an event. Veterans would have paraded through Belfast, including, I presume, my great-uncle Donald Clark, but it did not register with me at the time. Nor was the poppy the source of division it would become a few years later; yet, even at that time, few Catholics wore one. I recall only two people who did when I served as an altar boy at Mass on Remembrance Sunday: one was my father, the other a civil servant. When I asked our priest about commemorating the war dead, he replied that the Church remembered all the dead during the month of November. He may have been telling me the truth, but I still believe it was a fudge.

These differing experiences, and the discomfort they evoke, have accompanied me throughout my working life in journalism, especially as I covered the story we now call the 'Troubles'. There was one incident in particular where the present and the past collided head on: the IRA bombing of the Remembrance Sunday service at Enniskillen in 1987. A former garrison town, Enniskillen had a military history preceding the Battle of the Boyne. It was also a favourite place of mine as I had been married there. What happened that day was nothing short of sacrilege, and hurt me deeply. I still worked for the BBC in Northern Ireland at the time, and had been paying my own respects at the Cenotaph in Belfast when I heard about the bomb. The attack provoked moral outrage around the world; innocent people murdered while remembering the war dead. Though all those who were killed were Protestant, there were many Catholics at the war memorial, too. I knew some of them. They included the head of the local branch of the Royal British Legion, a Corkman who had settled in Enniskillen.

The tragedy turned the spotlight on Gordon Wilson, a local draper, originally from Leitrim, who had lost his daughter that day. It also prompted the singer Chris de Burgh to pen a song entitled 'At the war memorial', in which he referred to the last words of Marie Wilson to her father: 'Daddy, I love you very much':

And her words did more to make us one,
Than a hundred years of a bomb and gun,
Let the so-called patriots
See what they have done!

U2—then on a major tour of the United States—also responded vocally to the massacre at Enniskillen. On the day of the bombing, during a performance of 'Sunday Bloody Sunday', Bono condemned IRA violence during a furious rant in which he yelled 'Fuck the revolution'. Condemnation came from all parts of Ireland. The lord mayor of Dublin, Carmencita Hederman, broke down as she delivered a book of condolences to the town.

Even though the conflict had begun almost twenty years previously, the senselessness of the Enniskillen bombing genuinely shocked and horrified people from both sides of the divide. And although it tends to be forgotten, there could have been an even greater tragedy that same day, at Tullyhommon, fifteen miles away. This Fermanagh village sits on one side of the stream that marks the border with Pettigo, Co. Donegal. Members of the Boys' Brigade, Girls' Brigade and other youth organisations affiliated to the local Presbyterian, Methodist and Church of Ireland congregations assembled with veterans at a lay-by beside the main road before parading into the village and dispersing to their churches. Unknown to them, the IRA had planted a bomb that, had it exploded, would have wiped out a generation of Protestant children in this area. We only learned of this 'near miss' when the IRA contacted our newsroom that evening to say that a second bomb had not detonated. We subsequently discovered why: without knowing it, a farmer on a tractor had driven over the command wire and severed the connection. The terrorists, watching the children and veterans from the Donegal side of the border, would only have realised this when they attempted to detonate the bomb.

Having covered the Enniskillen atrocity, its immediate aftermath and subsequent commemorations, I was aware that this event had contributed to a change of attitude regarding remembrance in Northern Ireland. There was a great deal of reaching out on both sides. Catholics began to publicly remember relatives who had served in the Great War but whose memory had been kept within the confines of their family. Although few would have chosen to wear a poppy, they nevertheless became less uncomfortable with it, and began attending Remembrance Day events. In fact, the Enniskillen bombing marked a turning point in the Northern Ireland conflict, and should be seen as a milestone on the road to peace. During her inaugural address as Irish president ten years later, in November 1997, Mary McAleese referred to the horror of Enniskillen and the language of Gordon Wilson:

> His words of love and forgiveness shocked us as if we were hearing them for the very first time, as if they had not been uttered first two thousand years ago. His work, and the work of so many peacemakers who have risen above the awesome pain of loss to find a bridge to the other side, is work I want to help in every way I can. No side has a monopoly on pain. Each has suffered intensely.[1]

One year later, on 11 November 1998 (the eightieth anniversary of the end of the Great War), President McAleese and Queen Elizabeth stood side by side—as equal heads of state—at Messines in Belgium, where Irish soldiers, unionist and nationalist, Catholic and Protestant, had fought and died together in June 1917. Central to the Messines project were two men: Paddy Harte, a Donegal TD, and Glenn Barr, one of the leaders of the Ulster Workers' Council (UWC) strike of 1974, which, coincidentally, provided my baptism of fire in broadcast journalism. The UWC strike paralysed Northern Ireland, and brought down the power-sharing government that stemmed from the Sunningdale Agreement. Barr and Harte came from completely different backgrounds, but they could find common cause in attempting to understand the reasons why Irish soldiers, of different political complexions, had gone to war between 1914 and 1918. The Peace Park at Messines is a powerful testament to their efforts, and has been endorsed not only by two governments but, more importantly, by the Irish people.

Four years later, Alex Maskey became the first Sinn Féin lord mayor of Belfast. Maskey was keen to make a gesture of reconciliation on the occasion of the annual commemoration of the first day of the Battle of the Somme, 1 July. Attending the official ceremony organised by the Belfast City Council was still a step too far, so he instead went to the city hall Cenotaph two hours before the official service and laid a laurel (not a poppy) wreath. It was, he said, a tribute to all the men who had made the supreme sacrifice at the Somme and during the First World War. On a subsequent visit to the battlefields with the lord mayor of Dublin, both first citizens were offered a poppy to wear. Not surprisingly, Alex Maskey declined, but his counterpart, Dermot Lacey, accepted.

In recent years I have been encouraged by UTV (Ulster Television) in my work as a broadcaster to explore the differing attitudes to the poppy and to remembrance more generally. It has been a labour of love—one born of my own family experiences and my passion for history. I began by telling the story within a Northern Ireland context, focusing on the street battles of the early 1920s in Londonderry (Derry) when Catholic and Protestant ex-servicemen continued to fight their war, against each other, at rival commemorations. In Belfast, the Orange Order remembered—and remembered all too well—the sacrifice of the 36th (Ulster) Division at the Somme. In the end, Catholics stayed away, and, by default, remembrance became a one-sided affair. In fact, in those days, and until relatively recently, you could have been forgiven for thinking that it was only Ulster Protestants who fought and died for king and country during the Great War. The reality, of course, was that more Irish Catholics had fought and died in British uniforms than Protestants.

Once I had told the story of remembrance in Northern Ireland, I wanted to look beyond my own border to see how commemoration was viewed in the Republic. UTV reaches all of Ireland, and attitudes were changing in the Republic, too. My programmes met with a surprising, and encouraging, reaction, as people reclaimed the memory of the Great War. Even President McAleese agreed to be interviewed by me in this context. In one documentary, recorded on the former Western Front, it was hard not to be moved by the tears of a family visiting a war grave for the first time. These soldiers may have worn the uniform of the Crown, but that did not make them bad Irishmen.

However, not all stories had 'happy' endings. James Duffy, for example, from Gweedore, Co. Donegal, had enlisted in the Royal Inniskilling Fusiliers. He was serving as a stretcher-bearer in Palestine in 1917 when, alone and under heavy fire, he tended wounded men and brought them back to safety, undoubtedly saving their lives. He was awarded the Victoria Cross (VC) for 'conspicuous gallantry'. After the war, Duffy returned to Donegal and died in Letterkenny in 1969. When I interviewed his daughter Nelly, she told me that her father had kept his VC in a brown envelope in a drawer at home. It was, she said, 'a curse'. During remembrance time, he would walk the streets of Letterkenny selling poppies. People spat at him and only certain pubs would allow him onto their premises. His daughter remembered him wondering what he had done wrong. Given the political and cultural landscape in Ireland following the First World War, and the unfolding events only a few miles away in Northern Ireland, James Duffy may perhaps have wondered if he had fought on the wrong side.

In my formative years, the iconic moments in our history were fundamentalist. Commemorating the fiftieth anniversaries was fractious because many of the people who had 'been there' were still alive. But today our history is no longer understood in generational terms—as something handed down by parents or grandparents. These same events, half a century later, are viewed much more 'in the round' because so many of those who were alive in the 1960s are now dead. With the passage of time, it has become easier to remember this painful chapter.

Since its formation, Northern Ireland has always been unfinished business and disputed territory. Most people in the Irish Republic have been able to get on with their lives in the knowledge that the past is the past, where some battles were won and others lost. Until quite recently, this was not the case in Northern Ireland, which, for most of my life, has been trapped in its history with a large number of unresolved issues. This began to change in 1998. The Agreement—called either 'Good Friday' or 'Belfast', depending on your politics—helped put the cultural identities of both traditions on an equal footing. In the past, one person's victory was another person's defeat, and for that reason our commemorations were divisive. Today, that has changed because of a much-used phrase: 'parity of esteem'. Both sides can now look at these events in a different way without one being more legitimate than the other. Sinn Féin representatives now say they respect the wearing of the poppy by unionists. In return, they ask that loyalists respect the wearing of the Easter lily by republicans. They may not agree with each other's views or their symbols but both are given equal status, and there is a general recognition that neither side is going away.

This new dispensation in the North was underpinned by the visit of Queen Elizabeth to Dublin in May 2011. When the queen attended the Garden of Remembrance and paid her respects to the people commemorated there, she legitimised Easter 1916 and the subsequent War of Independence. It was raised to the same level as those commemorated at the Irish National War Memorial at Islandbridge. Just as within Northern Ireland, so between North and South two strands of history can be commemorated without either being seen as a victory or a defeat. The state visit laid down a marker that the British and Irish governments and the Northern Ireland Executive are keen to reinforce in the attempt to allow us all to break out of the prisons of our history.

In my own case, my views on commemoration have been informed over many years by the writings of Eoghan Harris and, particularly, Kevin Myers. They have ploughed their unique furrows for a long time. They have also reminded me that we cannot cherry-pick our history; we have to accept the palatable with the unpalatable. I have taken a keen interest in the work of Tom Burke and the Royal Dublin Fusiliers Association (RDFA) and its attempts to put the record straight by rehabilitating the memory of those men who for too long were written out of our history. As a member of the RDFA, my attention has been drawn to Seán Lemass. On the fiftieth anniversary of the Easter Rising, while Lemass was still taoiseach, he was the first 1916 leader to make a positive statement about Irishmen who fought in the Great War:

> In later years it was common—and I was also guilty in this respect—to question the motives of those who joined the new British Armies at the outbreak of the war, but it must in their honour and in fairness to their memory, be said that they were motivated by the highest purpose.[2]

Alas, in those days few people were listening. Ian Paisley even threw snowballs at Seán Lemass when he visited Stormont at the invitation of the then Northern Ireland premier, Captain Terence O'Neill, in an effort to thaw relations in Ireland's 'cold war'. More recently, the family of Seán Lemass has presented documents to Dublin City Library and Archive relating to two British soldiers—second cousins—who were in the trenches when Lemass was fighting the British in the GPO during the Rising. This is just one of the ways in which the old conservatism has been challenged as never before, and it is a timely reminder that in many Irish families young men fought in Flanders and Dublin, each with their own patriotic intentions.

Is it not now time to examine who we really are? Thanks to modern technology—in which I include my own medium, television—the world has become a smaller place, making us all neighbours. Perhaps, after all, our identity is not defined by others. In my own case, if I say I am British I don't want to say I am not Irish. I have found it is possible to be both. So is it not now time to allow ourselves to be who we are without condemning others for what they are not? Our history is more shared than we have ever been allowed to believe, and what matters as much as the two or more traditions to which we may belong are the places between.

Notes

1 *Irish Independent*, 12 Nov. 1997.
2 Anthony Quinn, *Wigs and guns. Irish barristers in the Great War* (Dublin, 2006), 128.

8

Church of Ireland Great War Remembrance in the South of Ireland: a Personal Reflection

Heather Jones

It is 1987 and I am nine years old. My mother is preparing Sunday lunch in our home in a Dublin suburb, after our Remembrance Sunday service. We are not long home; I still have my poppy. On the radio the news is on. My mother suddenly turns to me, shock pale, and says, 'There's been a big bomb in Enniskillen.' We listen to the news. Other people, wearing poppies like me, have been blown up and killed. I realise for the first time that remembrance can be dangerous. A Dublin Protestant child, I start to understand that, in the 1980s, poppies make us different. As an adult, I have since tried to understand why we persisted in wearing them; why it mattered so much that we remembered the world wars. It seems to me now that Great War remembrance within the Church of Ireland minority in the Irish Free State and later Republic was driven by three key characteristics: subversion, intimacy and ritual. Subversion and intimacy were central in the 1920s and 1930s, while in the 1980s, the decade of my own childhood, I experienced remembrance as forms of ritual.

Subversion: 1920s and 1930s

Until recently, to discuss the Irish in the Great War—from whatever background—was to subvert the dominant narrative that heroised 1916 and largely ignored the experience of Irish Great War soldiers. In school, in the early 1990s, just two pages of our Irish history book summarily discussed the First World War, while there were entire chapters on the Land League and home rule. Only recently has detailed scholarly research on Ireland's experience of the First World War begun to appear.[1] As a result, little has been written specifically on the Church of Ireland experience of the Great War.

In my case, I first learnt of the war as oral history. It was rarely explained directly, but there were allusions to it in adult conversations, followed by silences, creating a sense that some enormous, mysterious cataclysm had occurred. As a keen budding historian, I would ask elderly relatives who lived through the 1914–23 period to tell me what it was like, only to find a constant reluctance to talk about those years.

I can now understand this sense of taboo and disaster. For the Anglican minority in the south of Ireland following the change of state in 1922, the experience of the Great War blurred in folk memory with the subsequent turmoil of the War of Independence and the Civil War. The Great War experience was not one separate event but part of a series of disastrous upheavals between 1914 and 1923 that had a catastrophic demographic effect. There was a drop of thirty-four per cent in the Church of Ireland population in the whole of Ireland between the 1911 census (249,535) and the 1926 census (164,215). In the south of the country, Dublin saw a drop of thirty-one per cent, while provincial cities and smaller towns lost as much as fifty per cent of their Protestant populations.[2] The drop in the Catholic population for the same period was two per cent.[3] The change of state also necessitated a difficult cultural realignment, which led to the gradual abandonment of the traditional unionism and combined British-Irish identity formerly held by many Church of Ireland members.

The Great War remembrance practices that I experienced as a child had their origins not just in the war itself but also in these years of disaster for southern Anglicanism. As historians such as Peter Hart have shown, southern Protestants experienced intimidation and violence in the period 1919–23, predominantly from the IRA, which led them to emigrate in large numbers to Northern Ireland, Great Britain and the British overseas dominions—this migration chronologically paralleling the brutal, sectarian anti-Catholic ethnic-cleansing actions that were occurring in the North of Ireland during these years.[4] Southern Church of Ireland Great War commemoration was thus, in part, initially subversive, a response to the religious minority's traumatic experience of the change of state, a topic too taboo to be discussed even in the 1980s when, with the Northern Troubles ongoing, Southern Protestants generally feared drawing attention to themselves, and raising the ghosts of the change-of-state period was definitely something to be avoided.

It was only as an adult in the 1990s that I learned of the extent to which the War of Independence and Civil War was a time of insecurity for the Church of Ireland in the South; indeed, following the IRA killing of unarmed Protestant men at Dunmanway in 1922, the Church of Ireland felt under such threat that a special sitting of the Synod was held, and a deputation chosen 'to seek an interview with the Provisional Government in order to lay before them the dangers to which Protestants in the 26 counties are daily exposed'.[5] Among the delegation was the Church of Ireland archbishop of Dublin, J.A.F. Gregg, who asked Arthur Griffith if Protestants were to be 'permitted to live in Ireland or if it was desired that they should leave the country'.[6] Archive evidence reveals intimidation of religious minorities in 1919–23, driven by nationalism, the strategic imperatives of guerrilla warfare, and socio-economic grievance and rivalry; it was in this dangerous context that the majority of Church of Ireland Great War memorials were unveiled between 1919 and 1921.[7] Thus, Great War commemoration ceremonies in the Church of Ireland in the first decades of the new state were not just about the actual war dead themselves. These events were cultural manifestations of identity by a fearful community in significant demographic decline; the Church of Ireland population in the South of Ireland continued to drop after 1926, and only stabilised for the first time in the 1990s.

Growing up, there was constant existential anxiety about the minority's long-term demographic survival, and the Great War was definitely held up as a major cause of this.[8] In Church of Ireland folk memory, there was a belief that because Protestants had generally married other Protestants up to 1914, the impact of war casualties had affected the minority disproportionately. Within a small Church of Ireland population, the death of its young men at war meant that for the young women left behind it was often not possible to find a marriage partner, leading women to emigrate elsewhere in search of marriage, to 'marry out' by wedding a Roman Catholic, or to face spinsterhood—all of which caused minority population decline. It is not clear to what extent this belief was actually true as little research exists on how the war affected Irish marriage rates, but certainly 'marrying out' was a major factor in the decline of the Church of Ireland population after 1918, although mixed marriage was far more common among urban working-class Protestants than upper-class, middle-class or rural minority communities in the 1920s. The 1908 Roman Catholic *Ne Temere* decree, which predated the war, certainly played a key role in population decline. It declared that in any intermarriage between a Roman Catholic and a Protestant, the Protestant partner would have to give written affirmation that all children of the union would be raised as Roman Catholics. The belief that a whole generation of Protestant men was wiped out in the Great War remains, however, although interestingly new work by historians on wartime recruitment shows that Irish Protestants and Catholics volunteered during the first years of the war at relatively similar rates.[9]

Given this context, the Church of Ireland population's continued perseverance in commemorating the dead of the Great War, which, in the 1920s, was often accompanied by the symbols of the old regime, the Union Jack and the British national anthem (technically still legitimate as Ireland was a Free State dominion and not a republic), can be seen not only as an act of remembrance but also as a form of deliberate stubborn subversion—a refusal to adjust to the new Free State and an affirmation of a lingering cultural Britishness. However, by tacitly permitting this kind of commemorative subversion, the new state enabled its minority to peacefully come to terms with the transition to Irish independence and its own loss of status, and to establish new boundaries for what kinds of cultural 'difference' were publicly or privately acceptable. A significant factor in this stabilisation process was that throughout the 1920s, while it remained culturally insecure, the minority retained considerable economic influence, although some Church of Ireland members left after the change of state because their jobs were connected to the British administration. Others moved to Northern Ireland, such as my grandfather's primary-school teacher, who refused to accept the introduction of the obligatory teaching of Irish.

Just how important the subversive aspect of commemoration was for the minority is difficult to measure, however, because alongside specifically Church of Ireland acts of remembrance at this time, there were also public forms of remembrance in which Protestants and Catholics jointly participated. As Jane Leonard has shown, in the early 1920s, commemoration of the war in Ireland was not initially restricted to any one denomination.[10] Although it lacked state support, public commemoration of the Great War, uniting Protestant and Catholic veterans and bereaved, remained widespread on Armistice Day, despite radical republican protests and harassment, and many aspects of local Protestant minority commemorations of the war shared the characteristics of these wider events. Businesses, such as railway companies and banks, often erected non-denominational memorials that listed Protestant and Catholic dead together, and the British Legion held commemorative ceremonies that united Protestant and Catholic ex-servicemen. My mother recalls attending ceremonies of this kind, which continued well into the 1950s, although growing up in Crumlin she felt ambiguous about wearing the poppy because of its association with Britain. From the high participation rates of the 1920s, Catholic commemoration of the war decreased in the 1930s when Éamon de Valera came to power.[11] However, despite increasing state hostility to remembering the Irish dead of the Great War, it was really not until the late 1960s, with the impact of the fiftieth anniversary of the Easter Rising in 1966, the outbreak of the Troubles and the deaths of most Great War veterans, that older public forms of Great War commemoration in which Catholics and Protestants jointly participated largely disappeared. In contrast, the internal Church of Ireland commemoration practices continued.

Yet Church of Ireland commemoration in the South in the 1920s and 1930s was not just subversive in terms of the Free State, it also subverted the dominant Northern Irish narrative of the Great War, which promoted a particular version of Irish Protestant identity that came to dominate public perceptions. The Protestant majority in the North emphasised the experience of the Ulster unionist dead of the Great War in terms of a blood sacrifice made to defend Britain that validated the right of the six counties to remain within the United Kingdom. Within this narrative, there was little space either for those Catholic volunteers from all across Ireland who had fought in the Great War or for the Protestant minority in the newly independent Free State. The establishment of Northern Ireland split the Protestant minority across the whole island into a predominantly Presbyterian Protestant majority in Northern Ireland and a predominantly Church of Ireland tiny minority in the new Free State; these two populations subsequently increasingly culturally diverged, until by the end of the twentieth century the Southern minority was completely integrated into the Irish Republic. Church of Ireland Great War remembrance in the South had, by the 1980s, long lost all connection with unionism, thereby providing a different model of Irish Protestant commemoration that contrasted with the Northern unionist version.

Intimacy: 1920s and 1930s

The second characteristic that drove Church of Ireland commemoration in the 1920s and 1930s was intimacy. As a child, I wondered at the ubiquitous presence of war memorials in the many churches I visited, the majority planned, fund-raised for or unveiled during the War of Independence. A number of reasons explain this particularly intimate, local form of remembrance. First, due to the risk of harassment of public war remembrance during the upheavals of the War of Independence and Civil War, fearful and insecure Church of Ireland communities located acts of remembrance within the intimate, private sphere, retreating inside their own communal boundaries and erecting their own memorials to their war dead inside their churches. In contrast to war memorials in England, which are found both inside and outside of Church buildings and also at crossroads or in town centres, these Church of Ireland memorials were 'hidden' to all outside of the minority community.[12] By locating war memorials inside of Protestant churches, these memorials became physically invisible to the majority Roman Catholic population, which at the time was prohibited by a Catholic Church ban from entering a Protestant church. This generally protected the memorials from the risk of vandalism by radical republicans; it also hid Church of Ireland acts of commemoration from view, thereby avoiding negative attention.

As a consequence of denominational schooling in the Free State, interwar acts of Great War remembrance that took place in Protestant schools were also intimate and 'hidden'. Church of Ireland children were usually schooled in parish-run primary schools. These did not normally build their own war memorials; instead, school pupils would attend the Remembrance Sunday commemoration at the parish church, and would stand in silence at school at 11 a.m. on Armistice Day. My grandfather, George W. Smith, born in 1915, vividly recalled taking part as a child in this act of remembrance in St James's School, Dublin. Other sources corroborate that such acts of remembrance took place, sometimes with political overtones: in November 1921 the rector's Armistice address to St Matthew's parish school stated 'Fear God. Honour the King.'[13] In contrast, Protestant secondary schools did fund-raise and build memorials to their past pupils who fell in the conflict, as well as carrying out remembrance ceremonies, as did Trinity College, which, for much of the twentieth century, had a largely Protestant student and staff body. These became intimate memorials, for and by bereaved communities, for their own war dead.

The second key reason for the intimacy of Church of Ireland commemoration in the interwar years lies in the size of the community. Following partition, the Protestant minority in the Free State was now so small that intimate, local commemoration made sense both financially and emotionally. Placing war memorials within churches enhanced their intimate, emotional power, situating them in the building that was at the heart of all family rites of passage. Through this choice of location, Church of Ireland remembrance was firmly embedded in the spiritual and the familial, part of the sphere of prayer—the most intimate cultural sphere of the community—rather than the temporal, and increasingly unstable and hostile, civic realm of the state. Embedding the names of the war dead in a memorial on the wall of their parish church was intended to ensure permanency, that their names became part of history by being built into the oldest and most important community building. These intimate forms of remembrance offered consolation and attempted to reassert a sense of historical continuity at local parish level at what was in reality a time of great rupture.

The fact that the typical war memorial consisted of a list of names is also revealing. In Irish Protestantism, including the Church of Ireland, the Low Church tradition has long dominated, with biblical texts popular as church decoration. The Ten Commandments appear behind the altar, for example, at Coolbanagher Church in Co. Laois and Ballinatone Church in Co. Wicklow. Ostentatious iconography is not usually the norm, particularly in rural churches, although Georgian Protestant churches occasionally provide exceptions. The idea of the divine text is at the heart of the cultural understanding of the sacred space and its creation. In this way, by listing the names of the dead on church walls, contemporaries were actively sacralising them; the dead became a spiritual 'text'. Some parishes developed this idea even further by commissioning a roll of honour of those who had served. In the case of St Ann's church in Dawson Street, Dublin, the names of the war dead and their regiments were inscribed in gold lettering on panels behind the altar—precisely where the Ten Commandments often appeared in other churches. Although Low Church Protestants strictly opposed the idea of prayers to the dead or to saints or martyrs, there was clearly a need for the war bereaved to have a sense of spiritual comfort, particularly as these men were usually buried far away overseas where they fell. For those whose loved ones were listed simply as missing, the war memorial bearing their name in the local parish often served as an intimate substitute grave; the name remained where the man had been baptised and worshipped, and where his family continued to worship. The war memorial window—less common but to be found in several Dublin churches, such as St Ann's, Dawson Street, and St Philip's, Dartry—served a similar purpose.

This explains why decades later, in the 1970s and 1980s, when numerous Protestant churches were closed and deconsecrated, the war memorial was usually moved to another operational parish church and reinserted on its wall. This also helps to explain why annually, to this day, the war memorial lists of names are decorated with a wreath for Remembrance Sunday. Moreover, because Protestant intermarriage often resulted in particularly closed lines of denominational ancestry, especially in rural areas, names were often identifiably 'Protestant', designating precise community affiliation—a display of communal as well as individual loss.

The importance of 'naming' the dead was also expressed in the naming of children for men who fell in the war. I encountered this at first hand when told by Arthur Cronhelm that he was named for his uncle who fell on the Western Front; an example of the cultural transitions occurring within the Church of Ireland, he would later serve as a high-ranking officer in the Irish army. Ironically, his fellow parishioner Max Ingram told me he had been named after General Maxwell, who crushed the 1916 Easter Rising, because his mother went into labour on a doorstep when the upheaval of the Rising forced her to flee her home.

This adoption of 'intimate' forms of commemoration, however, was also about unifying a divided community. Southern Protestantism, although demoralised and disorientated in the new Free State, was not internally unified or homogeneous. There were political divisions between radical Protestant republicans, who supported 1916 and the War of Independence, and Protestant unionists, who lamented the old order; there were significant class divisions, ranging from working class to Anglo-Irish aristocracy; there were stark urban–rural cultural differences; and there were denominational divisions, particularly between Presbyterians, Methodists and Church of Ireland members.[14] As an all-island Church, the Church of Ireland also faced the fraught issue of how to deal with co-religionists in Northern Ireland. In other words, intimate forms of remembrance organised at local parish level were the least controversial approach; any kind of united or official 'Protestant' commemoration in the Free State in the 1920s or 1930s was simply not possible as the Protestant minority itself was too diverse. Moreover, with the departure or death during the 1914–23 upheavals of much of the Church of Ireland's traditional leadership caste, the Anglo-Irish aristocracy, the clergy now filled the leadership vacuum in the South, another factor that explains the predominance of memorials within churches rather than elsewhere. Intimate, local parish commemoration was thus logical and practical.

Ritual

In my childhood memories, ritual was the characteristic that dominated Church of Ireland Great War commemoration by the 1980s. By then, the original meanings of commemoration had disappeared, and although remembrance practices largely continued to resemble those of the past, they had become cultural rituals for the majority of Church of Ireland participants—traditions in their own right rather than about political subversion or intimate personal bereavement, as they had been in the interwar years. Moreover, remembrance during the 1980s was about the Second World War far more than the First—the veterans I saw as a child attending Remembrance Sunday services proudly wearing their British army medals, for whom remembrance remained personal, were commemorating 1939–45, not 1914–18. In fact, ritual to some extent had supplanted history; there was little real historical information in the commemorations about the Great War itself. It was usually not directly referred to; it remained an oblique, vaguely present cataclysm that no one wanted to talk about. War remembrance was now based around a general 'anti-war' Christian pacifist message; sermons warned of the horrors of all wars.

Above all, there was no sense that war remembrance had anything to do with Britain; rather, it was about a local Church of Ireland identity. Ironically, given how many Irish Catholics died in the Great War, the rituals of remembrance appeared to me as a child as simply one more element in a long list of things one did as an Irish Protestant that contrasted with the dominant Catholic culture—a marker of difference akin to going to Girls' Brigade or not making one's First Communion. The ritual of remembrance now served as a way of affirming and reconciling a unique Southern Protestant, hybrid Irish cultural identity within an explicitly moderate nationalist, not unionist, framework—an attempt to convey a sense of religious and cultural difference that was merged with a great pride in citizenship of the Irish Republic. This shift in internal commemorative meaning within the Church of Ireland helps to explain why many Protestants felt ongoing disappointment in the 1980s that the state dissuaded the president from attending the annual Remembrance Service at St Patrick's Cathedral. And it helps explain the shock felt by Church of Ireland members in the South at the 1987 Enniskillen bombing—a sudden, brutal reminder of the fact that elements in Irish society still saw commemoration of the world wars as a target for attack.

Today, I retain vivid childhood memories of our parish Remembrance Sunday service, with its obligatory quotation from Binyon—'They shall grow not old'—and the collective silence. I was fascinated to see elderly men and women I knew suddenly appear wearing medals; it hinted at past lives, griefs and adventures of which I had never suspected them. Poppies were worn, both at school and in church, although they remained such a controversial symbol in Dublin that they were always sold inside the church door or from under the counter in the case of one Church of Ireland bookshop. Initially, as a small child, I was mystified by this hostility to poppies because I was told that they were a peace symbol; I did not understand their link to Britain for many years. War memorials were simply part of the normal daily landscape, from the parish hall in Rathfarnham built to commemorate the Great War dead— where I went to Girl Guides—to the long list of names on the war memorial at secondary school in Wesley College, where at an annual commemorative assembly the poppy wreaths from the war memorial were solemnly carried to the podium by the head boy and head girl.

Ultimately, the success of remembrance as ritual perhaps explains the longevity of Great War commemoration in the Church of Ireland in the Irish Republic. For in 2012, it seems strange that it has lasted so long; there was nothing inevitable about these practices surviving, particularly as Catholic remembrance activities that had taken place in the early 1920s died out, and as Great War veterans and those who remembered them passed away, and a new cultural sense of Irish nationalism took hold in younger Church of Ireland generations from the 1950s on. Arguably, it was precisely because practices of Great War remembrance shifted to deeply local rituals of identity within the Church of Ireland that they continued. Commemoration became far less about the Church of Ireland's past than about its future—reaffirming its sense of a distinct hybrid identity and of minority cultural difference as a legitimate part of the Republic, and passing this on to new generations.

This suggests that commemoration evolved over time from something subversive that lamented the old regime into a rather benign anti-war ritual that affirmed a plural sense of identity. By the 1990s and into the 2000s, as the state became increasingly involved in commemorating the Irish dead of the Great War, of all denominations, the Southern Church of Ireland minority became increasingly secure in its sense of identity. The national narrative and the local minority narrative began to merge at the same time that increased cultural integration of the minority occurred. Today, commemoration of the Great War in the Republic has become interdenominational; the poppy no longer makes us 'different'. Here are some very positive lessons on the ways that war commemoration can evolve.

Notes

1   For example David Fitzpatrick (ed.), *Ireland and the First World War* (Dublin, 1986); Keith Jeffery, *Ireland and the Great War* (Cambridge, 2000; new edn 2011); Adrian Gregory and Senia Pašeta (eds), *Ireland and the Great War: 'a war to unite us all?'* (Manchester, 2002); Timothy Bowman, *The Irish regiments in the Great War: discipline and morale* (Manchester, 2003); John Horne (ed.), *Our war: Ireland and the Great War* (Dublin, 2008).

2   Kurt Bowen, *Protestants in a Catholic state: Ireland's privileged minority* (Kingston and Montreal, 1983), 20–1.

3   Bowen, *Protestants in a Catholic state*.

4   Peter Hart, 'The Protestant experience of revolution in Southern Ireland' in Richard English and Graham Walker (eds), *Unionism in modern Ireland: new perspectives on politics and culture* (Basingstoke, 1996), 81–98.

5   *Church of Ireland Gazette*, 12 May 1922.

6   Bowen, *Protestants in a Catholic state*, 24.

7   See the letters documenting cases of intimidation in the Irish National Archives, Department of the Taoiseach files, DT S 566, DT S 565 and the anonymous letters in D/J H5 377. See also Peter Hart, *The I.R.A. and its enemies: violence and community in Cork, 1916–1923* (Oxford, 1998); Gerard Murphy, *The year of disappearances: political killings in Cork, 1921–1922* (Dublin, 2011); David Fitzpatrick (ed.), *Terror in Ireland, 1916–1923* (Dublin, 2012).

8   Heather K. Crawford, *Outside the glow: Protestants and Irishness in independent Ireland* (Dublin, 2010).

9   David Fitzpatrick, 'The logic of collective sacrifice: Ireland and the British army, 1914–1918', *Historical Journal* 38 (4), 1017–30; Catriona Pennell, *A kingdom united: popular responses to the outbreak of the First World War in Britain and Ireland* (Oxford, 2012).

10   Jane Leonard, 'The twinge of memory: Armistice Day and Remembrance Sunday in Dublin since 1919' in English and Walker (eds), *Unionism in modern Ireland*, 99–114.

11   Leonard, 'The twinge of memory'.

12   On English memorials see Stefan Goebel, *The Great War and medieval memory: war, remembrance and medievalism in Britain and Germany, 1914–1940* (Cambridge, 2007).

13   Representative Church Body Library, Dublin, St Matthew's parish magazine, Dec. 1921.

14   On the Protestant working class see Martin Maguire, 'The Dublin Protestant working class, 1870–1932: economy, society, politics' (MA thesis, UCD, 1990).

9

The Long Road

Tom Hartley

It is often said that the journey is more important than arriving at the destination. Life as a political activist has posed many challenges, with many twists and turns, and it has often been uncomfortable. If there is one thread that holds this experience together, it is my political aspiration for a thirty-two-county united and independent Ireland. I cannot tell you when this aspiration entered my consciousness, yet it has always been there in my living memory, and it is probably fair to say that my own aspirations and political experience are reflective of the journey of the Northern nationalist community from the mid-1940s through to the present. My community felt powerless under the weight of discrimination and repression, but this changed in the 1960s as a result of a growing demand by the nationalist community for equality.

I was born into a large, working-class Northern Catholic family who lived off the Falls Road in west Belfast. I lived in a street where good neighbours played a key role in the day-to-day survival of the community. As I grew older, the politics of the Northern nationalist community began to seep into my consciousness. I became aware of difference. As an eight-year-old altar boy on the way to serve Mass in Clonard monastery, I was stopped by the RUC and my bag was searched. As a youngster, I was caught trying to take a Union Jack from a lamp post on the Springfield Road, then considered a Protestant area. In my teens, I watched the Orangemen march on the Falls Road from Broadway Presbyterian Church. The older I became, the more I heard stories of resentment about discrimination in employment and housing told by my elders. In these family conversations, combinations of key words emerged that later constituted the anchor terms of my historical analysis: the 1916 Rising, the Black and Tans, the Troubles, partition, pogroms, the McMahon murders, B-Specials, the Orange state, expulsion of Catholic workers from the shipyards, the Special Powers Act, state repression and discrimination.

By my late teens, my opinion of the Six Counties had crystallised. I lived in a unionist state built on three pillars: the Unionist Party, the RUC and the Orange Order. As a result of the systematic implementation of repressive legislation and the widespread use of structural discrimination, members of the Northern nationalist community were reduced to living out their lives as second-class citizens. The measures used by the unionists included a gerrymandered electoral system and discrimination in the workplace and in the allocation of housing. But these teen years were also a period of exciting new ideas and the construction of a world view that sought to challenge discrimination and repression. The Algerian War, the Vietnam War, the fight against South Africa's apartheid regime and the civil rights movement in the United States all impacted on my thinking. It seemed to me that struggles for independence and political rights across the globe arose from similar conditions that I faced as a young nationalist in the Northern state.

Between 1964 and 1969, my level of political consciousness was sharpened by the unfolding political crisis inside the Northern state. Riots in Belfast during the 1964 general election were a reminder of the tensions that existed below the surface. The riots triggered by the threat of Revd Ian Paisley to remove the tricolour from the window of the Sinn Féin election headquarters in Divis Street was for me an early introduction to Protestant political clerics. The backlash by elements of unionism and loyalism against the limited reforms introduced by the then unionist prime minister, Terence O'Neill, resulted in the death of Matilda Gould, a Shankill Road Protestant woman whose home was petrol-bombed when loyalists attempted to burn down the neighbouring Catholic-owned pub. One month after the attack on Matilda Gould, Patrick Scullion, a Catholic, was murdered by the same group of loyalists. This was a period when the rising expectations of the Northern nationalist community found a strong voice in the civil rights movement, which came into existence on 9 April 1967. While all of these experiences contributed to the development of my political consciousness and thinking, their impact on my political activity was limited. The near collapse of the Northern state in August 1969 on the streets of Derry and Belfast was to change this.

If there is one incident that moved me from being a spectator of events to being a political activist, it was the petrol-bombing of Bombay Street behind Clonard monastery on the night of 15 August 1969, when B-Specials and Shankill Road loyalists burned to the ground forty-five of the street's sixty-five houses. Against the backdrop of attacks on their homes, many nationalists perceived the deployment of the British army onto the streets of Derry and Belfast in August 1969 as a protective measure. However, this view of the army as protectors of the Catholic community quickly changed as a result of the tactics the British army employed during the Lower Falls curfew in July 1970; again, during the introduction of internment in August 1971; and on Bloody Sunday in Derry in January 1972. By this time, the nationalist community had become, for the most part, alienated from the British army. Prior to 1969, the British army was referred to as 'the army', but this changed after 1969, when the term 'British army' or 'Brits' entered the everyday political language of many in the nationalist community. Confronted by the presence of British soldiers on their streets, nationalists reflected the changed and hostile role of the army as a repressive, foreign and dominating force through language that moved from a historic ambivalence regarding the military to a language that expressed open hostility.

An enduring legacy of this period was a deep sense of being abandoned by the Irish government. This view fed into a strong undercurrent of nationalist memory in the Six Counties that, since partition, the Southern political establishment had turned its back on the plight of Northern nationalists, and had left them stranded and alone inside a repressive unionist state. This sense of despair was made more painful when Northern nationalists reflected on their contribution to the democratic struggles that shaped the course of Irish history. Belfast nationalists, the most vulnerable nationalist community in the Six Counties, were acutely aware of their role in the national struggle. Belfast was a gateway for the entry of republicanism into Ireland: on Cavehill, which overlooks the city from the north, the Society of the United Irishmen had been founded; Belfast had its Young Irelanders and its Fenians; Bulmer Hobson and Denis McCullough had reorganised the Irish Republican Brotherhood in the city; Parnell and Pearse were regular visitors. Alice Milligan and Anna Johnston (the poet Ethna Carbery) edited the literary-political journal *Shan Van Vocht*. One of the founders of the GAA was Peter McKay, a Belfast *Irish News* journalist. The memory of the Easter Rising and its personalities constituted a strong element of our historical memory. I knew that James Connolly had lived on the Falls Road, that Seán MacDermott had worked in Belfast, that Winnie Carney, a Belfast trade-union activist, had been Connolly's secretary and one of the few women to enter the GPO on Easter Monday 1916. In the years of the Tan War, Belfast nationalists suffered heavily as a result of the pogroms unleashed against them from July 1920. The historical totality of this memory is a reminder to Belfast nationalists that their participation in and contribution to the struggle for national independence had been an enduring theme in the political life of their city and their country from the 1798 Rebellion onwards.

This Belfast republican experience is located within a historical narrative in which the idea of an Irish nation is rooted in the concept of a self-conscious historical community that, in the face of domination by English governments, defined its claim to nationhood through its historical resistance to English governance. The concept of the nation was seen as the framework for a democratic resolution of the conflict between Ireland and Britain. After partition, this historical memory was absorbed into the aspiration for a united Ireland. This political goal contained the hope of delivery from British rule and the Orange state, and the achievement of our political, social, cultural and economic liberation.

For me, the 1970s were years of enormous change: I was now a full-time political activist. Between 1971 and 1972, I served a ten-month sentence in Crumlin Road Gaol, Belfast; in 1975 I was the manager of *Republican News* and manager of the Republican Press Centre, which was also a truce incident centre in 1975, and was at the very heart of the battle of words and concepts that was waged around the conflict. The ending of internment in 1975 and the subsequent attempt by the British government to criminalise republican prisoners triggered a protest in the H-Blocks of Long Kesh and Armagh women's prison. This protest and the subsequent hunger strike had far-reaching political implication for republicans. One of the first indications of this was a rethinking of the nature of public support required to underpin the prison protest. From the initial insistence that to support the prisoners one had to support the IRA, we pragmatically moved to building a broad-based solidarity movement that made a number of demands for prison reforms without actually using the term 'political status'. While this made it easier for broader support to emerge for the prisoners, it was also meant to make it easier for the British to compromise.

The election of Bobby Sands and, later, Owen Carron in Fermanagh and South Tyrone galvanised the drive towards an electoral strategy that saw important electoral gains between 1982—when we stood candidates in the Northern Assembly elections—and 1986, when the decision to drop abstentionism in the South was ratified by Sinn Féin's *ard fheis*. Since my election to Sinn Féin's *ard chomhairle* in 1979, I was involved in all of the discussions around strategy.

A significant political development took place in November 1985 when the Irish and British governments signed the Anglo-Irish Agreement. In Sinn Féin's view, one of the objectives of the agreement was to bolster the SDLP (Social Democratic Labour Party) and limit the growth of Sinn Féin. This move by the two governments to limit our political and electoral expansion coincided with our own review of our relationship with the SDLP. Prior to this reassessment, republicans saw the SDLP as a six-county party with a six-county agenda that needed to be robustly opposed. As a result of the review, our attitude towards the SDLP changed fundamentally: while still seeing the SDLP as a six-county party, we recognised the need to engage with it. As we saw it, whatever our differences, the SDLP, just like us, had a responsibility to outline how the conflict could be resolved. What followed was a private dialogue between Gerry Adams and John Hume that led to the early stage of a peace initiative. Talks between Sinn Féin and the SDLP also led to dialogue with the Irish government, the Irish-American community and the then US president, Bill Clinton. From this inter-party dialogue with the SDLP and the engagement with the Irish and US governments emerged a peace initiative within a loose political alliance of the two parties and the two governments. By creating the possibility of movement towards a resolution of the conflict, the alliance was strong enough to maintain a political momentum that eventually led to the IRA ceasefire of August 1994.

Other lines of communication began to open up as the peace initiative developed. For years, Sinn Féin had been frustrated by the unwillingness of political unionism to engage with us. With the development of our peace strategy and the greater potential for public dialogue, Sinn Féin sought to increase its level of engagement across a broad spectrum of opinion inside the Protestant community. This led us to enter into dialogue with the Protestant Churches, an engagement that brought its own insights. It challenged the assumption held by many inside the nationalist community that Protestants would only change if they found themselves in a united Ireland, when they would suddenly 'come to their senses'. As a result of the dialogue, I began to hear how unionists interpreted this view. In their eyes, we had made them a non-people robbed of their power to be a crucial component of the Irish political conflict and, indeed, to be a crucial element in the search for a just and lasting settlement on the island of Ireland. Another insight for republicans was to recognise how the infrastructure of Protestant religious thought processes defined the political language and structures of unionism. Having uncovered this hidden vein of thought, we looked for a similar undercurrent within our own political tradition.

Language has always constituted a major element of the political battleground. There was an assumption that as both communities speak English, they should at least understand one another. Not true. The political concepts of unionism, anchored in the thought processes of Protestantism, were not immediately understood by those of us from a Catholic and republican background. This was best summed up to me by Revd John Dunlop, a Presbyterian minister, when he described John Hume and Gerry Adams as two archbishops. His difficulty was that he did not know which one was the Pope! Here, John was reflecting on the hierarchical nature of the nationalist community, where the leader tends to speak in a collective way for all, whereas in the Presbyterian Church, the moderator is elected for a one-year term and speaks for no one but himself, reflecting the individualistic nature of Presbyterianism, and its emphasis on the power of the individual and on the independence of its congregations. So, while being raised in the Catholic community gave me a sense of belonging to every Catholic church in Belfast, Presbyterians tend to be rooted within their own local congregation. Protestants and unionists whom we met were deeply suspicious of the highly centralised structure of Sinn Féin, which ran contrary to the power of the individual within Protestantism and, by extension, unionism.

With the ceasefire of August 1994, new possibilities to broaden our outreach emerged. In 1995 the Irish government invited a representative of Sinn Féin to attend the VE Day and Holocaust memorial service at the Irish National War Memorial, Islandbridge. I was selected to represent our party. My attendance at this service was the first indicator of a change in Sinn Féin's attitude to world-war commemorations. On 1 July 2002 my party colleague Alex Maskey, as lord mayor of Belfast, laid a laurel wreath at the Cenotaph in Belfast on the anniversary of the Battle of the Somme. In the same period, Francie Molloy, Sinn Féin chairman of Dungannon Council, invited members of the British Legion into his parlour in Dungannon Council offices.

These political developments ran alongside my history work for Féile an Phobail, the festival based in west Belfast. When the festival began in 1988, I organised a history bus tour of the west of the city, which included a visit to the republican graves in Milltown Cemetery, the burial ground for Belfast Catholics. As a result of my political work with the Protestant Churches, I was intrigued by the way in which I seemed to have ignored Belfast City Cemetery, the largest municipal graveyard in Belfast, which was also located on the Falls Road, and thus on my doorstep, but where the majority of those buried are from the Protestant community. My blind spot to the history of that community was quickly exposed. As a way of confronting this lack of curiosity about the City Cemetery, I began an exploration of the headstones to be found there. In every sense, it was my work in the City Cemetery that introduced me to the historical complexity of the Belfast Protestant community. One example of this is the grave of Revd Richard Rutledge Kane, a Church of Ireland rector, a leading Orangeman in Belfast, and a unionist cleric who had led the opposition to Gladstone's first home rule bill. On his headstone he is described as 'A Faithful Pastor, Gifted Orator and Loyal Irish patriot'. Reputed to have been an Irish-speaker, he is recorded as being one of the patrons of the Belfast Gaelic League. His epitaph, which sets his loyalty to the Union within an Irish patriotic frame, still manages to challenge many visitors to his grave.

The knowledge gained in the City Cemetery combined with my knowledge of Milltown led me to organise a Féile an Phobail walking tour through Milltown and City cemeteries. This is the point where the history found in each site moved me very consciously to embrace the complexity of my Belfast history. In bringing the two cemeteries together in one tour, I was able to demonstrate that complexity. In the City Cemetery, I found the industrialists who made Belfast the Silicon Valley of its day alongside the historians who gave us the story of Belfast and Irish Presbyterianism. Unionist UVF gunrunners and political clerics are buried alongside the poor who laboured in the mills and shipyards. I also found members of the Gaelic League, Irish-speakers and republicans. In Milltown, I found a history of poverty, rebellion, assassinations, a very small Catholic middle class, and the mass expulsions of Catholics from the industrial centres of Belfast. I also found British soldiers and sailors, members of the RIC and a First World War soldier who is buried in the republican plot. At the start of every combined tour of these two big Belfast cemeteries, I suggest to those doing the tour with me that they can either like or dislike the history they are about to encounter, that they can agree or disagree with the politics of those who lie buried in the graves they are going to visit, but that these graves, be they Catholic or Protestant, unionist or republican, represent the complex history of Belfast. And for those of us born in Belfast, this is our history.

My interest in the City Cemetery had other consequences. As my research developed, I began to notice inscriptions on family headstones remembering soldiers, sailors and airmen, as well as two women who lost their lives during the First World War. To date, I have recorded 255 such family inscriptions. These inscriptions provided me with the opportunity to build a picture of the First World War and its battlegrounds. Belfast men and women died in every theatre of this war, fighting with the British, Australian, New Zealand, South African, Canadian, Indian and US armies. They can be found in a wide range of British army regiments, particularly those associated with the Irish diaspora. During the course of my research, I was told about 366 missing Commonwealth War Graves Commission (CWGC) headstones. In October 1979 headstones in the City Cemetery under the care of the CWGC had been vandalised. In response, Belfast City Council removed these headstones and stored them in Lady Dixon Park in south Belfast. Having lifted over 366 stones, and considering the politics of the conflict raging in west Belfast, the council's parks department found it difficult to decide when the stones should be reinstated. Twenty years later, my work in the cemetery brought me into contact with the local representative of the CWGC. Through my work as a city councillor, I met with a senior representative of the commission in September 2002. The nationalist communities who live in the vicinity of the graveyard have a deep respect for the dead, and abhor the desecration of any grave. My advice to the commission was to put the stones back. On 10 October 2002 six headstones were erected in the first phase of a reinstatement programme, and by 2006 all of the headstones were back in the cemetery. This desecration of the war-grave headstones was a reminder that our capacity to hurt the 'other' in the process of remembering our dead was a common-enough experience in a society in conflict. The vandalising and desecration of republican plots and British war graves and the use of abusive language to describe the fallen in different periods of our conflict have added further layers to our legacy of hurt. This can only be changed when all of us recognise the value of memory and remembrance to all of our citizens, and acknowledge that remembrance takes many forms.

Of course, older forms of historical hurt were experienced in the months and years that followed the end of the First World War. Irish soldiers from the nationalist community returning to Ireland were confronted with a political landscape that had been dramatically changed by the Easter Rising. This change drove their stories and experiences into the privacy of their homes, where they remained hidden until the end of the twentieth century. In my youth, I heard about family members who had fought in the Crimean War, about uncles who had been in the IRA in the 1920s and had then joined the Free State army, about my grandfather who had served with the British army in India and during the First World War, and about my uncle Davey who had served with the Royal Navy and had been torpedoed twice at Dunkirk. Yet none of this military history inside my family had any form of external, public recognition. Moreover, there was a widespread view among many nationalists that unionists in solely remembering the 36th (Ulster) Division failed to recognise those other Irish soldiers of the 10th and 16th (Irish) Divisions. There is also a historical view that in the pogroms against the Catholic community from July 1920 until August 1922, the unionists targeted Catholic ex-British servicemen because of their suspicion that these former soldiers, with their military training, were in a position to defend their community.

Clearly, when it comes to the topic of the British army, embracing the concept of 'our' history has brought its own dilemma. Being a soldier in that army has a long and continuing history in Ireland. The reasons for joining always were, and remain, varied and complex; military service did not automatically place the Irish soldier in a pro-Union frame. This story weaves like a thread through the narrative of our island history. We may reject the story but we cannot deny its existence. Yet for my generation, the experience of the British army is a bitter one and has left deep wounds. Campaigns to seek the truth about those shot dead by the British army in Ballymurphy during the first days of internment in August 1971 and the truth about the events in Derry on Bloody Sunday remind us of that wound.

However, contemporary attitudes about the British army have not stopped the nationalist community coming to terms with the historical complexity of family members who occupied those faraway trenches. In doing so, they are shedding new light on Irish soldiers and Irish regiments of the First World War. Families now look at their grandfathers and great-uncles in terms of their individual valour and sense of duty. They appreciate how poverty at home drove many of them into the ranks of the British army; a job and regular pay had its own attractions in the years leading up to the war. The process of publicly claiming a grandfather or great-uncle who served on the Western Front along-side a grandfather or great-uncle who served in the ranks of the IRA is well underway in many families. These unearthed memories easily embrace the complexity of the Irish soldiering experience.

In this decade of centenaries, there are choices to be made as to how the history of the turbulent years between 1912 and 1923 is to be remembered. My own journey continues as I look to the politics of the Reformation. This new dimension to my political consciousness finds its origin in my interest in the year 1912 and the genesis of the Ulster Covenant. This document, modelled on the 1643 Solemn League and Covenant, has awakened my interest in the radical politics of the English Civil War created by the political dynamics of the Reformation.

In this process of remembering, the sense of loyalty to one's own politi-cal view of history will be challenged by the task of taking ownership of the totality of our history. This is not an easy task, for such a challenge will surely alter the political perspective held by all who choose to disturb the foundations of their political opinions. In a journey to acknowledge the complexity of our history, we cannot avoid the contradictions that will be encountered. Will the choices we make act as another strain of divisiveness that diminishes the views of the other, or can we use this period as a way of enhancing a view of ourselves as the custodians of a history bursting with conflict and complexity, a history that reminds us that, as an island people, we have always been at that political interface where the battle of ideas has been waged and where political movements sought to change the world we live in? I believe there is a need to create a dialogue that facilitates a broad and progressive discourse, where we feel confident enough to lift our cultural and political anchors and engage with the complexity of our island history. We need to be dignified in our approach to others, and our engagement must create its own narrative of hospitality.

10

Somme Memories

Ian Adamson

William Sloan was born in Newtownards, Co. Down, in 1897. He was the only son of Anthony and Lizzie Sloan, who lived in Roseneath Cottage, Main Street, Conlig, Co. Down, near my father's shop at the corner of Tower Road; this leads past Clandeboye Golf Club to Helen's Tower. The couple were married on 24 August 1896 in Ballygilbert Presbyterian Church. Anthony worked as a general labourer, and his two nieces, Martha and Isabella, eventually became my two grannies. Anthony and Lizzie had two children, William and Lillah, to whom my grannies were therefore cousins. Shortly after the outbreak of the Great War, at the age of seventeen, William enlisted at Clandeboye without his parents' permission, and, like other young men from Conlig, came home already in uniform. He served with 11th Battalion, Royal Irish Rifles in 108th Brigade, 36th (Ulster) Division, and was killed in action on the first day of the Battle of the Somme, aged then only nineteen years. Initially, he was reported missing in action, but his mother Lizzie never accepted that he was dead, and until the day she died in January 1932, the front door of the cottage was left unlocked, day and night, just in case her son came home. He has no known grave and is commemorated at home in Conlig Presbyterian Church and in France on the Thiepval Memorial to the Missing of the Somme.

But the story does not end there. Following William's death, Lillah went with two of her cousins, my granny Isabella and her sister—my aunt Hannah, whose husband Herbie was in the 36th (Ulster) Division until the end of the war—to work on munitions at the Alfred Nobel dynamite factory at Ardeer in Ayrshire, Scotland. When I was a boy, I used to deliver daily newspapers to Lillah in Roseneath Cottage. We often talked about her brother, and she told me that we looked alike and that I reminded her of him—which is perhaps not surprising in view of the family connection. It was from Lillah, my granny Isabella and aunt Hannah that I learned most about the Great War. Granny helped inform my views on my identity as a British unionist, an Irish royalist and an Ulster loyalist, as well as my socialist principles. Always, she instructed, vote for the 'cloth cap'.

Only much later, however, did that interest in the war turn into something more active. In 1975 I was contacted by a leading French academic in the study of Ireland, Professor René Fréchet, following the publication of my book *The Cruthin: the ancient kindred* (Belfast, 1974). This was the beginning of a long and productive correspondence that lasted until René Fréchet's death in 1992. It is no exaggeration to say that as professor of English at the Sorbonne and the spirit behind the university's Institute of Irish Studies, set up in 1979, he served as guide and counsellor to the increasing number of French students engaged in research into Irish themes. His *Histoire de l'Irlande* (Paris, 1970) was only one facet of his numerous activities in the field of Irish studies. Apart from his love of Irish literature—his translation of the poetical works of Yeats (1989) is a model of precision and sensibility—he followed closely events in Northern Ireland, which he covered in a series of often outspoken articles published in the French Protestant weekly *Réforme*. An acute knowledge of facts as well as an indefectible affection for every aspect of life in the region guided his particular interest in the North. As a young lecturer, he had spent two years at Queen's University, Belfast. The experience he acquired and the long-lasting friendships he made at that time gave him an indisputable authority to comment on developments in the political situation there. There is no doubt that it was through him that the point of view of the Ulster Protestant found its most articulate and sympathetic spokesperson in France. His convictions and courageous declarations did much to counterbalance the often superficial representations of this community in the mainstream, essentially pro-republican French press.

I was greatly honoured that René Fréchet should take an interest in my work. Commenting on my *Identity of Ulster* (Bangor, 1982) he wrote:

> What an interesting, curious piece of work this is. Generally, if we are told it is not a question of a war of religion in Ulster, we are told about opposition between Catholics, whom people think of as mostly wishing for the unification of the island, and Protestants who want to remain British.
>
> Adamson, however, does not militate in favour of the bringing together of two quite distinct communities. He says that their division is artificial, that they are all more or less descendants of pre-Celtic peoples, and in particular of the Cruthin, who were constantly moving backwards and forwards between Ulster and Scotland, where they were called Picts, a fact that did not prevent their homeland becoming the most Gaelic part of Ireland. 'British', as far as he is concerned, takes on a meaning that Ulster people tend to forget. Here are some interesting phrases for comparison. '"Old British" was displaced in Ireland by Gaelic just as English displaced Gaelic'; 'the people of the Shankill Road speak an English which is almost a literal translation of Gaelic'; 'the majority of Scottish Gaelic speakers are Protestants'.
>
> In fact, Adamson is especially interested in Protestants, but those Protestants who have worked or are working towards reconciliation (could these even be the United Irishmen of the 1790s?), for a co-operative movement, for a kind of popular autonomy or self-management. He shows the paradoxical confusion of antagonistic, partly mythical traditions, and is trying to convince people of the fundamental unity of Ulster.[1]

Throughout the 1980s, René Fréchet followed my involvement in the creation of several community organisations to promote my ideals of mutual respect, common identity, cooperation and self-help. These included the Farset Youth Project. The idea behind the project was to bring together young people from both sides of the community and allow them to follow in the footsteps of St Columbanus from Bangor in the North of Ireland to Reims and Luxeuil in France, through St Gallen in Switzerland, to Bregenz in Austria, and finally on to Bobbio in Italy. In a country where violence was dividing the people, it was important to point to a shared past. This project became possible thanks in no small measure to the help of my friend Cardinal Tomás Ó Fiaich, whose foreword to the second edition of my book, *Bangor, light of the world* (Bangor, 1987) in 1987 is testimony to his commitment to the cross-community line we saw as so vital.[2] And as a result of Fréchet's interest, I republished *The narrow ground* by A.T.Q. Stewart in 1986, and first published *The cavalier duke* by J.C. Beckett in 1992.[3]

On our way back to Ulster during our first trip to France with young people from the Shankill and Falls Road areas of Belfast and from Tallaght and Inchicore in Dublin during the height of the Troubles, I asked the group to make a detour to the Ulster Memorial Tower to explain the part played by Irishmen of all persuasions in the First World War in France, Belgium and the Dardanelles. From our Farset Somme Project developed the idea of a Somme association, which was to be supported by an international organisation, Friends of the Somme.[4] This association took root at a press conference held under the auspices of the then lord mayor of Belfast, Sammy Wilson, and the lady mayoress, Rhonda Paisley, on the seventieth anniversary of the Battle of the Somme, 1 July 1986, when a Somme Commemoration Committee was initiated.

Having grown up in sight of Helen's Tower at Clandeboye, where the Belfast Brigade of the 36th (Ulster) Division had trained and on which the Ulster Memorial Tower at Thiepval had been modelled, I proposed that museum complexes close to both towers could be built, that Thiepval Wood could be purchased, and that Helen's Tower could be opened up to the public under the stewardship of the Dufferin family. Ian Paisley explained his own position as an MEP, and emphasised that this was a project to honour everyone who had fought at the Somme, both unionist and nationalist, Catholic and Protestant. He helped the project to achieve its aims through the good offices of the European Parliament, the French embassy and the Commonwealth War Graves Commission.

And so, on 1 July 1989, the Ulster Memorial Tower at Thiepval in France, the second Helen's Tower, built by public subscription and completed in 1922, was rededicated under the auspices of our Farset Somme Project by HRH Princess Alice, Duchess of Gloucester. Hundreds of pilgrims from Ulster made the journey, among them veterans of the 36th (Ulster) Division and public representatives from throughout Northern Ireland. We were delighted that the duchess continued to be associated with our work by consenting to becoming the first president of the Somme Association, formally established in 1990, and that her son Prince Richard agreed to follow her in this role following her death in October 2004. He had opened our Somme Heritage Centre at Whitespots, Conlig, Co. Down, in 1994. This also contains an exhibition on nationalist and republican Ireland, centring on the Easter Rising of 1916, to show both sides of the story as part of our shared history.

As founding chairman of the Somme Association, I have travelled to France and Belgium every year since its inception to remember the ordinary soldiers from throughout Ireland who fought and died there. Prince Richard has accompanied us many times, officiating at our ceremonies of remembrance in both France and Gallipoli, and meeting with President Mary McAleese in Turkey. In commemorating the ninetieth anniversary of the end of the First World War in 2008, I was especially privileged to attend three services of remembrance in Belgium and France. The first took place on Sunday 29 June at the memorial at Wytschaete (Belgium) for the 16th (Irish) Division, the Catholic and largely nationalist division that had fought there alongside the loyalist 36th (Ulster) Division at the Battle of Messines in June 1917. Dr Ian and Baroness Eileen Paisley attended this service, and Dr Paisley laid a wreath at the grave of Major Willie Redmond at Locre—where I myself had first laid a wreath when it was overgrown and generally forgotten in 1989—as well as at the 16th (Irish) Division Memorial Cross at Wytschaete during our service there. On 1 July we attended the British and French service at the Thiepval Memorial led by the then secretary of state, the Right Honourable Sean Woodward. As chairman of the Somme Association, I also officiated at the Ulster Tower service in memory of the 36th (Ulster) Division and of their comrades-in-arms who had fought there at the Battle of the Somme. On Sunday 7 September 2008 the association held a further service of remembrance at the 16th (Irish) Division memorial at Guillemont in honour of its members who fought at Guillemont and Ginchy during the Battle of the Somme in September 1916. This service was attended by Councillor Gerard Diver, mayor of Derry, and by dignitaries from throughout Northern Ireland.

Helen's Tower at Clandeboye contains a beautiful room in which are inscribed poems by Lady Helen Dufferin, Alfred, Lord Tennyson and Rudyard Kipling, amongst others. Tennyson's verse reads:

> Helen's Tower here I stand,
> Dominant over sea and land.
> Son's love built me, and I hold
> Mother's love in letter'd gold.
> Love is in and out of time,
> I am mortal stone and lime.
> Would my granite girth were strong
> As either love, to last as long
> I would wear my crown entire
> To and thro' the Doomsday fire,
> And be found of angel eyes
> In earth's recurring Paradise.

This poem is replicated in the Ulster Tower at Thiepval, but slightly altered to make it a fitting tribute to the sons of Ulster and their comrades-in-arms who fought and died in the First World War:

> Helen's Tower here I stand
> Dominant over sea and land

> Son's love built me, and I hold
> Ulster's love in letter'd gold.

This suggested to me the importance of literature as a means of understanding the experience of those who fought in the Great War, and of paying tribute to them. To this end, I established the Somme Association's *Battlelines* journal. This regular publication also kept the Friends of the Somme and general public informed as to developments within our organisation, and included interviews with First World War veterans, biographies of Irish VC holders, features on cemeteries and memorials, reprints of prominent newspaper headlines, and general historical articles. Amongst the soldier authors so remembered were Tom Kettle, journalist and professor at the National University of Ireland, who died as a lieutenant with the 9th Battalion, Royal Dublin Fusiliers at Ginchy in September 1916, and Francis Ledwidge, who was killed while labouring with a working party in Flanders on 31 July 1917. These two poets were specially remembered at our services in 2008. Captain Lord Dunsany, Ledwidge's patron and senior officer in the Royal Inniskillings, wrote at the time: 'I gave my opinion that if Ledwidge had lived, this lover of all seasons in which the blackbird sings would have surpassed even Burns, and Ireland would lawfully have claimed, as she may do even yet, the greatest of the peasant singers.'[5]

In September of that year, we also remembered J.R.R. Tolkien and his two groups of friends, the first in the pre-war Tea Club and Barrovian Society (TCBS), and the second after the war in the Inklings, the latter including C.S. Lewis, from Belfast. Tolkien never forgot what he called the 'animal horror of trench warfare'. The sights that he witnessed at the Somme, the images, sounds and the people he met stayed with him until his death in 1973. But from that horror came the inspiration of his great works, including *The Lord of the Rings*.

During the war, Tolkien served as a second lieutenant with the 11th Lancashire Fusiliers, and took part in the Battle of the Somme. Tolkien's battalion disembarked in Amiens, the capital of the Somme, and marched to a hamlet called Rubempré ten miles away. On 30 June they moved near to the front line. The great offensive began early the next morning, but the men of Tolkien's battalion were held in reserve. They were to go into battle several days later when, if all had gone according to plan, the German line would have been smashed open and the Allied troops would have penetrated deep into enemy territory. In reality, of course, the British went over the top at 7.30 a.m. on 1 July to be met by a storm of unsuppressed German fire. The famous 36th (Ulster) Division attacked from Thiepval Wood. Soon, the awful truth dawned that on the first day of battle the British had 57,000 casualties (5,500 from the 36th (Ulster) Division), with 20,000 of them dead. Rob Gilson, a close school friend of Tolkien's and a member of the TCBS, had been killed at La Boisselle, where a great mine had been detonated in no-man's-land. Aided by unusually effective artillery fire, the men of the 36th (Ulster) Division managed to penetrate further than any other British unit, reaching the formidable Schwaben redoubt.

When Tolkien went into action with the 11th Lancashire Fusiliers on 14 July in an unsuccessful attack on the ruined hamlet of Ovillers, many men of his battalion were killed around him. Day followed day in the same pattern—a rest period, back to the trenches, and more attacks. Tolkien was among those in the support at the eventually successful storming of the Schwaben redoubt, upon which Northern Ireland's national war memorial—the Ulster Tower—now stands. He was rescued in the end by 'trench fever', a highly infectious disease carried by lice, and invalided back to England in early November. Sadly, however, his other friend from the TCBS, Geoffrey Bache Smith of the Salford Pals, was killed in the last days of the battle.

C.S. Lewis arrived at the front-line trenches on his nineteenth birthday, 29 November 1917. Lewis also suffered from trench fever at the beginning of February 1918, but returned to the front on 28 February. The Germans launched their great spring offensive on 21 March, utilising additional troops that had been withdrawn from the Eastern Front following the Russian Revolution. During the first Battle of Arras, from 21–28 March 1918, Lewis was in or near the front line, and next saw action in the Battle of Hazebrouck, from 12–15 April, when he was wounded by a British shell exploding behind him. The Medical Board described his wounds thus: 'shell fragments caused three wounds in the left side of his chest, his left wrist and left leg', and on 25 May 1918 he arrived on a stretcher in London.[6]

The experiences of the First World War drew Tolkien and Lewis together in Oxford in a legendary friendship that culminated in the Inklings, a new literary club to replace the vanished TCBS and in which Lewis substituted for both Gilson and Smith. Tolkien's first story, written early in 1917 during his convalescence, was 'Fall of Gondolin', which deals with the assault of the last elvish stronghold by Morgoth, the prime power of evil. These are the elves that form the basis of the Silmarillion in the *Lord of the Rings*. Many years later, Tolkien remarked of one of his principal characters: 'My Sam Gamgee is indeed a reflection of the English soldier, of the privates and batmen I knew in the 1914 war, and recognised as so far superior to myself.'[7]

Although the centenary of the Great War is upon us, the great works of Tolkien and Lewis have left us an extraordinary evocation of the atmosphere of pre-battle tension and watchfulness, the plunge from peace into terrifying peril, the mass movement of thousands of men, and the love, comradeship and wonderful courage of ordinary people on a battlefield that was dominated by great machines and swept by airborne killers, ruthless and without pity. This understanding of the war has been at the heart of the work undertaken by the Somme Heritage Association, work that has borne important fruit over the years, not least in reconciliation within the island of Ireland.

On 10 September 2007, Dr Paisley, as First Minister of Northern Ireland, and President Mary McAleese, as head of state of the Irish Republic, shook hands for the first time—another symbolic milestone on Ireland's road to rec-onciliation—on the occasion of an exhibition held at the Somme Heritage Centre on the role of the 16th (Irish) Division and its largely Catholic and nationalist soldiers in the Battle of the Somme. President McAleese paid tribute both to the event and to the museum, stating that:

It is an honour to be here at the opening of this exhibition commemorating the Battles of Guillemont and Ginchy, part of the heroic struggle of the Battle of the Somme fought over ninety years ago. Congratulations to Dr Ian Adamson, Carol Walker and all the members of the Somme Association for this labour of love, which allows the stories of those who fought and died to be honoured and respected and better known by a new generation.[8]

As Dr Paisley's adviser on history and culture, this gave me the greatest of pleasure. The event also helped pave the way for the visit of Her Majesty the Queen to the Irish National War Memorial at Islandbridge, Dublin, on 18 May 2011, where I felt no less honoured to be presented to her by President McAleese on behalf of our association. I knew that William, Lillah and Granny Kerr would have been pleased.

Notes

1   Ian Adamson, *The identity of Ulster: the land, the language and the people* (Bangor, 1982) reviewed by René Frechet in *Réforme* 1,811 (Apr. 1982).
2   Ian Adamson, *Bangor, light of the world* (Belfast, 1979).
3   A.T.Q. Stewart, *The narrow ground: patterns of Ulster history* (Belfast, 1986); J.C. Beckett, *The cavalier duke* (Belfast, 1992).
4   See *Battle Lines: Journal of the Somme Association* 1 (1990).
5   Arthur St John Adcock, *For remembrance: soldier poets who have fallen in the war* (London, 1918), 59.
6   Roger Lancelyn Green and Walter Hooper, *C.S. Lewis: a biography* (London, 2002), 44.
7   John Garth Harper, *Tolkien and the Great War: the threshold of Middle-earth* (London, 2003), 310.
8   Mary McAleese, *Building bridges: selected speeches and statements* (Dublin, 2011), 262.

11

Rediscovery and Reconciliation: the Royal Dublin Fusiliers Association

Tom Burke

During the opening of the exhibition *Let Ireland remember*, organised by the Royal Dublin Fusiliers Association (RDFA) at the Dublin Civic Museum in November 1998, Pat Cummins took my hand and said to me, 'Thank you for remembering my father.' Pat was named after his father, Paddy Cummins, who was a transport sergeant in the 6th Royal Dublin Fusiliers (RDF). Paddy was a married man when he enlisted. His wife Winifred lost her brother when he was killed while serving with the Highland Light Infantry during the Battle of the Somme in 1916. After the war, Paddy returned to Dublin and his pre-war job as a baker in Kennedy's Bakery in Parnell Street. Together, Paddy and Winifred had six children, one of whom was Pat, who in adult life worked in Dublin Gas Company and served as a Fianna Fáil TD between 1958 and 1965. Sergeant Paddy Cummins died of lung cancer in 1955 at the age of sixty-seven, and was buried in Glasnevin Cemetery. Winifred died in 1961 at the age of seventy-five. She, too, was buried in Glasnevin.

For many years, Pat Cummins spoke to few people about his father. When I first met him in 1997 he was a bit reluctant to open up. It was not until we got to know each other better that he began to talk about his father. As to the reason for Pat's shyness, he informed me that for many years he had felt embarrassment about his father's past. Being the son of a British soldier, particularly a British soldier who served during that iconic year of 1916, and as a Fianna Fáil junior minister under Taoiseach Seán Lemass simply did not fit the model of an Irish republican TD. His journey to thanking me for remembering his father was Pat's personal journey of reconciliation between himself and his father—a journey that took him from embarrassment to pride. Pat is just one of the hundreds of people I have met since 1996 who have travelled their own journey in rediscovering their relative's past and the role they played in the First World War. In many ways, Pat's journey was a microcosm of Ireland's coming to terms with its role in the First World War. It was through the efforts of such people that the RDFA was established.

I cannot recall exactly when I began my own journey of discovery about Ireland and the First World War; there was no divine moment of inspiration. Looking back now, all I can say is that since the moment my journey began, my life was utterly changed. I had no interest in military history, and although I lived near the ex-servicemen's housing estate in Killester on Dublin's northside, I had no relatives who served in the British forces during the war. Perhaps the spark that lit the fuse was ignited when in November 1993, while out on a Sunday-afternoon cycle, I stopped off at St Patrick's Cathedral in Dublin and went in. There was a remembrance service on at the time, and I had never been to one before. I was amazed to see such a service in Dublin, with men wearing medals and poppies, and British standards hanging from the walls of the cathedral. To me, this was a contradiction, the contradiction of Irishmen remembering Irishmen who died in the world wars serving in British forces. Perhaps it was divine intervention after all, because from then on I wanted to learn more and explain this contradiction to myself. There were very few books on Irishmen in the British army at the time. What shocked me was the gap in my education about Ireland and the First World War. What shocked me even more was the high number of Irishmen who served with the British in the war. I was moved by their suffering and misery, and most of all by their small place in Irish historic memory compared to the men of Easter 1916. I felt this was a terrible injustice that needed to be redressed, and that this should take the form of a human story in an exhibition. On 10 November 1995 I duly wrote to Noel Carroll, PRO at Dublin Corporation, and informed him that 1996 would mark the eightieth anniversary of the Easter Rising but also the eightieth anniversary of the Battle of the Somme. I asked him if it would be possible for the corporation to commemorate the latter event through an exhibition dedicated to the Dublin men who fought and died, or, indeed, came back to their city after the war. My objective was to create awareness on the island of Ireland, particularly in the Republic, about the tragic, and I believed forgotten, history of the Irishmen and women who took part in the First World War.

The reply from Dublin Corporation was positive. At that time, there was no Royal Dublin Fusiliers Association. The previous association had long since passed away. The formation of the present-day RDFA is a story in itself. Suffice to say that a group of people, mainly collectors of militaria, came together on 23 March 1996 at the Teacher's Club in Dublin and formed a committee to present the first exhibition. The exhibition aimed to tell the story of the individual soldier, preferably a Dublin Fusilier, who took part in the war. I felt the war was a human tragedy, and this was the central theme of the exhibition. By focusing on the human/personal dimension, I believed the public could identify with the exhibits, which had three basic components intended to bring the exhibition to life: a photograph of the soldier, a script of his life story, and an item of his military memorabilia such as a medal, a diary or a cap badge. I believed the public could identify with the exhibition in this format. From the outset, I had no intentions of telling the history of an Irish regiment of the British army; I was neither qualified nor interested in doing so. I believe this human-story approach was crucial to the success of the entire project. The IRA and loyalist ceasefires had been declared in 1995, and the peace process was in its infancy. Conscious of the delicate political situation on the island, I knew that if I had decided to present an exhibition in Dublin with a very British, militaristic theme, the project would have failed utterly. In 1996 the Irish public and political establishment were not ready for such an exhibition.

On 19 November 1996 the tánaiste and minister for foreign affairs, Dick Spring TD, and the British ambassador, Veronica Sutherland, jointly opened that first exhibition at the Dublin Civic Museum in South William Street. In attendance were executive members of Dublin Corporation and members of the Ulster Unionist Party. Kevin Myers, then of the *Irish Times*, gave a brief talk on the history of the RDF in the First World War.

The exhibition was a great success and, using the names from the first visitors' book, a meeting was called to form the RDFA as a history society. The meeting took place in the Civic Museum on 25 January 1997. Over eighty people attended, and it was decided to build on the success of the exhibition by presenting a series of public lectures and exhibitions. From 19 November 1996 to 5 November 2011, the RDFA delivered no less than sixty-one public lectures on the First World War, with topics ranging across the political, military, social and economic history of the war and its impact on Ireland. There was an average attendance of seventy people. The purpose of the lectures was to educate ourselves and the general public, and to reawaken an interest in the First World War at a public, as distinct from an academic, level. To achieve this, we invited Irish historians and writers who had published on these topics.[1] Membership of the association grew over the same period from 166 to a maximum of 547 in 2005, and in 2011 stood at 376, averaging 400 a year. By February 2012 some 1,251 persons from the Republic of Ireland, Northern Ireland, Britain, Europe, the US, Canada and Australia had expressed an interest in joining the RDFA. Much like the old regiment itself, the bulk of the membership of the RDFA came from a cross-section of Irish society.

On the application form to join, we invited applicants to state the reasons for their interest in the regiment. The answers to this question offered an interesting insight into Irish attitudes regarding the First World War across the crucial fifteen years in which the public memory of the conflict was recovered in the Republic. In general, the answers fell into three broad categories. First, interest in military history, specifically in Irish regiments of the British army disbanded in 1922; second, genealogical curiosity regarding family involvement in the First World War; and third, a desire to redress a version of Irish history that many applicants felt had been unkind to their relatives. This last category was the largest, and it yields some of the most moving insights into the changing attitudes towards Dublin, and Irish, involvement in the war.

One applicant noted: '[The men of the RDF] have been airbrushed out of history. This should be reversed.' Another applicant's grandfather was killed during the German gas attack on the 2nd RDF at Mouse Trap Farm near St Julien in May 1915, which prompted the wish (or was it a prayer) 'May he rest in peace with his comrades now that they are home.' The ambivalence of 'home' suggests that he was also welcoming his grandfather 'home' into the consciousness of his native city. One woman joined up because she had found letters in a biscuit tin in her attic written by an uncle she never knew. He had served with the 7th RDF in Salonika, and had survived the war. Another prospective member wrote that his maternal grandfather was of Ulster Presbyterian stock and had fought with the British army during the war, but that his paternal grandfather joined Seán Mac Eoin in the north Longford flying column in the War of Independence. This particular applicant attended one of the lectures in 1997, and joined the association because he 'was impressed by the ethos of reconciliation and non-glorification of war which [it] promotes'. Some of the applicants expressed pride in their relative, and welcomed the opportunity to express that pride. One wrote:

> My late father…was a Sergeant with the 2nd RDF from 1914 to his discharge in 1919. I feel at last that recognition is being given to all Irish men that fought in that terrible conflict and I thank the Association for doing so. Their reasons were noble, their courage unsurpassed, they should not be forgotten.

On the same theme, another applicant—who lived in Cahir, Co. Tipperary, and tended the war memorial in the town for years—wrote on his application form:

> The Dublin Fusiliers suffered great hardships, just like my father's regiment, The Royal Irish Regt. Four Cahir men died with the Dubs in World War 1 and are remembered with respect with their Regts name on the Cahir war memorial…They should all be remembered with pride. They are Irish!

Another man simply wrote: 'My father, God be good to him, was a member of the Royal Dublin Fusiliers.'

One applicant, whose grandfather served in the RDF, expressed a sense of shame arising from what he perceived as the ill-treatment Irish veterans of the war received on their return home. He was 'embarrassed about the treatment of veterans over the last 80 years and would like to be part of any organisation that is working to turn around years of neglect/avoidance'. Another applicant was an ex-British soldier himself whose relative was killed on the first day of the Somme offensive in 1916. 'As an exile', he noted,

> we treated the King's 8th Irish, the Liverpool Irish, as our own and it was normal to be comfortable with Nationalism and service to the Crown. Above all I feel that our Irish dead should be written back into the history books and remembered.

Interestingly, one applicant had been a member of, and kept the books for, the original RDF Old Comrades' Association.

From reading the responses on the RDFA application forms, especially those written by people whose fathers had served in the RDF during the war, one gets a sense that people were drawn to the association because they wanted their relatives' names placed in the landscape of recent Irish history and their memory respected. A similar longing for restoration in Irish history also emerged in the taped interviews that I conducted with many of the members whose fathers had served in the RDF during the war. I never gained much of an insight into military history from these interviews, but I did learn what it was like to be the son or daughter of a Dublin Fusilier growing up in the Ireland of the 1930s and 1940s. Many of these people, like Paddy Cummins, never spoke about their fathers' past. One member from Ballyfermot, whose father and two uncles were in the RDF, actually had a shrine to them placed on the mantelpiece over his fireplace, with flowers, candles and pictures. Sadly, he died not long after I interviewed him in August 1997.

The association staged dozens of exhibitions throughout Ireland and in Belgium between 1996 and 2001. The number of visitors to the exhibitions is listed in table 1. Not all the visitors signed the visitors' books, so the minimum numbers are recorded, whilst the true totals are somewhat larger. The books provided an opportunity for the public to have their say anonymously about the content of the exhibitions, and so yield an insight into a larger spectrum of public opinion than that recorded by the membership applications of the RDFA, which so often drew on a family connection. The overwhelming public reaction was favourable. Of the almost five thousand who signed the visitors' books between November 1996 and May 2001, only two or three made comments that were negative or in any way derogatory. Of course, this public was still self-selected in that it had to be sufficiently interested to visit the exhibitions. Nonetheless, one can only conclude that what the exhibition said about Ireland and the First World War—and especially how it said it, by emphasising the human dimension—was overwhelmingly accepted by this wider segment of the Irish public.

Table 1: *Royal Dublin Fusiliers Association exhibitions, 22 Nov. 1996–31 May 2002*

Location	Period of exhibition(s)	No. of signatories in visitors' books	No. of days of exhibition (5-day week)	Average (approx.) no. of signatories per day
Civic Museum, Dublin	22 Nov. 1996–19 Mar. 1997	1,466	80	19
Phoenix Park Visitors' Centre 1, Dublin	5 Apr. 1997–24 July 1997	876	79	11
County Museum, Dundalk, Co. Louth	29 Sept. 1997–1 Dec. 1997	220	45	5
Bank of Ireland Arts Centre, Dublin	13 Jan. 1998–31 Jan. 1998	148	15	10
Raheny Public Library, Dublin	5 Feb. 1998–14 Mar. 1998	178	28	7
Rathmines Public Library, Dublin	1 Apr. 1998–30 Apr. 1998	80	22	4
Ardgillan Castle, Co. Dublin	3 Feb. 2000–15 May 2000	627	76	8
Dungarvan Museum, Co. Waterford	July 2000–Aug. 2000	38	44	1
Phoenix Park Visitors' Centre 2, Dublin	3 Feb. 2001–2 Sept. 2001	1,146	153	8
ILAC Library, Dublin	2 May 2002–31 May 2002	46	22	2
Total	22 Nov. 1996–31 May 2002	4,825	564	8

Thus, of the 1,466 personal comments in the visitors' book for the first exhibition, which ran from November 1996 to March 1997, none were negative or abusive. The following are representative examples: 'Magnificent, a fitting tribute'; 'Memories of my grandfather'; 'Very interesting'; 'Very important that we remember'; 'Enlightening—About time'; 'Recognition to very brave men'; 'The hidden history of Ireland uncovered'; 'My great uncle died in 1915—Thank you'; 'Excellent, I hope it becomes a permanent exhibition somewhere here in Dublin—well done'. One Australian tourist noted: 'The personal stories have made history come alive for me. Thank you.' Several visitors left comments in Irish, including 'An suimiúil (very interesting); 'An spéisiúil' (very special); 'Ní bheidh a leithéad arís ann' (the likes of him will not be seen again) and 'Go raibh maith agat' (thank you).

Following the Civic Museum in 1996, the exhibition was added to and taken to other venues, mainly in Dublin but also in Dundalk and Dungarvan. The comments in the Dundalk visitors' book were positive. Since the town was associated with republican activities during the Troubles, it was interesting to see that no derogatory remarks were made. Schoolchildren visited many of the exhibition venues around Dublin, and, again, the vast majority of the remarks were positive.

In the Raheny Library exhibition, a note of ambiguity crept in as one man signed his name in Irish and noted: 'O had they died by Pearse's side'. Towards the end of this exhibition, another man commented, 'Stupid'. But directly beneath his comment, another man glossed it with 'Narrow minded git—Interesting history'. Another commentator recalled the all-important role of family history in preserving the memory of the RDF and other Irish soldiers of the Great War: 'Reminded me of stories from my mother'.

The exhibition in Rathmines Library produced the first truly negative comments since the project began. A female visitor wrote: 'Aren't all the Brits...for putting our brave lads through WW1 and the famine. All illegal immigrants should be expelled for sponging...Red sky at night Sheppard's [*sic*] delight. Red sky morning it's a Communist takeover'. I think these comments speak for themselves and the confused individual who wrote them. However, Rathmines produced an interesting comment from a visitor from Belfast who linked the exhibition to the Good Friday agreement.

> Let us now all move forward like civilised human beings. God gave no man the right to take another man's life—neither in war or peacetime. This [exhibition] is a cruel reminder of man's inhumanity to man...Long live the Good Friday agreement—we all owe it to future generations in these small islands. A very good exhibition. Thank you.

Of the 627 signatories at the exhibition in Ardgillan Castle in north Co. Dublin, none were negative. School teachers arranged visits for local schoolchildren to help them with their history projects.

The ILAC Library exhibition in Dublin's Moore Street also proved successful. However, one man—who signed his name in Irish—noted 'For what died the sons of Roisin?'

Over the last decade, the RDFA has become an established part of the commemorative landscape of the Great War in Ireland. On 26 April 2001 the taoiseach, Bertie Ahern TD, launched the RDFA website (www.greatwar.ie) at a state reception in Dublin Castle. Each year, visitors to the website have generated between two and three hundred requests for assistance in tracing relatives who had served in the regiment, once more indicating the importance of family history not only in the preservation of the memory of the RDF but also now in its recovery for a wider public. In May 2001 the *Irish Times* recommended the site to Leaving Cert students, stating: 'Those studying history in the Leaving Cert will find it particularly useful. A fine site and a credit to the Association.'[2] Newspapers more generally and journals such as *History Ireland* have covered the exhibitions and lectures, as have television and radio stations such as RTÉ, UTV and BBC Northern Ireland. I can also honestly say that had it not been for the genuine assistance of the Irish government and senior civil servants, the work of the RDFA in creating an awareness of the First World War in Irish society would never have been as successful as it has been. With the qualified exception of Sinn Féin, moreover, political support for the work of the RDFA was cross-party. Beginning with Dick Spring's willingness to open the first exhibition in November 1996, right up to President McAleese's visit to Gallipoli in March 2006—when I had the honour of being her official guide—regardless of which political party was in power, the Irish government's support for this project has been second to none.

No doubt all this reflects the changed political climate, in which the Belfast Peace Agreement of 1998 placed a premium on the understanding and accommodating of the different histories and traditions of both parts of Ireland, for the link between the First World War and the Irish peace process was the commonality between Irish nationalism and unionism in sharing the tragic history of the First World War. But that in no way detracts from the personal commitment of those involved. This helped the work of the association in exploring and presenting this shared history in the Republic, and in doing so helped build a bridge between nationalism and unionism, between North and South. It is an interesting historical fact that the Good Friday Agreement, the opening of the Peace Park in Messines, the RDFA exhibition *Let Ireland remember*, and, sadly, the Omagh bombing all occurred in the same year of 1998. The early work of the RDFA was carried out amidst a sea change in the memory of the Great War within the Republic, and it contributed in a significant way to the recovery of that memory. Only on that basis could reconciliation, which is still ongoing, be attempted.

Notes

1 A full list of lecture titles and speakers, and exhibitions for the period November 1996 to November 2008, is contained in the RDFA journal, *The Blue Cap* 15 (Dec. 1998).
2 *Irish Times*, 8 May 2001.

12

Charley Bourne, Jack Ford and the Green Fields of France

Brian Hanley

On 21 March 1918 the German armies launched a huge offensive that drove the Allies back across the former Somme battlefields. An estimated twenty thousand soldiers lost their lives that day. Among them was Private Michael Leahy of the Royal Irish Regiment. From Caherconlish in east Limerick, Leahy was thirty-nine and left a widow, Ellen, of Portlaw, Co. Waterford.[1] Four years later, his nephew, nineteen-year-old Thomas Leahy, also from Caherconlish, would die while serving with the new Irish National Army. Thomas was accidentally shot by one of his comrades while guarding Cahir Castle in Co. Tipperary. He had joined the Free State army on 7 October 1922, when the Civil War was just four months old.[2] Though there had been clashes around Caherconlish during July 1922, by then the worst of the fighting in Limerick was over. He left behind a mother, a brother and two sisters—my grandmother Bridget and grand-aunt Winnie. It was from them that I first heard stories of their brother and uncle. Historians argue about the possibility of assigning motive, of understanding why men like Michael and Thomas Leahy made the choices they did. My grandmother and grand-aunt recalled Thomas telling his mother that he would be home for Christmas 'if Dinny Lacey [the Tipperary IRA leader] didn't get him first', and they remembered seeing his coffin being brought back to Caherconlish in December 1922. But as to why he had joined the army in the first place they were vague, as they were about his uncle's reasons for joining the British army.

I also heard stories about other relatives from my grandfather's side of the family. These involved the O'Brien brothers, Thomas and Michael, from Fedamore, who served with the IRA's Mid-Limerick Brigade during the War of Independence. Thomas spent a period on hunger strike whilst in gaol in Belfast, while Michael, a doctor, was medical officer to the volunteers. Both men were captured by British forces just after Christmas 1920 at Caherguillmore House, near Bruff. On 27 December 1920 republicans took over the unoccupied mansion for a fund-raising dance. However, troops and police surrounded them, and in the ensuing battle five IRA volunteers and one Black and Tan were killed. The republicans surrendered; what happened next was recounted to me in terms similar to those used in *Limerick's fighting story*: 'male guests ran the gauntlet of Black and Tans…who used clubbed rifles, table legs and portions of stair banisters to lay upon skulls, smash in teeth and deal savage punishment to all. Men subsequently found by the enemy to be without wounds were quickly put on a par with the others. An inquisition took place, too, but despite the beatings no information was given to the British.'[3] The

O'Brien brothers were jailed in England until after the Anglo-Irish Treaty. Michael died in 1923, and there was no doubt the injuries he sustained at Caherguillmore House contributed to his early demise. But there had been vengeance, as within a month 'a three-to-one toll of the Tans was exacted at Dromkeen'. In February 1921 eleven police and Black and Tans were killed there in an IRA ambush.[4] Among those who took part was Seán Clifford, commander of the 4th Battalion of the Mid-Limerick IRA, and another relative of my grandfather.[5]

An extended family tree that includes IRA volunteers together with British and Free State soldiers is not unusual in Ireland.[6] But it meant that in my childhood, war, and the War of Independence in particular, was very real. My grandparents had actually *seen* Black and Tans. My grandfather, Jack Clifford, had been questioned by them while he carried messages for the IRA in his shoes. He was a staunch Fianna Fáil supporter who only read the *Irish Press* and whose distrust of the British extended to a dislike of 'their' sports, especially soccer. A fine hurler, he was once praised in the *Limerick Leader* for his 'very plucky and sporting game', despite rough treatment, against an Ahane team that included the famous Mackey brothers.[7] I remember as a child hearing him speak about the War of Independence, but I do not recall him ever suggesting that my grandmother's relatives had been less patriotic or less noble for serving in the British or Free State armies (the Civil War breakdown among various relatives being far from clear-cut anyway). In general, however, I heard less about them than I did about those who had served with the IRA.

What I broadly understood from both school and from listening to adults when they discussed history was that the British had ruled Ireland for eight hundred years. At Easter 1916 a group of idealists, led by Patrick Pearse, began a rebellion, without any hope of success, in order to reawaken the Irish people. Though defeated, their execution enraged the Irish people so much that a new rebellion began. The IRA, led by Michael Collins, renewed the struggle, this time as a guerilla war. Despite their unleashing of the Black and Tans, the British were eventually forced into talks. But the subsequent Treaty divided the Irish people and led to a tragic Civil War. What was clear to me (though school teachers differed in their emphases and enthusiasms) was that the violence used in the fight for independence had been justified, and had the support of the Irish people. This was no longer the case, and the modern IRA, as one school textbook explained, was 'not to be confused with the "Old IRA"...the men who fought for Irish freedom between 1916 and 1923'.[8] That was a crucial distinction, and one that was reinforced at home by my parents.

Nobody growing up during the 1970s and 1980s could avoid the war in Northern Ireland. It was always there, casting a shadow over every discussion about 1916 or the War of Independence. I hope I am not misremembering or misrepresenting my parents' and grandparents' opinions, but they seemed to me to combine distrust of the British and hostility towards the unionists (especially Ian Paisley) with confusion about the IRA. (My grandmother's reaction to the IRA's rejection of John Paul II's plea for peace in 1979 was to conclude

'Ah, sure, they can't be the real IRA at all.') My grandfather dismissed any suggestion that he should be 'ashamed' because of the Provisional IRA's activities, and was decidedly unsympathetic when British soldiers featured on news broadcasts about Northern Ireland. But it was he who also bought me British war comics every week. It was from these, rather than at school or at home, that I first formed views about the Great War.

I was far from the only Irish child reading comics that celebrated the British military during the 1970s. *Warlord*, *Victor* and the various *Commando* books were devoured by my contemporaries. Movies like the *Guns of Navarone* were shown regularly on RTÉ, along with TV series such as *Dad's army*. Bedroom walls featured posters of Spitfires and Hurricanes alongside others for Manchester United and Liverpool. My favourite comic was *Warlord*, which advertised the modern British military in-between the adventures of characters like Lord Peter Flint. But as I grew slightly older, I began to read *Battle Action*, a comic whose style was grittier and seemed more realistic. *Battle* featured a First World War story, 'Charley's war', about Charley Bourne, a teenager who in 1916 lies about his age in order to join the British army. Charley's career saw him at the Somme, Passchendaele, Ypres and Cambrai, before ending up in Russia fighting the Bolsheviks in 1919. Artistic licence permitted author Pat Mills and artist Joe Colquhoun to include in the stories everything from gas attacks to Zeppelin raids and mutinies. Regular characters included Sergeant Tozer, a veteran of the Battle of Mons, 'Ginger' Jones, Charley's best friend, the pompous upper-class officer Captain Snell, and a variety of traumatised men, such as 'Budgie', 'Weeper Watkins' and 'the Scholar'.[9] They were reasonably complex and not all likeable. In contrast to their depiction in *Warlord*, the Germans were not crude caricatures but men suffering similar problems to their British enemies. Whatever about the Second World War, by the time I was a teenager I was sure that the Great War had been a horrible waste of life, and it was a British comic that helped convince me of this.[10]

This view was reinforced by a range of cultural influences. I enjoyed, without understanding all of its references, the TV series *When the boat comes in*. This starred James Bolam as Sergeant Jack Ford, a Great War veteran who returns to north-east England and is thrown into the political and industrial turmoil of the post-war years. While sympathetic to the ordinary fighting men, the tone of the series was cynical about the generals and authority in general. It was clear that the veterans had not returned to a 'land fit for heroes'. In one episode, Ford is offered a chance to join the Black and Tans, but declines in deference to an Irish friend, Paddy Boyle (who, it transpires, is an IRA man). Another influential television series, this time home-made, was *Strumpet City*, an evocative production of James Plunkett's novel about Dublin during the 1913 Lockout. Fitz (played by Bryan Murray), a striking foundry worker, was one of its most likeable characters; in the aftermath of the workers' defeat, he is shown in British uniform sailing off to France. The point that the beaten Dublin workers had nowhere to go but the trenches was well made. Several popular songs also dwelt on the horror of the Great War. 'The band played waltzing Matilda', written by Eric Bogle, had been a hit for Tommy Makem and the Clancy Brothers in 1977. Even more popular was The Fureys and Davey Arthur's version of another Bogle song, 'The green fields of France', which seemed to be played on radio constantly during the summer holidays of 1979. The song recounted how 'the suffering, the sorrow, the pain…the killing, the dying, was all done in vain'. I saw a school production of *Oh, what a lovely war!*, while the movie *All quiet on the Western Front* was shown to us in class. As a result, I was familiar with many images of the war, especially those of rat-infested trenches and men being mown down after going over the top. The 1914 Christmas truce, when British and German soldiers had played football in no-man's-land, featured in the video for Paul McCartney's 'Pipes of peace', a number one during December 1983.[11] I did not like the song, but I understood the message, which was similar to that of The Jam's 'Little boy soldiers', The Pogues' version of 'The band played waltzing Matilda', and Elvis Costello's 'Oliver's army', all of which I did like. In secondary-school English, we also read Siegfried Sassoon, in whose poems 'scarlet Majors' sped 'glum heroes up the line to death'.[12] The majority of what I knew about the Great War, and my own views on it, were thus far more informed by British and international popular culture than by any form of Irish nationalism.

At school, the war was taught as part of European history. I do not recall Irish participation being dealt with in any detail. We did touch on the conflict in English classes through the poetry of one of the Irish war dead, Francis Ledwidge, whose 'Thomas McDonagh' began with the memorable lines 'He shall not hear the bittern cry, in the wild sky, where he is lain'.[13] The poem, however, was contextualised in terms of the Easter Rising far more than Ledwidge's war service. Despite enjoying Peter Weir's movie *Gallipoli*, I would have been surprised to hear that Irish soldiers suffered huge casualties in that campaign, along with the Anzacs and Turks. I knew there was a war memorial in Limerick's Pery Square, but was not aware of commemorations being held there. I never saw anyone wearing a poppy, and would not have known what that meant until the mid-1980s. Any awareness I had of this practice came when Margaret Thatcher condemned peace campaigners for producing white poppies in 1986. Ulster unionist politicians weighed in, criticising those who wore the white flower for insulting the war dead. Though I had no intention of wearing either symbol, my sympathies lay with the peace campaigners, whose desire to commemorate but not celebrate seemed perfectly sensible to me. By then I was attracted to socialist politics, and if there was any position on the Great War I agreed with, it was contained in the slogan displayed on Dublin's Liberty Hall in 1914 asserting 'We serve neither King nor Kaiser but Ireland'. When I read how the major European socialist parties had collapsed into support for their nations' war efforts in 1914, I felt proud that at least James Connolly had maintained his opposition to imperialist slaughter.

What was more relevant to me by that stage was that the Irish state seemed to have great problems with commemorating 1916. Though I was unaware of the debates that had been taking place among historians, anyone who paid attention could see that there had been a perceptible change in how the Rising was viewed. There was now a palpable air of embarrassment at celebrating what one former minister for education referred to as a 'blood cult'.[14] The official commemorations of the seventieth and seventy-fifth anniversaries of 1916 were remarkably low-key.[15] Patrick Pearse came in for particular criticism, often depicted as a fanatic bent on sacrificial violence, and whose writings glorified bloodshed.[16] Some commentators were even holding the 1916 rebels responsible for the conflict in Northern Ireland. John Redmond and the home rule party were increasingly held up as moderate, peaceful alternatives to violent republicanism. There was also now far more attention paid to Irish participation in the Great War. The relatively small number of rebels was contrasted unfavourably with the 'fifty thousand' Irishmen who had died in British army uniform.[17] Some suggested that the joint sacrifice of Irish nationalists and unionists in the war might have helped avoid partition and further conflict, only for the impact of the Easter Rising.[18]

I rejected much of this instinctively, though not because I thought Irish-nationalist history sacred. I agreed with Eamonn McCann's view that many Irish people paid far more attention to 'a mixture of half-truths and folk mythology about the past' than they did to actual history.[19] But what seemed to be happening was an attempt not just to remember but justify, and indeed embrace, the First World War. Many of those promoting remembrance of the war seemed contemptuous of Irish republicanism, and eager to mock its faults while ignoring those of the imperial powers. During 1991, when government commemoration of the Easter Rising was confined to a brief wreath-laying ceremony, I took part in the alternative events organised by the Reclaim the Spirit of 1916 group.[20] I agreed with Joe Lee's assertion that it was

> curious that many who deplore the violence of 1916 should simultaneously demand we now commemorate the sacrifice of all Irishmen who died in the First World War...commemorating the victims of the Great War is not a celebration of non-violence. More Irishmen killed and died in the First World War than in any conflict fought on Irish soil.[21]

What seemed clear was that remembrance of the Irish Revolution and the Great War were mutually exclusive. You could only have one, it seemed, at the expense of the other.

My own understanding of Irish involvement in the war deepened when I studied history at Trinity in the mid-1990s. I found that historians had revised downward the number of Irish dead to perhaps thirty thousand. I learned that the war had never been very popular in much of Ireland, and that recruitment levels had fallen off quite early. To my surprise, the make-up of the Irish recruits was much more socially diverse than I had imagined. Similarly, the reasons men enlisted varied, with friendship and fraternity often as important as ideology (though had I read my republican classics more closely, particularly Tom Barry and Ernie O'Malley, I should have known this already).[22] Unionist and nationalist recruits had joined for opposing reasons, and there was little evidence to suggest they abandoned their mutual antipathy post-war. Veterans would confront each other as IRA volunteers, Black and Tans, B-Specials and

Free State soldiers.[23] More intriguingly, the home rule party was not the caricature depicted by both detractors and latter-day supporters: many of its MPs
were former Fenians, and its rhetoric was often viscerally anti-British. The
decision to back the war effort did not come naturally to many home rulers;
nationalist intellectuals, such as Tom Kettle, and labour activists, such as Francis
Ledwidge, grappled with many of the same worries as those of contemporary
European socialists. I was less happy to discover that Connolly's position was
rather more pro-German than the 'neither king nor Kaiser' slogan implied.[24]
I also had to accept that the Great War and Irish Revolution could not be
discussed separately. The Rising took place *because* Britain was at war, and any
hopes of military success that the rebels had were dependent on German aid. A
serious shortage of manpower in 1918 forced the British to consider introduc-
ing conscription in Ireland, a move that radicalised Irish nationalist opinion
to an unprecedented degree. Éamon de Valera and Arthur Griffith—inspired
by the idea that in a new world order small nations would be entitled to self-
determination—made gaining recognition for Ireland at the post-war peace
conference a central plank of Sinn Féin policy.

Regarding the Great War as a central part of the Irish experience was
less and less a controversial idea, however. A new culture of commemoration,
entwined with the peace process, had emerged by the late 1990s. One of the
most significant aspects of this was the decision by the republican movement
to recognise and, to a degree, participate in commemoration of the Irish dead
of the world wars.[25] A minor but suggestive example of this was the change in
republican attitudes to the wearing of poppies by Irish entertainers in Britain.
In 1999 an endorsement by the boy band Westlife of the Royal British Legion
Poppy Appeal was condemned by Sinn Féin as an insult to the victims of the
British army in Ireland.[26] By 2008 Irish contestants on shows such as *The
X factor* were routinely wearing poppies—and some even taking part in fund-
raising in support of British military charities—without a hint of mainstream
republican condemnation.[27]

At best, this new atmosphere contributed to a deeper understanding of the
impact of the Great War on Ireland. At worst, however, it has suggested a commemorative trade-off whereby nationalists celebrate Easter 1916, unionists the
Somme, and both sides congratulate each other on their maturity. The very real
issues that divided Irish people in 1914 are glossed over, and the role of Britain
virtually ignored. While we cannot understand the Irish Revolution without
reference to the Great War, neither can we understand Irish participation in
the war without reference to Ireland's relationship with Britain. When John
Redmond appealed for nationalist support for the war effort, he did so as the
leader of a minority political party in Westminster, not as head of an Irish
executive. There was no Irish parliament to authorise 'our' participation.
Ultimately, these life-and-death decisions were taken by a British government
that ruled Ireland, in the last resort, by its ability to deploy force.[28] The lack of
democratic legitimacy for British rule in Ireland must be considered when
discussing Ireland's role in the war.

Being critical of Irish involvement does not mean having to dismiss the memory of those who served. Those tempted to do so should consider Ernie O'Malley's reaction to such attitudes among his fellow volunteers:

> we dismissed the agony, blood, and misery of the trenches as we dismiss anoth-er's sorrow. There is an Irish proverb: 'It's easy to sleep on another man's wound.' When I read the casualty lists for news of my brother I found friends and acquaintances amongst the killed and wounded. I could see mother's face when she read the morning paper and a hand involuntarily going to her throat if there came a sharp knocking at the door. It might be a telegram: 'We regret…'[29]

It should be possible—as those who have been involved in a project inves-tigating the service of Belfast nationalists in the Connaught Rangers have asserted—to work on remembrance that is 'by no means a contribution to the glorification of the senseless slaughter of the First World War'.[30]

But it is also valid to ask why war should be commemorated and whether the nature of commemoration implies that war is justified and normal. Certainly, the manner in which the poppy is now central to British remem-brance (and, therefore, to Irish remembrance as well) is problematic. Worn from early October onwards, embroidered on football jerseys and practically compulsory for those in the public eye, many now see the poppy as expressing support for the British military, not simply commemoration of past conflicts.[31] It is hard to disagree with the British veterans who recently complained that the build-up to Armistice Day now amounts to 'a month-long drum roll of support for current wars'.[32] This has not always been the case. Historian Pádraig Yeates remembers how his father, who fought in the Second World War, 'never wore a poppy and anyone I knew who served with him never wore a poppy. They regarded it, and the British Legion, as symbolizing all that was worst, most jingoistic and reactionary in the British establishment.'[33] In Ireland, the use of the symbol is even more problematic, commemorating as it does *all* British military losses, not just those of the world wars.

Ironically, the peace process has also allowed the Irish government (at least partly for reasons of political advantage) to renew commemoration of the Easter Rising. While undoubtedly popular, commemoration of the revolu-tion as primarily a military event risks missing important features of it. The general strike against conscription during April 1918, for example, was not just part of the movement for Irish self-determination but an expression of the wider movement across Europe against war and for change. The leaders of the strike certainly saw the parallels with revolution in Russia and else-where.[34] Remembering the war also means commemorating those who resisted participation in it, and those who hoped that a new world might emerge in which such slaughter would never be seen again. In November 1934 former servicemen took part in demonstrations in Dublin organised by the left-wing Republican Congress. Veterans of Flanders and the Middle East joined ex-IRA members in alternative Armistice Day events. They marched under the banner 'Honour the dead by fighting for the living'—a slogan with resonance for the present as well as for commemoration of the past.[35]

Notes

1   *Ireland's memorial records, 1914–1918* (Dublin, 1923), 79.
2   Thomas Leahy's records show he 'attested for service in the National Army on 10 October 1922…died on 7 December 1922'. Commandant P.B. Brennan, Military Archives, to author, 17 Dec. 2002.
3   *Limerick's fighting story* [anonymous, published by *The Kerryman*] (Tralee, 1948), 103–4.
4   J. O'Callaghan, *Revolutionary Limerick: the republican campaign for independence in Limerick, 1913–1921* (Dublin, 2010), 137–42.
5   Seán Clifford contributed an interesting statement to the Bureau of Military History: witness statement 1279 (National Archives of Ireland).
6   There were other relatives who served in one or other of these forces in my extended family.
7   *Limerick Leader*, 3 Sept. 1932.
8   Mark Tierney and Margaret MacCurtain, *The birth of modern Ireland* (Dublin, 1969), 188.
9   The names of many of the characters in 'Charley's war' were inspired by those in Frederic Manning's *Her privates we*, a gritty and, for its time, quite graphic novel, first published as *The middle parts of fortune* in 1929 (New York). The novel was based largely on the Australian author's own experience of service in the ranks of the British army on the Western Front.
10   Which was one of the objectives of Pat Mills, though of course I had no idea about that at the time.
11   The Christmas truce is also the theme of The Farm's 1990 hit 'All together now'.
12   J.J. Carey and A. Martin (eds), *Exploring English 3* (Dublin, 1969), 160–1.
13   Carey and Martin (eds), *Exploring English 3*, 236.
14   Gemma Hussey, *Irish Independent*, 29 Mar. 1991.
15   *Irish Press*, 31 Mar. 1986; *Irish Times*, 9 Mar. 1991.
16   See Joost Augusteijn, 'Patrick Pearse: proto-fascist eccentric or mainstream European thinker?', *History Ireland*, Nov./Dec. 2010.
17   Though incorrect, this figure remains widely in use. See 'Is it time to start wearing the poppy?', *TheJournal.ie*, 10 Nov. 2011, http://www.thejournal.ie/readme/column-is-it-time-to-start-wearing-the-poppy-275814-Nov2011 (accessed 17 Jan. 2013).
18   Popular attitudes remained far more enthusiastic about the Rising, however. See opinion poll in *Irish Independent*, 29 Mar. 1991.
19   Eamonn McCann, *War and an Irish town* (London, 1980), 117.
20   For a flavour of these debates see Theo Dorgan and Máirín Ní Dhonnchadha (eds), *Revising the Rising* (Derry, 1991), 25.
21   *Irish Independent*, 29 Mar. 1991.
22   Tom Barry, *Guerilla days in Ireland* (Dublin, 1971), 8; Ernie O'Malley, *On another man's wound* (Dublin, 1979), 28.
23   For discussion of many of these themes see John Horne (ed.), *Our war: Ireland and the Great War* (Dublin, 2008).
24   For a defence of Connolly's position see Manus O'Riordan and Francis Devine, 'The justification of James Connolly' in *James Connolly, Liberty Hall and the 1916 Rising* (Dublin, 2006).
25   See Richard Grayson, *Belfast boys: how unionists and nationalists fought and died together in the First World War* (London, 2009), 180–4.
26   *Irish Times*, 3 Nov. 1999.
27   Though republican critics of Sinn Féin continued to complain about this. *Derry Journal*, 4 Nov. 2008.
28   J.J. Lee, 'The background: Anglo-Irish relations, 1898–1921' in Anne Dolan and Cormac O'Malley, *'No surrender here!' The Civil War papers of Ernie O'Malley, 1922–1924* (Dublin, 2007), xi–xxxii.
29   O'Malley, *On another man's wound*, 59.
30   6th Connaught Rangers Research Project, *The 6th Connaught Rangers: Belfast nationalists and the Great War* (Belfast, 2011).

31 Nationalists in Northern Ireland are very aware that the BBC, for example, requires its staff to wear poppies on screen. *Irish Times*, 11 Nov. 1995.
32 *Guardian*, 5 Nov. 2010.
33 *Irish Times*, 17 Nov. 2006.
34 See Tom Johnson's article, 'If the Bolsheviks came to Ireland' in *Irish Opinion*, 23 Feb. 1918.
35 *Republican Congress*, 17 Nov. 1934.

Commemorations

13

Irish Varieties of Great War Commemoration

Keith Jeffery

The First World War has been, and is, 'remembered' and commemorated in Ireland in an extraordinary range of ways. Over recent years, moreover, the intensity of this commemoration appears to have increased, as the events themselves have receded. This is especially true in independent Ireland, where commemoration has ebbed and flowed since the end of the war itself, but where now engagement with the war and its commemoration has become especially striking and prevalent. And over the coming years, during which the centenary of the First World War will be marked, this trend is likely to be further intensified. It is, therefore, worth our while to review the existing history and patterns of Great War commemoration in Ireland since 1918, for it is only by contemplating where we have come from that we might usefully hazard where we may be going to in the matter of future commemoration.

I want first to sketch out the general pattern of Irish commemoration over the past ninety or so years, for there has been a widespread assumption that the more recent intensification of commemoration (particularly in independent Ireland and among the nationalist community, both North and South) has, as it were, sprung out of a blank canvas: that alleged 'national amnesia' identified by F.X. Martin in a famous essay, '1916—myth, fact and mystery', published in the academic journal *Studia Hibernica* in 1967.[1] Explicitly linking the First World War with the 1916 Easter Rising—a conjunction which has now become extremely common in matters of official Irish First World War commemoration—Martin observed that in independent Ireland it was 'difficult to find men and women who will acknowledge that they are children of the men who were serving during 1916 in the British Army'. This, he wrote, was 'the "Great Oblivion", an example of national amnesia'. This notion of a 'national amnesia' has had considerable currency, but on closer examination of the historical record we find that the 'amnesia' that Martin identified, and which may have existed in the Republic of Ireland in the 1960s, was by no means a consistent or constant feature of Irish public and community life from the 1920s onwards.

Broadly speaking, in independent Ireland, the two decades between the end of the First World War and the outbreak of the Second were ones of widespread and active commemoration, culminating with the construction of an Irish National War Memorial park at Islandbridge by the River Liffey on the then western edge of Dublin. During the Second World War, when independent Ireland remained neutral, commemoration was actively suppressed, as there were concerns that remembering the dead of the First World War would be conflated with service in the British army, navy or air force in the Second. After 1945 public commemoration ceremonies did not return on anything like the scale they had been before 1939, and for thirty years or so there was a marked decline in Great War commemoration (which was now linked with that of the 1939–45 war). This trend was powerfully reinforced after the outbreak of the Troubles in Northern Ireland from the late 1960s, and for another twenty years the practice of war commemoration was perceived to have become highly politicised. There was, indeed, a striking withdrawal of public political engagement with such ceremonies as continued to be held in the Republic. This tendency, however, was reversed from the late 1980s, and dramatically so in conjunction with the peace process that brought the political violence almost completely to an end. The pattern of commemoration in Northern Ireland, especially within the unionist community, was rather different, with much less of a dip in the practice following 1945. The Troubles, nevertheless, had a significant impact, and unionists in Northern Ireland have with their nationalist compatriots shared in a remarkable growth of commemoration since the 1990s.

In the immediate aftermath of the First World War, the combination of personal and public mourning and commemoration was at its most intense, as communities and individuals strove to come to terms with the dreadful losses of the war. This was a period of well-attended Armistice Day and remembrance ceremonies, accompanied by the commissioning and dedication of public, institutional and church war memorials across the whole island. Although historians have only patchily explored the story of war commemoration in Southern Ireland, pioneering work by Jane Leonard (among others) has confirmed that during the interwar years there were extensive and well-attended public demonstrations on Armistice Day (11 November) and at other times in many places across Ireland. In November 1924, for example, an estimated twenty thousand veterans and a crowd of fifty thousand gathered at College Green in Dublin. There was official involvement by successive Irish governments, too. In the 1920s official Irish representatives laid wreaths at the London Cenotaph, and Éamon de Valera's Fianna Fáil government after 1932 provided a publicly acknowledged state subsidy for the completion of the Irish National War Memorial, with de Valera himself agreeing in principle to attend the opening of the memorial (though the onset of the Second World War prevented this).[2]

Accompanying the annual commemorations was the erection and dedication of war memorials, which in many cases reflect the wide public engagement of all sorts of Irish people, nationalists as well as unionists, in the commemoration of the war. The inscriptions on some Irish war memorials tell their own story. The Great Southern and Western Railway Company's memorial at Dublin's Heuston Station commemorates those who 'laid down their lives for their country in the Great War'. While 'country' in this context might be ambiguous, the Celtic cross in Castlebellingham, Co. Louth, is more explicit, as it remembers men 'who died for Ireland in the Great International War', and the memorial on South Mall in the centre of Cork is dedicated to those who 'fell in the Great War fighting for the freedom of small nations'.[3] These inscriptions tell us two things. First, they simply reflect the fact that more Irish nationalists than unionists died fighting in the British army in the Great War;

and second, they confirm that the commemoration of Irish war dead was by no means restricted to unionists.

It is true, however, that there was a noticeable difference between developments in independent Ireland and those in Northern Ireland, where unionists were more engaged in commemoration than nationalists, and also more inclined to relate the war service of soldiers to the establishment of the new Northern state and the maintenance of the precious unionist link with the rest of the United Kingdom. Powerfully underpinning this was the experience of the 36th (Ulster) Division, a predominantly Protestant and unionist formation that had suffered grievous losses on the first day of the Battle of the Somme, 1 July 1916. At the dedication of the war memorial in Coleraine in November 1922, Sir James Craig, the first prime minister of Northern Ireland, asserted that 'those who have passed away have left behind a great message… to stand firm, and to give away none of Ulster's soil'.[4] Craig was evidently able to get away with this unchallenged, despite the fact that Catholic, as well as Protestant, dead were named on the memorial. But this pattern was by no means consistent. In November 1925, at the unveiling of the memorial in Portadown, Co. Armagh (a town with a reputation for sectarian antagonisms), wreaths were laid not only by the Orange Order but also by the Ancient Order of Hibernians, demonstrating that it was a monument for the whole community.

The community dimension of these Great War memorials is among the most important and resonant in any consideration of commemoration in contemporary Ireland, and here the Portadown memorial is as good an example as any. In cities, towns and villages throughout Ireland—North and South—there are war memorials in urban centres, parks, at roadsides, in many churches and other places, such as schools, banks, hospitals and so on. We may pass them every day with scarcely a thought about their history and the histories of those they commemorate. Portadown's impressive angel with a dying soldier is perhaps more difficult to miss than some, but few people these days will pause to contemplate what seems to be no more than a bald list of names. Yet each of these individuals has a story to tell; each of them had a family left behind to mourn, for whom that very monument may effectively be the only gravestone they have for a loved husband, father, brother or sweetheart. One is struck by the variety of age, situation and experience to be found among the men (and one woman—a nurse) on the memorial at Portadown. Although the great majority of the three hundred-odd First World War dead fell on the Western Front in France and Belgium, and fully seventy men died in that terrible July of 1916 during the Battle of the Somme, there are Portadown men who lie in Turkey, Greece, Serbia, Israel and Iraq. There are heartbreaking stories of family tragedy: the two Abraham brothers killed together on 1 July 1916, and another brother killed the following year; John Hayes, who also died on 1 July, and his two brothers who were killed later in the war; William Cooke, who left four children, and William Malcomson, a weaver, who left seven; Edward Jones, killed in Belgium, whose widow named their yet-to-be-born son Edward Ypres Jones after his dead father and the place where he had died. There are stories of high heroism, too, but not all the men on that memorial were heroes in the conventional sense. One man, serving in the Scottish Rifles, had an extremely chequered military career, being charged with 'disorderly behaviour while drunk', 'not being shaved on parade', and even desertion, for which he got six months' detention in 1915. Another, serving with the Australian forces (and there are a fair number of Portadown men who had emigrated to Australia and Canada who came back to serve), appears to have been murdered by a fellow-soldier. Two men died while prisoners-of-war in Germany, and are buried in Berlin. Another failed the medical for the British army and became an ambulance driver for the French Red Cross, and lies forever in Serbia.[5]

After 1945 the Portadown war memorial, like most First World War memorials throughout the world, was adapted to cover the Second World War as well. This occurred in Ireland as elsewhere, though sometimes only very minimally. The memorial in Nenagh, Co. Tipperary, was altered by the simple expedient of adding an *s* to the phrase 'who fell in the Great War', along with the dates '1914–1918 and 1939–1945'. But even the addition of just one letter could alter the political significance of the service commemorated, since engagement in the Second World War challenged the neutral position of the Dublin government. Inscriptions on more recent war memorials have also carried distinct, if sometimes only implicit, political messages. A memorial erected at the Loughshore Park in Newtownabbey, Co. Antrim, in November 1982 (and since removed) was dedicated 'in memory of the members of H.M. Forces who gave their lives in the two World Wars…and in subsequent conflicts', a formulation which, while non-specific, could be understood to include men and women who had served in the British armed forces (including local recruits in the Ulster Defence Regiment and the Royal Irish Regiment), as well as police personnel (serving in the Royal Ulster Constabulary). A more politically explicit combining of First World War memorial with the Troubles exists in a monument erected by the loyalist paramilitary Ulster Defence Association in 1997 in Ballymacarrett, east Belfast. Created as the East Belfast Brigade roll of honour, it commemorates 'members of the 2nd Battalion Willowfield, East Belfast Regiment, Ulster Volunteer Force who died in the First World War', replicating a plaque which had existed in the local Orange Hall but had been lost when the hall was demolished in 1983. The new memorial combined the First World War commemoration with that of 'Fallen Volunteers of 3rd Battalion, East Belfast Brigade, Ulster Volunteer Force, who lost their lives during the Troubles'.[6] Republican paramilitary memorials also closely follow the pattern of conventional war memorials first generally established in the aftermath of the First World War.

Inevitably, during the Troubles the association of war memorial ceremonies with the Northern Ireland state, and the involvement of serving military personnel as well as police and ex-servicemen and women, led some republicans to consider the memorials themselves and events surrounding them, to be legitimate targets for attack. War memorials in various places have been damaged by vandalism and worse. The Limerick memorial was blown up by republicans in August 1957. The one in Drogheda was vandalised on a number of occasions, and the head of the military trumpeter at the memorial in The Moy, Co. Tyrone, was knocked off in the early 1990s. Such thinking lay behind the bombing by a unit of the Provisional IRA of the Remembrance Sunday ceremony at the Enniskillen war memorial on 8 November 1987, when eleven people were killed. This 'Poppy Day bombing', widely regarded as one of the very worst attacks of the Troubles, had a devastating effect on attitudes towards the IRA, especially in the Republic, where widespread revulsion and condemnation undermined any residual mainstream support for militant republican violence, and fed into efforts to find a peaceful solution to the conflict. Following Enniskillen, indeed, there was increased participation across Ireland in Remembrance Day ceremonies. One remarkable public effect of the event was a sharp rise in the number of poppies sold and worn in the South. Before street sales of poppies in the Republic were given up in 1971, approximately twenty-five thousand had been sold annually. When they were resumed in 1988, some forty-five thousand poppies were sold.[7]

From the late 1980s, there was a marked revival of interest in Ireland's involvement with the First World War. This reflected wider trends in Britain and elsewhere, which were partly due to a sense that the last veterans would not survive for very much longer. In part, too, it was a manifestation of a growing popular interest in genealogy and family history, which, combined with the facts that the Great War was the first mass national war and that participation was very well recorded, made it irresistibly fascinating. Some public commentators, too—notably the journalist Kevin Myers in Dublin—had begun to raise the subject of Ireland's role in the First World War, and its widespread neglect in popular memory.

In 1990 the Somme Association was established in Northern Ireland 'to ensure that the efforts of Irishmen to preserve world peace between 1914 and 1919 are remembered and understood'. From the start, there was an admirable, though clearly political, cross-community agenda: 'to co-ordinate research into Ireland's part in the First World War and to provide a basis for the two communities in Northern Ireland to come together to learn of their common heritage'.[8] The significant aspect of the Somme Association was not the interest in the Somme, which for decades had been the central focus of Ulster unionist war commemoration, but the widening of its scope beyond the Protestant and unionist community, a trend that began to surface in the South, too. In 1992 a Royal Munster Fusiliers Association was founded with the aim of perpetuating 'the memory and traditions of the regiment', a British army formation disbanded in 1922 after Irish independence. Such a development could not have happened in times when the British army was seen as an enemy of 'the Irish people', and it reflected a progressive normalisation of relations between Ireland and Britain. The notion that a common heritage for Irish people from differing political standpoints might be found in British army service suggested that the recovery of this particular slice of Irish history might contribute towards the improvement of relations between nationalists and unionists. In 1997 a Royal Dublin Fusiliers Association was established to remember 'those who have been forgotten for a long time, particularly the tens of thousands of Irishmen and indeed many women, who fell in the First World War'.[9]

As people in the Irish Republic began to rediscover the involvement of forebears in the First World War, the commemoration of that war started to be integrated into public life much more fully than ever before, or at least ever since the late 1930s. In 1993, for the first time the head of state, President Mary Robinson, attended a Remembrance Day service in St Patrick's (Protestant) Cathedral in Dublin. First World War memorials in the Republic began to be refurbished, starting with the Irish National War Memorial, which had fallen into some disrepair. Under a Fianna Fáil government it was restored and declared open in 1994 by the then minister for finance, Bertie Ahern. Commemoration of the First World War began to be drawn into a wider, more general commemoration of all Irish people who had died in war. The Great War memorial in Cahir, Co. Tipperary, was rededicated in 1995 'to commemorate the men and women of this district who fought and died in all military conflicts worldwide'. In 1996, marking the seventy-fifth anniversary of the Battle of the Somme as well as the traditional 1 July events in Northern Ireland to mark the involvement of the Ulster Division, a service was held at the Irish National War Memorial on 8 September to commemorate the largely nationalist 16th (Irish) Division's part in the battle.

The most outstanding manifestation of this new engagement with Irish Great War commemoration was the Island of Ireland Peace Tower, erected in Belgium close to the site of the Battle of Messines in 1917, where the 36th (Ulster) and the 16th (Irish) Divisions fought alongside each other. Inspired by a cross-community reconciliation project based in Derry and led by Paddy Harte, a Fine Gael TD, and Glenn Barr, a former paramilitary and loyalist politician, the tower was dedicated on 11 November 1998 by President Mary McAleese, Queen Elizabeth II and Albert II, King of the Belgians. It was the first time the heads of the Irish state and the United Kingdom had participated together in any sort of war commemoration, reflecting the way in which the First World War could be used for purposes of national as well as local reconciliation. Currently, the Peace Tower sits at the centre of a Peace Park, which contains a very ambitious 128-bed Peace Village and International School for Peace Studies, which opened in June 2006. It comprises part of the Messines Vision, and is substantially funded by the European Union Programme for Peace and Reconciliation. The aim is to host courses for groups from divided communities from Europe and beyond with 'a uniquely experiential learning programme' that 'uses the events of the Great War...to engage participants in learning about their shared history, cultural heritage, peace and reconciliation, and the futility of war'.[10]

There is no sign of any slackening in the pace of Irish Great War commemoration. Astonishingly, memorials are still being erected in Ireland. In Killarney, on 24 September 2009, an entirely new memorial was 'erected in memory of those from Killarney and surrounding areas who served and died in the 1914–1918 war'. It was unveiled by President McAleese, who congratulated the war memorial committee for 'healing' the memory of Killarney's Great War dead 'and drawing them back into memory and drawing them back into the community'.[11] Illustrating the increased Irish interest in the conflict, the event was attended by members of the Irish Great War Society, a kind of re-enactment group, dressed in replica First World War uniforms. On 24 March 2010 President McAleese unveiled another brand new memorial, at Green Hill cemetery by Suvla Bay in Gallipoli dedicated to soldiers of the 10th (Irish) Division. President McAleese referred to a 'deficit of remembrance' that had afflicted Irishmen who had fought 'for the British Empire' but who had returned to Ireland to 'considerable ambivalence and even hostility about their role and their sacrifice'. Now, however, 'distance of time and changing historical context' allowed a contribution to be made 'to the much needed healing of memory on our own divided island'.[12]

Not all of this renewed memorial building is without criticism. Republican Sinn Féin described the unveiling of the new Killarney memorial 'to Irishmen who fought and died in the British Army…as an insult to the many Irishmen who were executed by the same British Army'. The local Republican Sinn Féin chairman, John Sheehy, from Listowel, said: 'It would be a far more meaningful gesture for those behind this project to consider a memorial to the Irishmen who ignited the flame of liberty for Ireland during those years. This event', he added, 'smacks of historical revisionism or else it is another stunt devised to lure tourists to the Killarney area. Either way this ceremony should be boycotted by all nationally minded people.'[13]

Much of this enhanced First World War commemoration draws on a belief that shared military experience and the shared human costs of that experience might transcend local Irish political and sectarian differences. This theme has strongly emerged in recent years, and is evident in the way Ireland's involvement with the First World War has been 'remembered' and commemorated. But if we look at our more domestic Irish conflicts, the situation has been, and in some cases remains, rather different. In sharp contrast to any notion of common suffering and common experience across the whole community, the Northern Troubles that flared up from the late 1960s produced an intensified polarisation of society that has helped entrench (a handy military metaphor) political attitudes. One thing largely absent (to our great cost) from what we might call the 'civil war' of the Troubles is any sustained sense that shared military experience on each side of the conflict might have any sort of reconciling potential. And the same can be said of 1916. If we are serious about trying to extract some good from common suffering in 1914–18, then we must also seriously contemplate the possibility that some good might be extracted from an understanding of the common suffering and loss not just on the battlefields of continental Europe but also here at home.

It has to be admitted, however, that the impulse to enlist Ireland's First World War experience in a kind of benign military mobilisation, occupying a moral high ground where *all* sections of the community might find a place, has indeed helped undermine the barriers of mutual communal ignorance that sustain much of the continuing social antagonisms on our island. In *Ireland*

and the Great War I celebrated the achievement, for example, of the Island of Ireland Peace Tower in November 1998.[14] Although criticisms can be made of the whole scheme, its imaginative harnessing of shared memory and shared experience and the drawing together of the now fairly distant past with the altogether more contentious and hazardous present, provides an opportunity for differing interpretations of what the Irish people involved believed to have been their duty to be accommodated in a creative rather than destructive fashion. Ireland's domestic (and not just recent) past is perhaps so painful that we may require the more remote experience of, for example, the First World War to help us come to terms with it.

There is a final speculation that might be advanced concerning the commemorative attraction in Ireland (especially nationalist Ireland) of the First World War. This is suggested by the circumstances of the dedication of the memorial in Enniskillen on 25 October 1922. One of the very last public engagements of the very last chief governor of all Ireland occurred here, when Lord FitzAlan, the last viceroy, did the dedicating. Six weeks later, his position had been abolished. Paul Bew has written of 'pre-partition history' (and he is especially interesting when reviewing the period from the start of the war to the Rising).[15] Commemoration of the First World War enables Irish people to reach back to a politically united Ireland. It is perhaps an irony that the great aim towards which Irish nationalist politics aspires only now exists in the sort of historical re-enactment manifest at the dedication of a newly minted First World War memorial in Killarney.

Notes

1 F.X. Martin, '1916—myth, fact, and mystery', *Studia Hibernica* 7 (1967), 7–126.
2 Keith Jeffery, *Ireland and the Great War* (Cambridge, 2000), 109–23; Jane Leonard, 'The twinge of memory: Armistice Day and Remembrance Sunday in Dublin since 1919' in Richard English and Graham Walker (eds), *Unionism in modern Ireland: new perspectives on politics and culture* (Basingstoke, 1996), 99–114.
3 A wonderful resource for Irish war memorials is the website www.irishwarmemorials.ie. See also another useful site: www.ulsterwarmemorials.net/index.html (both sites accessed 21 Jan. 2013)
4 *Belfast Telegraph*, 11 Nov. 1922.
5 These details are drawn from James S. Kane, *Portadown heroes* (Newtownabbey, 2007). A significant and rewarding demonstration of interest in Ireland's engagement with the First World War is the production in recent years of books such as this, containing biographical lists of the fallen from various localities; see for example William Henry, *Forgotten heroes: Galway soldiers of the Great War, 1914–1918* (Cork, 2007); Robert Thompson, *Bushmills' heroes 1914–1918* (Coleraine, 1995); Colin Moffett, *Newry's war dead* (Newry, 2002); and Donal Hall, *The unreturned army: County Louth dead in the Great War 1914–1918* (Dundalk, 2005). The series of 'books of honour' being collated mostly on a county basis is a related phenomenon. The first of these, the *County Donegal book of honour*, was published in 2002.
6 Details of this, and other loyalist and republican memorials, will be found on CAIN, the University of Ulster's most valuable 'Conflict Archive on the INternet': http://cain.ulst.ac.uk/index.html (accessed 21 Jan. 2013).
7 Leonard, 'The twinge of memory', 110.

8 Quotations from Somme Association Development Appeal brochure, *c.*1994.

9 Jeffery, *Ireland and the Great War*, 137.

10 Quotes from www.schoolforpeace.com (accessed 21 Jan. 2013).

11 *Irish Times*, 25 Sept. 2009.

12 For the full text of President McAleese's speech, see http://archive-ie.com/page/10148/ 2012-05-16/http://www.president.ie/index.php?section=53&speech=781&lang=eng (accessed 7 Jan. 2013).

13 Statement issued on 10 Sept. 2009, http://admin2.7.forumer.com/viewtopic.php (accessed 21 Jan. 2013).

14 This starry-eyed attitude attracted some critical comment in reviews of the book; see Michael Hopkinson in *Twentieth Century British History* xv (2), 204–6: 5, and Timothy Bowman in *War in History* xi (3), 369–71: 370.

15 See for example Paul Bew, *Ideology and the Irish question* (Oxford, 1994).

14

Historians and the Commemoration of Irish Conflicts, 1912–23

David Fitzpatrick

1

History and commemoration are not incompatible, but the proper relationship between these two pursuits is contested and uneasy. As participants in the public debates and manifestations associated with the current 'decade [*sic*] of commemorations', historians should warn planners against the perils of adopting bad history when designing their commemorative programmes. Though many may reject the very concept of 'good history', few would deny that historical research is capable of identifying elements of falsification, distortion and undue political influence in the way that past events are narrated. Academic historians are not privileged arbiters of historical truth, but they should be better equipped than most people to detect appealing but flawed narratives. Let us first consider certain aspects of current and potential commemorative practice that seem to me to embody bad history.

One of the strongest and most admirable impulses behind public commemoration in contemporary Ireland, North and South, is the desire for pluralism. Who would cavil at the notion that we should commemorate victims as well as victors, unionists as well as nationalists, women as well as men, 'ordinary' folk as well as public figures? Yet it is all too easy to achieve the spurious appearance of 'inclusivity' in commemorative ceremonies, events or exhibitions by adopting simplistic and misleading dichotomies. If concentration on these dichotomies involves the marginalisation of other groups, historians should try to complicate the picture. For example, though it is better to commemorate the 16th (Irish) and 36th (Ulster) divisions in tandem rather than individually, this dual focus does a grave injustice to members of the 10th (Irish) Division, still often ignored, as well as the one-third of Irish servicemen who had no connection with any Irish unit.

A connected problem is excessive focus on 1916, the year of the first Battle of the Somme and the Dublin insurrection, or rebellion. Since Easter Monday and 1 July have long figured so prominently and divisively in the commemorative calendars of Irish republicans and Ulster unionists respectively, the idea of weaving these episodes into a seamless sacrificial narrative is almost irresistible. Yet by concentrating on a single year marked by massive casualties on the Western Front for the 16th as well as the 36th Divisions, the broader legacies of the war are neglected. The dramatic character of the rebellion and the first day's battle on the Somme, though splendid material for graphic commemoration, fails to convey the slow and messy course of political change in Ireland or the monotony and attrition of trench warfare. Concentration on 1916 also lends excessive weight to the patriotic idealism of those experiencing armed conflict for the first time, whether in Dublin or on the Somme. The story of the last two years of the Great War, when conscription applied in every part of the United Kingdom except Ireland, is grimmer and less heroic than that of 1916, awful though the carnage was in that year. Likewise, the high-mindedness of many of the Easter rebels is at odds with the more practical and often ruthless outlook of the guerrilla fighters of 1920–21 or the 'irregulars' of 1922–23. To sideline the seamier aspects of the past is to distort public understanding of history. It is not enough to glamorise heroes or even to ennoble victims from 'both sides'; somehow, the drama of set-piece confrontations must be balanced by evocation of the mundane and repellent facets of conflict.

Another tempting but dubious stratagem for commemorators is the notion of equality of suffering between perpetrators and victims of political violence. Though projects such as 'The Dead of the Irish Revolution' justifiably incorporate all detected fatalities—whether of republicans, loyalists, the Crown forces or civilians—it is bad history to suspend moral judgement when trying to give meaning to human losses. Combatants delivered and also courted death, whereas non-combatant civilians (the great majority of fatalities in 1916 and almost half of those killed between 1917 and 1921) did neither. The lives of both perpetrators and victims should be remembered, but not in the same way. Far from avoiding all forms of judgement, historians should try to add moral intensity to the ways in which we commemorate and comprehend the past. Morally neutral commemoration is a dangerous deception, inviting abuse by partisans seeking to exonerate those responsible for past atrocities. We should not unquestioningly applaud the motives of those who participated in revolution or fought 'for' the British Empire any more than the motives of complacent staff officers or opportunist politicians. Commemoration, like good history, should help us to understand what forces impelled people to commit terrible as well as courageous acts. Though the outcome of such investigations is often contentious and morally unsettling, it is preferable to a bland recitation of general blamelessness.

The issue of motivation points to a further form of bad history often reflected in commemorative practices. Commemoration lends itself to crude stereotyping, whereby home rulers enlisted for wartime service because they were deluded into fighting for the freedom of small nations, or unemployed workers were driven into the trenches by domestic poverty. Yet scholars have long since demonstrated the inadequacy of such caricatures. Wartime enlistment cannot be explained by economic motives since self-interest could never be served by voluntarily accepting a high risk of death rather than choosing continued existence, however comfortless. National feeling and patriotism, though providing essential spiritual succour for those who did enlist, would seldom have caused a man to accept the King's shilling in the absence of peer-group or family pressures enabling the recruit to act outside the limits of normal rationality.

Yet another alluring but misleading assumption should be avoided when trying to incorporate the Crown forces into Ireland's commemorative programmes. No Irish political or administrative body is likely to portray the Black and Tans as patriotic idealists, but a psychological platitude is sometimes invoked to depoliticise the issue. Being ex-servicemen, the paramilitary forces of the Crown may glibly be dismissed as victims of 'brutalisation', warped by their fearful experiences in the trenches. Yet recent studies of policing and reprisals have suggested that the Black and Tans and Auxiliaries were no more brutalised than the bulk of Europe's surviving male population. The atrocities they committed against civilians, like many of the civilian murders perpetrated by the IRA, were largely the result of weakness of central control compounded by paranoia arising from ignorance of their opponents. Ignorance generated irrational suspicion of all those belonging to alien groups, whether reputed 'loyalists', in the case of the IRA, or Irish civilians in general, in the case of newly arrived soldiers or paramilitary police. This suggests a psychological problem, inviting common commemoration, arising not from prior brutalisation but from shared fear, ignorance and indiscipline.

Ninety years on, with the Northern conflict largely demilitarised, many would prefer to remember constructive rather than violent aspects of the revolutionary epoch. Parallel celebrations of the evolution of the Free State and devolution in Northern Ireland would arouse little enthusiasm, partly because Northern home rule is now generally regarded, even by unionists, as a failed experiment in majoritarian supremacy. Nor is it easy to devise a truthful narrative incorporating supporters and opponents of the Anglo-Irish Treaty in a common enterprise of democratic state-building in the South, given the performance of both parties in the Civil War. Faced with this conundrum, many historians as well as politicians have portrayed those who actively supported the Treaty as democrats acting in accordance with the will of the majority, and their opponents in the Civil War as idealists. Yet on close inspection this is a spurious comparison: there were idealists on both sides but very few genuine 'democrats' in either party until it became apparent, after the Civil War, that the constitutional framework of the Free State offered practical opportunities for all factions. In 1922–23 the dominant figures on both sides were elitists accustomed to working through a secret fraternity—the Irish Republican Brotherhood (IRB)—to control myriad revolutionary organisations, and to engineer popular acceptance of their actions.

Nor is it historically acceptable to portray Ulster unionists as unswerving imperialists and opponents of home rule. It does not require a degree in history to notice that Ulster unionists came close to rebellion against the Crown in 1912–14, that the leaders were notably slow to throw their followers into the imperial war effort, and that they went on to accept and control a home rule state in Northern Ireland. Once again, the leadership was sustained by a powerful fraternity, the Loyal Orange Institution, which was even more effective than the IRB in controlling political machines and whipping up popular support. Good commemoration would stress the common influence of fraternity and solidarity in nationalist and unionist Ireland rather than the strength of political idealism. Yet the implication of that approach is to bring into question the motives and sincerity of many Irish political leaders of all factions.

As official or unofficial advisers to those planning commemorations, historians should draw lessons from the experience of previous commemorative programmes. The Southern bicentennial festivities in 1998 celebrated the shared involvement of Catholics and Protestants in the United Irish movement, but paid scant attention to their shared mobilisation in loyal units of the militia and the yeomanry. Until recently, little attempt was made to acknowledge the civilians, let alone the Crown forces, who died or suffered in 1916. Historians should do their best to avoid the use of simplistic and exclusive dichotomies or facile attributions of motive; they should raise awkward issues and, above all, seek to broaden the terms of debate in the interminable round of national soul-searching that we now face.

2

During the period of war and revolution, the Irish conflict was internationalised as never before. Irish loyalties were translated and tested on foreign battlefields, where there was no avoiding personal contact with British soldiers and foreign civilians. The post-war peace conference and carving up of defeated empires encouraged republicans to extend their appeal to a global audience, and to initiate a daring crusade for international recognition in Europe, Australasia, South America and (most spectacularly) the United States. This campaign provoked a mimetic campaign by Ulster propagandists, who also proved resourceful in securing financial and moral support from emigrants and their descendants, from co-religionists and from political sympathisers in the US. The international perspective would inevitably underline the primacy of the Great War as a destabilising force, creating the conditions for political turmoil and reorganisation in Ireland as elsewhere. The translation of parochial disputes to a global stage is a theme that, if carefully handled, might provide a worthy basis for public commemoration. Yet, as always, there are snags for those hoping to depict the Irish conflict as one step in the long march towards globalisation.

In the search for a supranational narrative incorporating all protagonists in Irish conflicts between 1912 and 1923, it is often suggested that commemoration should focus on Ireland's struggle for decolonisation. The theme of decolonisation easily lends itself to international comparisons, raising glittering prospects for funding, collaborative studies, exchanges with foreign scholars, and links with other states or political movements emerging from, or contributing to, the collapse of Eurocentric empires. This theme also promises a 'holistic' narrative, readily bringing together the participation of nationalists and unionists in the Great War, the struggle for independence, and the subsequent fracturing of republicanism. After all, despite their conflicting terminologies and political affiliations, both separatist and unionist interpreters viewed the Anglo-Irish struggle as a challenge to Ireland's involvement in the Empire. A programme affirming this underlying affinity might help contemporary republicans and unionists to treat each other's historical legacy with greater empathy and respect.

For republicans, pre-war Ireland was not an integral part of the United Kingdom but a colony occupied by 'the English garrison' with the connivance of alien 'settlers' (*colons*), mainly Protestants of British stock. Most nationalists as well as republicans aimed ultimately for decolonisation—equated with ending political subjection to Britain—though the means and timescale for achieving decolonisation were matters of bitter contention. Irish unionism was a reactionary movement for maintaining the subjection to Britain of the 'native Irish', mainly Catholics. The formation of unionist and then nationalist paramilitary forces in 1914 initiated a gradual transition from political debate about decolonisation towards armed conflict. The wartime participation of both nationalists and unionists, though deplored by republicans, was excused if not validated by the notion that both groups were driven by patriotic ideals: nationalists were fighting for home rule while unionists fought for the Crown. The 'War of Independence' and subsequent civil conflicts, both Southern and Northern, were viewed as the outcome of increasing polarisation on the issues of decolonisation and partition. Republican interpreters stressed the crucial role of unionist Ulster's successful pre-war resistance against the imposition of home rule and the resultant menace of partition in radicalising nationalist opinion and popularising strategies that validated the violence that led to revolution.

It is not difficult to translate this vision of Irish history between 1912 and 1923 into unionist terminology. Ireland had never been fully assimilated into the Union because the native Irish were primitive, deluded by priests, and manipulated by unscrupulous and corrupt politicians. Though they might eventually be enlightened through mass education and preferably religious conversion, abetted by gradual realisation of the economic benefits of the Union, Irish Catholics remained fundamentally disloyal and therefore unworthy of full citizenship. Nationalism was a reactionary movement against economic and social progress as embodied in unionist ideology and practice. Though some unionists interpreted Catholic enlistment in the wartime forces as welcome evidence that a broader imperial patriotism was at last eroding Irish parochialism, most doubted the extent and sincerity of the change. Like their republican adversaries, unionist and Orange leaders interpreted the Southern 'rebellions' of 1916 and 1919–21 as a sign of intensified communal polarisation directed (in their view) as much against the Protestant minority as against Britain. Though the creation of the Free State offered some hope of Irish accommodation with the Empire, most unionists shared the belief of the Treaty's republican opponents that the Irish remained at heart antipathetic to any British connection beyond mutual coexistence.

Despite the republican–unionist consensus that decolonisation was central to all Irish conflicts between 1912 and 1923, historical scholarship has raised so many objections to this model that it cannot safely be adopted as the basis for inclusive commemoration. Economic, social, cultural and political studies point towards much deeper assimilation of Irish Catholics into the United Kingdom than either group of contemporaries was prepared to acknowledge. Despite persistent inequality and discrimination in both the public and private sectors, Catholics dominated local and parliamentary representation, were increasingly well represented in the civil service, the magistracy and the professions, and included a rapidly growing social elite moulded by Church-controlled schooling and the accretion of wealth by Catholic businessmen. Irish Catholics also played a major part in peopling, administering and policing the Empire. Catholic Ireland, though formerly in some senses a colony, was rapidly taking on metropolitan attributes.

Contrary to the decolonisation model, the dominant strain in nationalism before 1916 envisaged home rule within the evolving British Commonwealth rather than secession and independence. Redmond sought a measure of freedom similar to that of the 'white' dominions, and his separatist opponents were increasingly marginalised until catapulted unpredictably into public favour after the rebellion. Over the same period, Ulster unionism had moved away from defence of the existing Constitution towards acceptance of special provision for all or part of Ulster, with several possible outcomes ranging from installation of a rebel 'provisional government' to provincial home rule. The two main parties up to 1916 were no longer local players in a global battle between decolonisers and colonists but contestants for territorial control under several possible constitutional frameworks.

The common involvement of nationalists and unionists in the Great War did not necessarily intensify their competing allegiances to Ireland and the Empire. Indeed, many leaders in both camps believed that the comradeship of the trenches and participation in a shared struggle would have the opposite effect, eroding the antagonisms arising from mutual ignorance and suspicion, and thus weakening the impulse for decolonisation. Though no generally acceptable compromise was in fact agreed, there were several moments during the war, even after the rebellion, when it seemed quite practicable. While the rebellion was undoubtedly followed by political radicalisation on both sides, and an explosion of anti-imperial sentiment among nationalists, many studies of the period have suggested that the 'transformation' of public opinion was skin-deep, and that a settlement within the imperial framework remained the most likely outcome of Sinn Féin's campaign for a republic. In short, the triumph of anti-colonial rhetoric masked a surprising degree of flexibility. On the other side, Ulster unionists appropriated the republican slogan of 'self-determination', emphasising that their first loyalty was to Ulster rather than Britain.

The strongest argument against the decolonisation model is the outcome of the conflict: home rule for six Ulster counties and dominion status for the rest. In many respects, the result of the republican campaign was the Redmondite solution under a new name, admittedly with greater autonomy than home rule had ever offered. Political independence was not achieved, even partially, until the Treaty had been dismantled by Éamon de Valera and a twenty-six-county 'republic' installed by his opponents. That republic remained overwhelmingly reliant on British trade and investment until access to the European Common Market changed the focus of dependency. As for cultural decolonisation, some would maintain that it has scarcely begun. These lingering signs of dependency explain the otherwise puzzling fact that the rhetoric and terminology of decolonisation and anti-imperialism remained until very recently a common feature of Southern Irish political discourse for all major parties, and that even today it shapes the archaic polemic of Sinn Féin. Despite the disintegration of the British Empire and rapidly intensifying political, cultural, economic and financial immersion in Europe, the two Irelands have yet to erase their British colonial imprint.

This analysis suggests that the pre-war confrontation of political and paramilitary factions was between Commonwealthers and potential 'unionist' secessionists, not between nationalist secessionists and loyal imperialists; that the war experience promoted, at least temporarily, communal reconciliation rather than antagonism; that post-rebellion polarisation never eliminated the likelihood of a political settlement within the imperial framework; and that this is precisely what was achieved in 1921–22. It would be tendentious and misleading to conflate Irish political conflicts before and after the 1916 rebellion as a continuing and intensifying struggle over decolonisation. Though the Irish case cannot be detached from the broader convulsions associated with European war and post-war reorganisation, these are better treated as accelerants of moderate constitutional change rather than as agents of precipitate decolonisation. A more convincing 'holistic' narrative for Irish political history between 1912 and 1923 would concentrate on the persistent opportunities for compromise and reconciliation, never extinguished even in the darkest periods of Anglo-Irish and civil conflict.

3

Some have argued that historical scholarship and commemoration differ so much in their rationale that historians should avoid personal involvement in commemorative projects. Whereas good historians try to establish what happened, how and why (no matter how painful and depressing their findings may be), good commemorators use 'history' to pursue meritorious political, social or therapeutic objectives. Though often morally desirable, the use of history to promote intercommunal or international reconciliation may involve the suppression of ugly or inconvenient facts. As I have suggested, it may nevertheless be possible in the Irish case, without unduly twisting the record, to highlight events and alliances pointing towards compromise rather than confrontation. If so, the moral imperative of the commemorator and the heuristic imperative of the scholar may prove to be compatible after all.

Yet one problem remains. Public commemoration is futile unless driven by the conviction that it will bring social dividends, whether for those still troubled by the legacy of past conflicts or for future generations. By contrast, state-sponsored programmes 'choreographed' by indifferent bureaucrats and performed by well-funded hypocrites are both wasteful and potentially divisive, though they may benefit participants and political interests. The problem with allowing academic historians an active part is that so few of them are driven by social or moral passion. History is a dry discipline in which moral and social judgements are more often rhetorical devices than expressions of personal conviction. The moralising amoralist asserting authority from alleged historical research is particularly unsuited to involvement in commemoration. Let us hope that, somewhere amidst our diverse but generically callous profession there are a few truly 'good' historians with sufficient knowledge, judgement, impartiality, altruism and passion combined with sound political instincts to make 'good' commemorators. The rest of us should remain interested bystanders, offering critical dissections of whatever emerges. After all, it is the essence of the profession that we are always too late.

15

Beyond Glory? Cultural Divergences in Remembering the Great War in Ireland, Britain and France

Jay Winter

1 Passive suffering and the poetry of war

In 1936 William Butler Yeats explained the omission of the poetry of Wilfred Owen from his *Oxford book of modern verse* in these terms:

> I have a distaste for certain poems written in the midst of the great war; they are in all anthologies, but I have substituted Herbert Read's 'End of the War' written long after. The writers of these poems were invariably officers of exceptional courage and capacity, one a man constantly selected for dangerous work, all, I think, had the Military Cross; their letters are vivid and humorous, they were not without joy—for all skill is joyful—but felt bound, in the words of the best known, to plead the suffering of their men. In poems that had for a time considerable fame, written in the first person, they made that suffering their own. I have rejected these poems for the same reason that made Arnold withdraw his 'Empedocles on Etna' from circulation; passive suffering is not a theme for poetry. In all the great tragedies, tragedy is a joy to the man who dies; in Greece the tragic chorus danced.[1]

When he learned that some were shocked at his Olympian disdain for Owen, he replied:

> My anthology continues to sell, & the critics get more & more angry. When I excluded Wilfred Owen, whom I consider unworthy of the poets' corner of a country newspaper, I did not know I was excluding a revered sandwich-board Man of the revolution & that somebody has put his worst & most famous poem in a glass-case in the British Museum—however if I had known it I would have excluded him just the same. He is all blood, dirt & sucked sugar stick (look at the selection in Faber's Anthology—he calls poets 'bards,' a girl a 'maid,' & talks about 'Titanic wars'). There is every excuse for him but none for those who like him…[2]

I want to suggest that the 'excuse' for those who like Owen in Britain is that they use a linguistic grammar and register of emotion different from that of Yeats. I term this British register 'beyond glory' or, in Yeats's language, beyond the 'tragic joy' he believed to be at the heart of poetry.[3] 'Tragic joy' was not the register of Owen or British war poetry. Of that we can be certain.

I want to suggest that the best way to understand Yeats's point of view is to situate him in a poetic and literary space closer to that found in France than to that found in Britain during and after the war. Both Irish and French writers still saw 'glory' in war, in part because both adapted a revolutionary rhetoric to the issues of the day, and in part because they drew on a long tradition of Catholic writing on 'glory' configured very differently in Protestant Britain.

The word 'glory' is a touchstone for different ways of talking about war and the loss of life in war. These modes of expression are broadly national in character, though it would be foolish to suggest that they were uniform or ubiquitous. All war writing is multi-vocal, but some voices are louder than others. I will discuss the different ways British and French patterns of remembrance addressed the sacred domain of glory, and then I will try to align Yeats the Protestant Irish patriot with the French approach to this term redolent with Catholic inflections of a cultural rather than a catechistic kind. Finally, I will qualify the argument by referring to dissident voices, including those in *The silver tassie*, Sean O'Casey's play, which also suffered Yeats's opprobrium. No interpretation of cultural responses to the Great War is universally true, but I hold that some are truer than others.

2 Glory

Now for glory. In a talk broadcast by the BBC on 8 September 1940, the text of which he asked thirty-five years later to be placed in his coffin, the distinguished republican jurist René Cassin recalled the villages in flames in which he had fought, and his comrades who fell beside him near St Mihiel in October 1914. Herewith the French:

> Je vous reconnais bien, Capitaine Woignier, catholique lorrain à l'âme ardente, qui avez fermé les yeux en contemplant votre terre natale, et vous, Vandendalle et Pellegrino, sans peur et sans reproche, paisibles horticulteurs au sang vermeil, comme vos belles fleurs. Je te reconnais Garrus, humble journalier des collines du Var, toi le braconnier libre penseur, volontaire pour les patrouilles dangereuses, et vous, Samama, juge d'instruction qui aviez tenu, parce que juif, à ne pas rallier à un poste moins exposé...[4]

My rendering of this passage in English is as follows:

> I recognise you very well, Captain Woignier, Catholic from Lorraine with an ardent soul, whose last sight was that of your native soil, and you, Vandendalle and Pellegrino, without fear or fault, whose blood shone as red as your beautiful flowers. I recognise you Garrus, humble labourer of the hills of the Var, you the game poacher and free thinker, always ready to volunteer for dangerous patrols, and you Samama, examining magistrate who, because you were a Jew, would not accept a less dangerous position...

I start with this text because it illustrates my first point. Remembering the Great War in France frequently entails speech acts of a different kind and character from those attending remembrance in Britain. There is a florid, high-toned, romantic resonance to many contemporary French accounts of the war that I believe goes beyond the Big Words of High Diction on which Anglo-Saxon writers from Robert Graves to Paul Fussell have focused.[5] My claim is not that ponderous and plodding prose was unknown in Britain; on the contrary. It is rather that the kind of rhetoric used to honour the living and the dead who went through the war is different in France and in Britain.

I have no settled views on why this is so, but offer two suggestions. The first is to note the enduring force of the Jacobin equation of military service with citizenship, and the way the heady words of the 'Marseillaise' and the cult of Napoleon affirmed, *pace* Waterloo, their proud martial tradition. Secondly, we must recognise the power of the King James version of the Bible, which has no equivalent in France, as having framed the vernacular of the language. Separating the language of Church and state in France produced republican pomposity that had a different timbre, operating in different registers, than did British prose.

Let me try to make the point in another way. I want to suggest that the French word *gloire* is not the same as the English word 'glory'. And here the difference may arise from the distinction between Catholic and Protestant usages and connotations. Here (Fig. 1) is a plaque from the village church at Auvers-sur-Oise, a church made immortal by Van Gogh's rendering of it. The plaque captures the voice of the village priest:

> Hommage d'affectueuse reconnaissance à mes chers enfants que j'ai élévés dans l'amour de Dieu et de la Patrie, ils sont tombés glorieusement au champ d'Honneur.
> Gloire à DIEU!
> Gloire à notre France immortelle!
> Gloire ici bas et là Haut à ceux qui sont morts pour elle.
> Ceux qui pieusement sont morts pour la Patrie
> Ont droit qu'à leur tombeau la foule vienne et prie,
> Entre les plus beaux noms leur nom est le plus beau!
> Reposez en paix, mes chers enfants.
> Dormez dans la Gloire!!!
> Votre vieux curé bien fier de vous,
> Qui n'a jamais désespéré de la victoire.

I hesitate to translate this passage, since my intention is to compare and not to ridicule.[6]

Perhaps one way to see the force of the cultural divide I want to explore is to compare this French inscription—one of thousands—with the inscription on the Cenotaph in Whitehall: 'The Glorious Dead'. To be sure, we are comparing Britain's central war memorial with one in an obscure parish church, but the setting matters less than the language used in them. The term 'The Glorious Dead' was chosen by Kipling, a man who used language to talk about war in a much more ambivalent and subtle manner than he is usually given credit for. Why does the word 'glorious' carry less heightened emotion than the word 'glory' or its French equivalent, *gloire*? Simply because the noun

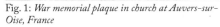

Fig. 1: *War memorial plaque in church at Auvers-sur-Oise, France*

Fig. 2: *War memorial in church at Auvers-sur-Oise, France*

gloire denotes a state, an elevated rank, something important gained, and the adjective covers it perhaps a bit more delicately, like a shawl, leading to the word 'dead', unmistakably something lost, by them and by us, the survivors. In addition, by sticking to an adjective, Kipling subtly bypassed the realm of the religious, which was precisely what Lutyens had intended to do in designing the Cenotaph as an ecumenical, and not as a Christian, site of memory. In a way, Kipling and Lutyens together showed how to glorify those who die in war without glorifying war itself. This suggests a paradox: Britain, with an established Church, may have had a somewhat more secularised language of remembrance than republican France, which went to war in 1914 less than a decade after the end of a nasty battle over the separation of state and Church.

And yet it is evident that the two French cases we have cited—that of an assimilated Jewish republican veteran born in Bayonne and raised in Nice, a man who almost died of his wounds in 1914, and that of a Catholic cleric from the rural hinterland near Paris—highlight one of the central contrasts of the cultural history of the Great War. The English language works differently from the French language when it comes to heightened eloquence; consequently, memories expressed in the two languages in the period of the war and in recollecting the war may never be the same, and may always remain at a tangent to each other.

Let me try to add a further nuance to this argument, using another image from the village of Auvers-sur-Oise. Here (Fig. 2) is an unusual war memorial, one in the village church itself. It is literally next to the curé's paean to the dead but it offers a very different message. The bas-relief shows a young woman kneeling down beside a cross with the laurel wreath of victory resting on the ground. In the background a cock is crowing at the day of victory in November 1918. Her hand is on her head, presenting the classical pose of melancholy—her head is heavy with grief and her eyes have the eternal stare of the inconsolable.

I want to consider this plaque as a counterpoint to the noble rhetoric of the clergyman just to the left of it. The first point of difference is the gendering of mourning. The priest speaks to his fellow men about the nobility of their sacrifice, instilled in them in church and in school during their early years, and bearing its fruit in their wartime sacrifice. The woman speaks to other women, to her fellow mourners, wives, mothers, sisters, daughters, perhaps a majority of the *pratiquants* who gathered there in prayer or reflection. Gendering the message changes it radically. And here there may be more convergences than divergences in the representation of loss of life in the Great War in France and Britain. By this I mean that writing about the sacrifices of war showed striking cultural differences, whereas configuring the same theme in sculptural form may have enabled messages to cross language barriers. Writing war (or memories of war) and configuring war are not identical or even parallel acts. The visual arts may blunt differences that language preserves.

I want to emphasise the tentativeness of this assertion. Mourning in prose or poetry and mourning in stone and colour follow different patterns. And when we consider monumental sculpture, we can see, following Antoine Prost, the choices available to artists and artisans.[7] There are those who try to configure glory, and those who, like Lutyens, sidestepped the obvious or the clichéd and searched for symbolic indirection.

The Cenotaph undercut triumphalism; perhaps that is why it became the national point of reference for remembrance, and it fits well within the funerary category, one of the three Prost delineates in his typology of war memorials—the classical, the patriotic and the funerary. All three are there in both countries' sculptural repertoire. It is this undercutting of triumphalism—vividly portrayed in the Auvers-sur-Oise bas-relief—which points to some commonalities between British and French ways of remembering the Great War and those who died in it.

3 Glory and commemorative forms

Let me turn for a moment to spatial expressions of cultural difference. Funerary horticulture and design are strikingly different in different national and cultural settings. Taking the British and French cases alone, it is evident that war cemeteries reflect the difference between a conscript army fighting on its own soil and a volunteer army (until 1916) fighting and dying on foreign soil. That the Imperial (now Commonwealth) War Graves Commission chose small-scale cemeteries rather than the massive French or American equivalents requires explanation.

Here are a few illustrations of this distinction from a less well-known venue, that of Gallipoli. This was a combined French and British operation, though one with less than an indelible impression on French writing on the war. Just consider the contrast between these two cemeteries at Gallipoli. The first (Fig. 3) is a British and New Zealand cemetery at Suvla Bay in the north of the peninsula. The site is small and well tended even in these barren salt

Fig. 3: *British and New Zealand cemetery, Suvla Bay*

Fig. 4: *Plaque at British and New Zealand cemetery, Suvla Bay*

Fig. 5: *French military cemetery, Gallipoli peninsula*

Fig. 6: *Memorial at French military cemetery, Gallipoli peninsula*

marshes. Notice, too, the plaque (Fig. 4) to one man, Lance Corporal J.M. Brown of the Derbyshire Yeomanry, who died there on 22 August 1915, as the inscription his family chose states, not for 'glory but a purpose'. And compare it to the French military cemetery (Fig. 5) right at the tip of the Gallipoli peninsula. The scale is grand and each tomb is austere. Its individuality is limited to a name on a wrought-iron cross, easier to anchor in this soil than a stone. The serried ranks of the French dead present an entirely different narrative: in the French case (Fig. 6) the man is embraced in the nation, whose army remains, as it were, at attention. In the British (or more precisely, imperial) case the individual stands apart, a civilian in uniform mourned by his family rather than a citizen-soldier honoured by the state.

For comparative purposes let us consider a few images of Irish commemorative sculpture. The choice I have made is arbitrary, but it may help to show the multivalent character of Irish commemorative language, even in stone, borrowing, I believe, as much from the kind of Catholic and revolutionary archive evident in France as it does from the British First World War sculptural and horticultural language, especially with reference to Ulstermen who died in the war. It may well be that the bombing of the Enniskillen war memorial in 1987 was an attack on a British—rather than an Irish—way of framing remembrance in stone. But the overlap between the two languages of commemoration in stone is evident as well.

That said, let us consider first the heroic posture, more French than British in my view. Have a look at Eamon O'Doherty's James Connolly memorial of

Fig. 7: *James Connolly memorial, Beresford Place, Dublin*

Fig. 8: *Michael Collins bust, Merrion Square, Dublin*

Fig. 9: *IRA memorial, Pettigo, Co. Donegal*

1995 (Beresford Place, Dublin; Fig. 7). The martyr of the Irish uprising is also the tribune of labour, standing defiant beside Liberty Hall. A bust of Michael Collins (Merrion Square, Dublin; Fig. 8) provided him with the dignity his assassination seemed to have denied him. Similarly heroic, though anonymous, is the IRA memorial to four men who died in 1922 in Pettigo, Co. Donegal (Fig. 9).

We should be as little surprised at the use, either centrally or in a more muted form, of Catholic notation and forms in Irish commemorative sculpture. The IRA memorial in Herbert Park in Dublin (Fig. 10) sacralises the dead by urging passers-by to consider their souls as residing in the right hand of the Lord. The Celtic cross was used in Victorian times and after to mark the centenary of the 1798 uprising, giving this form a romantic inflection of a very Irish kind.[8] The Doyle memorial in the Church of St Columbanus and St Gall on Milltown Road in Dublin (Fig. 11) offers a more explicit set of ecclesiastical motifs. The enduring power of the Catholic figurative tradition is evident in the Kevin Barry stained-glass window, the work of Richard King in 1934, placed in 2011 on permanent display in the Belfield campus of University College, Dublin (Fig. 12), where Barry was a medical student before becoming the first Irish Volunteer to be executed by the British after the initial executions of the leaders of the 1916 uprising. But, as Stefan Goebel has shown, stained-glass windows were British and French (and German) forms used to locate modern wars in medieval settings.[9] Here, we confront overlaps between commemorative forms in Catholic and Protestant communities.

4 Calendars of commemoration: the Irish case

My fundamental claim is that language frames memory. Different linguistic forms and conventions provide cultural boundaries separating to some degree acts of remembrance concerning the war in different countries. Now it should be apparent why I have placed the Irish case between the British and the French. The shadow of Catholicism and the mixed legacy of the 1916

Fig. 10: *IRA memorial, Herbert Park, Dublin*

Fig. 11: *Doyle memorial, Church of St Columbanus and St Gall, Dublin*

Fig. 12: *Kevin Barry memorial window, University College, Dublin*

insurrection tend to resuscitate glory at the very moment it went into some disfavour in the British lexicon of war.

And yet there were dissident voices. Let us for just a moment compare two of Yeats's most celebrated poems with that other rejected text, *The silver tassie*, to show the stakes of contestation over the 'glory' of war or the 'glorious dead'. Perhaps we can start with the reverie Yeats wrote in memory of Major Gregory, 'An Irish airman foresees his death'. In it, he gives an account of a knight of the air, a death-defying man of honour; we all know the verse:

> Nor law, nor duty bade me fight,
> Nor public men, nor cheering crowds,
> A lonely impulse of delight
> Drove to this tumult in the clouds;
> I balanced all, brought all to mind,
> The years to come seemed waste of breath,
> A waste of breath the years behind
> In balance with this life, this death.

Glory marks the space beyond the mundane, 'the waste of breath' of ordinary life, when men died lamely, ingloriously, one at a time.

And we all know, too, how the language of sacrifice, while subjected to doubt, still sweeps all before it in 'Easter 1916'. Glory lies in the transubstantiation of the names, changed utterly, 'wherever green is worn', giving birth to 'a terrible beauty', the aesthetic redemption of bloodshed yielding glory.

I cite the last poem not for purposes of surprising anyone. I rather use it to bring us back to where I started. The language of glory, the language of sacrifice survived the war in some places and not in others, and Yeats was one of those who made it survive.

Is it surprising that the rhetoric of two Catholic countries convulsed time and again by revolutionary acts and revolutionary failures seems to have more cultural affinities with each other's than each does with the different rhetoric of the Protestant island between them? Perhaps what is more surprising is the case of those who did not agree. And that brings us to *The silver tassie*, famously rejected by Yeats for presentation in the Abbey Theatre in 1928. On five occasions in the play, O'Casey sends up the notion of 'glory' by putting the word in the mouth of Susie Monican and then reducing it to lip service of the worst kind.

Susie: Sinners that jeer often add to the glory of God: going out, she gives you, Sylvester, and you, Simon, another few moments, precious moments—oh, how precious, for once gone, they are gone for ever—to listen to the warning from heaven.

[…]

Susie: Oh, Syl, oh, Simon, don't try to veil the face of God with an evasion. You can't, you can't cod God. This may be your last chance before the pains of hell encompass the two of you. Hope is passing by; salvation is passing by, and glory arm-in-arm with her. In the quietness left to you go down on your knees and pray that they come into your hearts and abide with you for ever…[*With fervour, placing her left hand on Simon's shoulder and her right hand on Sylvester's, and shaking them*] Get down on your knees, get down on your knees, get down on your knees and pray for conviction of sin, lest your portion in David become as the portion of the Canaanites, the Amorites, the Perizzites, and the Jebusites!

[…]

Sylvester: If she'd only confine her glory-to-God business to the festivals, Christmas, now, or even Easter, Simon, it would be recommendable; for a few days before Christmas, like the quiet raisin' of a curtain, an' a few days after, like the gentle lowerin' of one…

then he could put up with it. But enough is enough. 'I always get a curious, sickenin' feeling', Sylvester says, 'when I hear the name of the Supreme Bein' tossed into the quietness of a sensible conversation.' Could it be that the subject of 'glory' and its poetic or dramatic representation was what really separated the 'sensible conversations' of Yeats and O'Casey?

When Yeats's hauteur moved him to dismiss O'Casey as 'a Dublin slum author who in tackling the subject of the Great War and imagining scenes in France was writing beyond his social range and knowledge',[10] perhaps he was covering up some of his own nakedness with respect to knowledge of the ugliness and mechanical stupidity of the war. And perhaps that nakedness was intolerable, too, when he read Owen's poems; the two men he detested knew and spoke of things remote from him. Owen's poem 'Disabled' clearly inspired O'Casey's characterisation of Harry in act III, in his wheelchair watching, like Owen's crippled man, the gaze of young women moving to men who still were whole. That fact makes us suspect Yeats's real motives when he wrote his rejection letter to O'Casey in these terms. *The plough and the stars*, says Yeats, was admirable, written

> out of your own amusement with life or with sense of its tragedy…But you were not interested in the Great War; you never stood on the battlefield or walked its hospitals, and so write out of your opinions…your great power of the past has been the creation of some unique character who dominated all about him and was himself a main impulse in some action that filled the play from beginning to end.

O'Casey was irate, and scoffed: '"Not interested" to one who talked and walked and smoked and sang with blue-suited wounded men fresh from the front; to one who had been among the armless, the legless, the blind, the gassed and the shell shocked'.[11] While this was true enough, he did not seem to catch what may have been the real yawning gap between Yeats and himself—their different views about glory and the religious trappings of the language that venerated it, especially in wartime. What O'Casey saw was that the Great War was not the place to find 'some unique character' dominating the world around him. That romantic view of war was an obscenity after the Somme and Passchendaele, though Yeats apparently thought otherwise.

I am not of the view that Yeats wanted to silence war talk;[12] instead, perhaps through a tendentious reading of Nietzsche, he refused during and after the war to give up the notion of 'glory' and the strong personalities prepared to give their lives in quest of it, be it for a 'lonely impulse of delight', for Ireland's independence, or for some more contested act of violence or self-sacrifice in the civil war that followed 1916. In this sense, Yeats the Protestant Irish patriot was aligning himself with a French and not a British cultural and rhetorical form, one central to our understanding of the very different rhetorical registers in which remembrance unfolded in the decades after the armistice.

I have entitled this chapter 'Beyond glory' for a reason. While in all three countries some went 'beyond glory,' others still basked in its traditional illumination. Here we return to the point where I started. It has required generations to take the shine off the 'glory' of violence in Ireland; in a hesitant way, perhaps cultural historians have clues as to why it has taken so long. Language frames memory in a host of ways, and both language and memory can be lethal.

Notes

1   W.B. Yeats, *Oxford book of modern verse* (Oxford, 1936), xxxiv.
2   W.B. Yeats, *Letters on poetry from W.B. Yeats to Dorothy Wellesley* (Oxford, 1964), 113.
3   Roy Foster, *W.B. Yeats: a life. II: the arch-poet* (Oxford, 2003), 555–8.
4   *Cahiers de l'Union Fédérale* 377 (Nov. 1987), 'René Cassin au panthéon', Archives Nationales (Paris), Fonds Cassin, 382 AP 185.
5   Paul Fussell, *The Great War and modern memory* (New York, 1975).
6   If one were to try, however, it might read as follows:
    > In homage and affectionate acknowledgement of my dear children whom I raised in the love of God and of the Fatherland, and who have fallen gloriously on the field of honour.
    > Glory to GOD!
    > Glory to our immortal France!
    > Glory here on earth below and in heaven above to those who died for her.
    > Since they died in piety for the Fatherland,
    > it is only right that their graves should be thronged with those who have come to pray;
    > Their names are the brightest of the brightest!
    > Rest in peace, my dear children.
    > Sleep in Glory!!!
    > Your old priest, who never despaired of victory,
    > Is deeply proud of you.
7   Antoine Prost, 'Monuments to the dead' in Pierre Nora (ed.), *Realms of memory: the construction of the French past* (1992; trans. from French, New York, 1997), 307–30.
8   Thanks are due to John Horne for drawing my attention to this point.
9   Stefan Goebel, *The Great War and medieval memory: war, remembrance and medievalism in Britain and Germany, 1914–1940* (Cambridge, 2007).
10 Máire Sexton, 'W.B. Yeats, Wilfred Owen and Sean O'Casey', *Studies: An Irish Quarterly Review* lxx (277) (spring 1981), 88–95: 91.
11 Sexton, 'W.B. Yeats, Wilfred Owen and Sean O'Casey', 92.
12 Terence Brown, 'Writing the war' in John Horne (ed.), *Our war: Ireland and the Great War* (Dublin, 2008), 244.

16

Divisions and Divisions and Divisions: Who to Commemorate?

Anne Dolan

In June 1928 Cavan Circuit Court made Philip Smith pay £10 damages to a Mrs Galligan for calling her virtue into disrepute.[1] Whether she was as chaste as she might have been is another matter, but in the exchange of words between the two, Smith added that Galligan's husband 'ought to be shot for thatching Soraghan's house'.[2] The Soraghans were murdered in December 1923: husband and wife shot in their own home in Cavan several months after the end of the Irish Civil War.[3] It had been described as 'the most atrocious murder ever committed in this country', perhaps because of the daughter found crawling in a pool of her mother's blood.[4] It was shocking because Mary Anne Soraghan was four months pregnant, carrying a son, as her post-mortem revealed; it was shocking because the idea of men coming to the door in the evening, forcing their way in, was all supposed to be done and gone by the end of 1923. The Soraghans died over land; about eight acres altogether—eight acres and two cows and four pigs.[5] They died because after four years of war and civil war, family rows could be settled in this way. The two men who forced their way in and shot the couple left behind an old revolver of 'bull-dog pattern and of British make'; the man who may well have charged them with the task, Bernard Briody, was described as 'a well-known Gael'.[6] Briody was a good 'Gael', a 'goalkeeper for the county team ten years ago' who perhaps knew the right people with an old revolver at the bitter end of 1923.[7] Politics and the personal blurred, and the consequences of what war unleashed did not come to a neat and tidy end just because war was over in May 1923.

No one would buy hay or oats from the farm in 1924. Soraghan's brother preferred to face court in 1925 rather than deal with his relatives' debts, too afraid to have anything to do with the farm or whatever money Soraghan left.[8] Nearly five years after these deaths, the charge of thatching their roof was as bad as 'slut' or 'whore' or whatever aspersion Philip Smith could cast on a married woman's virtue; it was still part of the winning and the losing of a small, local row, still part of the cruel banter of the back-roads that said Cavan had no intention of burying its hatreds with its dead.

This is a small example; it is not of war or revolution or rebellion or even civil war, though it is perhaps one of their small consequences (what brought a big British bulldog revolver to the end of Cavan? What made and shaped the men who now knew how to use it?). It is not of war or revolution or even civil war, at least as we have been encouraged to know or remember them. Commemoration has no time for the sordid afterthoughts of war, but the Soraghans' case suggests that commemoration is about far more than just choosing to remember and forget. Commemoration casts the awkward, the unspoken, the silenced into sharp relief, and the centenaries present the same questions of what can and cannot be countenanced, about what will or will not be overlooked. This example is not the stuff of big events that prompt a decade of commemoration, and I do not intend it to be; Homer's ghost is not whispering as it did to Patrick Kavanagh that 'I made the Iliad from such a local row'.[9] There are many obvious awkwardnesses and divisions that we could all point to in the years and events of 1912–23 without counting maybe one of war's sordid costs in December 1923; that we cannot even agree on what to call our wars is strikingly suggestive of that.[10] Yet while we can continue to contest those familiar divisions, I want this small case to suggest some other divisions that we may not seem so willing to see. What do we do with the detail of these kinds of deaths. What do we do with the hatreds and the extremes of violence when the time comes to commemorate? Do we draw a neat dividing line between what can and cannot be written about, between the evidence and what we might want to know, between that which is deemed virtuous and that which is viewed as profane according to whoever plays the commemorative tune? Is it about admitting the divide between the purposes of history and commemoration altogether?

The sources possibly present the first problem for those who are not so keen to dwell on divisions past. If we can detail the divisions of one family feud, if we can quote the man who shot Soraghan with his 'Let him take that lest he is not done in', think how easy it is to document the hatreds and divisions of more significant wars than the Soraghans' and Briody's.[11] So much of the material now available, and, perhaps more importantly, the kinds of questions historians are now asking of it, points to the very essence of division. While there has been considerable political will towards uncovering our 'shared history' across events during the period of centenaries, hatred in its many expressions is probably the one thing we are more certain of discovering in the records.[12] Peter Hart felt the fury of those who did not want to hear what IRA veterans had to say about themselves, and now we seem to be faced with the question of how to find a 'shared history' in a period of our past that very quickly runs out of common ground.[13] The question is where is the place for hatred and division—whether it is the old divisions of nationalism and unionism, of North and South, of Britain and Ireland, or the smaller hatreds of family or community—if the centenaries clamour for something more conciliatory instead? The political will, as mentioned, is to use these commemorations, in the words of Micheál Martin, as 'opportunities for fresh insights…and a deeper mutual understanding among people of different traditions on the island', and it is very easy to find similarly trite quotations to echo that.[14]

But what if work like Peter Hart's, like Tim Wilson's on the McMahon murders in Belfast, like Eunan O'Halpin's and Daithí Ó Corráin's project on the dead of the Irish Revolution, my own work on killing in this period, potentially present the raw material for another generation to polarise itself around the old worn prejudices and assumptions, whatever our intentions?[15] More and more people are looking at violence and its nature and consequences in this period in an Irish context, echoing, in so doing, the scholars who have led this field in European history, and perhaps that research agenda is at odds with a political impetus driven by far bigger questions of peace and reconciliation.[16] But what is to be done? If the Northern Troubles were felt to act as a muzzle on certain kinds of historical inquiry about this period throughout the life of the revisionist debate, is there a risk, if inquiry is now driven by the politics of peace, that we are simply exchanging a muzzle for a straightjacket?[17] Resolution to more contemporary divisions will not be found in the past, particularly if that past is being remade in the image of more recent problems, if 1912–23 is mocked up like a shabby caricature of the Troubles.[18] The sense that what was fixed then can be fixed now makes something of a mockery of it all. One solution might be to balance the dirty deeds of all sides, in all conflicts, and hope that casting a kind of plague on all their houses might be the most equitable solution of all. But the records do not always present us with a neat and tidy accumulation; our books will probably not balance because there are winners and losers. There are the marginalised and the minorities Peter Hart wrote of; there are the Soraghans who fall from far baser motives than we might want to expect, and we have to be able to write of the perpetrators of violence and of the worsted in game without being held up as proponents or opponents of what was and was not done then as well as now.[19]

There is, or maybe there should be, a clear division between the historians' view of this period and the political expectations or aspirations for these commemorations. The historians who ably assisted in the remoulding of the 1798 rebellion in 1998 as a European moment, as the coming together of Catholic, Protestant and dissenter, who adhered to a political agenda that had no wish to seek or find sectarianism in the past when solutions were being sought for the problems caused by marches at Drumcree, have since been harshly treated by those who felt the historians' role required a little more rigour than that. We might all do well, however we perceive them, to dwell upon the kinds of criticisms Roy Foster and others have levelled at those who were thought to be too eager to fatten at the commemorative feast in 1998.[20] Maybe when the decade is done we might be shown to our cost the division between those who had something original to say and those who simply felt obliged to say something, anything to be part of all the fuss.

Shortly before leaving office in 2010, Taoiseach Brian Cowen mused on 'the important theme of commemorating our shared history' in the decade ahead:

> For too long we have concentrated on our differences…A space has now opened for a new and inclusive discussion of our foundation stories. This coming decade of commemorations, if well prepared and carefully considered, should enable all of us on this island to complete the journey we have started towards lasting peace and reconciliation…we should not allow ourselves to be history's slaves…we believe that mutual respect should be central to all commemorative events and that historical accuracy should be paramount.[21]

He felt it was time to 'banish that "giant albatross" of history from around our necks, and replace it with a garland of hope for our better future.'[22] However ham-fisted with his garlands and his albatrosses, his sentiments are little different to more recent statements by Enda Kenny.[23] A statement in July 2011 on behalf of the cross-party committee in the South to consider the commemorations promised that 'it will be fittingly commemorated when the time comes'.[24] And maybe it will be. In many respects it is too easy and too lazy to find fault with this instinct. Politicians using the past to justify their present actions are probably just good politicians. Their job is to get re-elected, to keep the peace, and if the past works just as well as promises on the economy, on education, on anything and everything else, then so be it. It is not their job to be accurate or maybe even ethical about the past. It is their choice to use it to crusade for change, to make or sustain peace, to bring recompense where recompense is due. It is their option to use it to fight dirty as well as fair. And it is in this way that the past needs to fulfil a purpose for politics, in the way in which it is rarely undertaken on its own terms; that is the very point at which it is easiest to see the division between political necessity and the historian's practice.[25]

In an article published in 2003, Roy Foster admitted that he was 'not sure whether reconciliation is the historian's business'.[26] He might well have gone further. Historians have neither the training nor perhaps the temperament to make, let alone keep, peace. It would also be foolish and incredibly arrogant to ascribe to them more importance, more powers of influence, than they actually have. If a peace process cannot survive the revelations of some of the past's discontents and hatreds, then it is perhaps a rather nervous, hollow peace. Political pressure may be there to find the things that unite us all, but the challenge has to be to write as openly as possible about our disconnections, to understand them as much if not more so than our obvious connections, to write about our violence, our shared wars, our wars amongst ourselves without feeling an obligation to do our bit for peace. Seeking out shared traditions only makes sense in the context of examining the hatreds and the bigotries, the silences and the disconnections that countered them. Looking at them in isolation is like praising the stitching but never admitting there was once a tear.

That said, these are quite smug and easy statements to make at the historian's remove. For those who have a responsibility for the safety and the security of the present, how much does or should the integrity of the past count? Should certain sleeping dogs be allowed to just snooze on? Are the reckonings of old wrongs any more or less important than resolving grievances now? Are there certain things that we still just do not need or want to know? The danger of the political project, of the 'shared history', is the assumption, or maybe just the implication, that the past can somehow fix us, or at least contribute to our improvement. And, again, this is where the divide opens between the 'right' way to remember and the historian's task, the difference between reconciliation and simply uncovering the past, between judging the past and just exploring it without some moral compunction to forgive and to forget.[27] At the same time, there cannot be any abdication of responsibility on the historian's part this time around, even if the reasons for shying away now—this search for a shared, slightly selective past—are far more anodyne than the fear during the Troubles of the 1970s and 1980s, and beyond that the history of 1912–23 could encourage the paramilitarism of all sides. Because there are those who still thrive on what this period can lend them, because there are those who are certain who the heroes and the villains were, who want to paint a very particular picture of 1912–23 to sharpen the focus of a generation that cannot now remember troubles of any kind, there is scope for much to be done, scope for complexity and confusion to be crowded into something that should never be cast in simple black and white. The division is perhaps between those who want to arbitrate between right and wrong and those who want to find instead a multiplicity of motivations and interpretations, who see beyond heroes and villains, and look instead to people just doing what they did as they saw it to get by.

Yet for all those who have an interest in perpetuating the divisions, who define themselves by the victories and the losses of the past, for those who need and hold onto a past populated by heroes and villains, who hold on despite or in spite of all the years of conferences and footnotes and advances within the historiography, there are also those who dread the coming decade for what it might stir up. Do they create a divide between what can and cannot be written about? Is silence for some still the most fitting response? If history can only uncover divides, never fix them, should this give pause for thought before we rush in armed and sanctimonious about the authenticity of the records, rush in just because it is the hundredth anniversary when it is no different really from the ninety-seventh, the ninety-eighth or the ninety-ninth? There are certain views held dear, certain causes sacred, certain individuals cherished, not necessarily out of any malign or political ends but from pride in a past constructed makeshift from snatches of schoolbook facts and family remembrances. It is pride in a version that makes sentimental sense, that swells chests and sets the pulse racing to the beat of whatever nation's anthem, and to tamper with it, to arrogantly correct it should give pause for thought. The right to define hero from villain is a cherished one, and how the historian chooses to interfere in that process can dictate if their ideas fall on fallow or on fertile public ground. Perhaps one of the clearest divisions likely to emerge from the decade of centenaries is going to be the division between the historians' versions of the past and the far more popular, and often polarised, versions of events. How those versions encounter each other may well dictate the spirit of the next few years.

We might also ask whether the divisions we default to are far too simple. The convenient ones are caricatured and cultivated, the more awkward ones overlooked. We divide people too easily along lines of definition and allegiance, we resort far too readily to phrases that mark apart a society that was far more complex, far more messy and unsightly, as the Soraghans and others might attest. Party labels, allegiances, groups of all and any kind harbour within them a confusion of impulses and motivations, and that has to blur the edges of the divisions we assume. Joseph Dunne, who took the pro-Treaty side in the Irish Civil War, admitted to doing so because he was fed up risking his life for his benighted country, that all he wanted was a job, that he had no faith in the new Free State; it was something to be going on with, nothing more.[28]

His practicality, his need to get by, to make ends meet, his faith in the anti-Treaty cause give way, get lost, are drowned out by the certainty that we can call him soldier, and as a soldier in the National Army we plot for him only a simple straightforward course. If we allow this alone to define him, we miss the glorious uncertainty of it all. Similarly, as David Fitzpatrick has shown, 'the revolutionary unrest of 1919–21 did not dissuade over 20,000 men from enlisting', and the Irish proportion of the British army 'was almost as large in 1921 as in 1913'.[29] Too many examples defy the simplicity of the divides we impose upon them for us to be so sure of them any more. In similar ways, we divide the war dead, whatever the war, too easily from the veterans. The dead can be crafted, moulded, turned to many ends; the veterans survive in all their awkward glory demanding to be listened to or left alone, to be rewarded and recompensed, to defy what we want to assume they stood for, and accuse all who reneged on the cause once fought for.

And what if the divides were far more base, far more mundane than we may have assumed? What does that do to those caricatures of right and wrong, of them and us? My small war in Cavan was about land and greed; and land and greed, envy and opportunism, have their part to play in this as in any other war and revolution. P.S. O'Hegarty could see in 1924 that civil war had revealed the Irish to be, as he put it, as base as any other nation; his illusions were all taken and gone.[30] We might ask why we have preferred to define divisions along more noble, or more idealistic lines, as time has gone on. Indeed, it might be asked why it has taken so long for the historiography to acknowledge certain kinds of more difficult divisions, some that participants at the time had no qualms about conceding. Why has it taken so long, for example, for the existence of sectarianism in the South to be acknowledged, and why was that acknowledgement accompanied by such a vitriolic debate? These kinds of issues—sectarianism, greed, land, punishments, intimidations—often prompt a quite clear division between those who examine this period with a view to judging the past and those who want to understand it whatever its terms. There is too much of the air of the comfortable parlour game about acclaiming or condemning at a century's remove. If land was there to be grabbed in the midst of civil war, if it was easier to shoot than to run, easier to run than to shoot, to shun than to stand by the most vulnerable, why should the passage of a century give us the right to pass judgement when each one of us might just as easily or as equally fail or succeed in living up to standards we, too, readily exact from the past. We should be surprised and exasperated and disappointed, just as we will no doubt surprise and exasperate and disappoint those who will follow us here in a century's time.

Why has so much of this period the capacity to cause such division still? During September and October 2011, prompted by some of the discussions of Martin McGuinness's candidacy for president, Seán Farren of the SDLP felt the need to clearly restate the differences between the old IRA and the Provisionals.[31] However, the more we know and see of the nature and the methods of the old IRA, that distinction becomes more and more difficult to outline. With men ordered to kill to keep them silent, with others implicated to 'keep our weak ones right', with problems solved by dirty deeds, the moral high ground seems to be levelling out.[32] Foul and fair deeds were committed by all sides in the name of states and separatism and allegiances of all kinds; the need to divide Troubles then from Troubles now possibly enforced one of the most trenchant divisions, one that insisted on seeing the violence of one period as somehow more sacrosanct, more noble, more worthy than the other. For many, there is something terrifying still in admitting some of the sameness: some of the parallels of experience, the same talk of sweat and blood, the same instincts of fear and pleasure and shame, whether volunteer, soldier, paramilitary, then or now.[33]

Although I began in the byroads of Cavan, I want to suggest that one of the greatest and most unhelpful divisions has been the way the Irish case has been separated from its European context. The thought of placing the Irish story within a wider European narrative, of sacrificing Irish exceptionalism, still seems frightening for some, and we might consider why. Arguably, from the road to war—the arming, the obsession with militarism—through the Great War, through the Troubles that followed, it is possible that Ireland was rarely so European. From the trenches dug in St Stephen's Green during the Rising, to the appeal to Versailles for recognition, to the Treaty that placed the Irish Free State at the heart of the Commonwealth, defined and defining itself according to the status of Canada and Australia, even to the South's Constitution drafted with an eye to every Constitution in the world that its authors could find, Ireland was part of a European story. Why few have chosen to read it in that way for so long is another kind of division that has to be considered. In a European context, Ireland had small wars, few casualties, a remarkably quick return to stability and peace. Yet if we admit that, do we undermine all the importance that so many have placed on those small wars for so long? Or do we find that instead of being ruled and ruined by our divisions, we actually dealt with them relatively peacefully; that given the conditions, there could or should have been more deaths, more spite and sectarianism, more envy and avarice? While that is of little consolation to those who paid the price of those divisions, the Soraghans' deaths perhaps give us a glimpse of what might have been as much as what was. Our massacres and atrocities were measured in these kinds of small numbers, and we probably should not lose sight of that.

Yet if we overstate certain divisions, we certainly seem happy to overlook others. Class divisions are among the most striking of this period in Ireland as elsewhere, yet no one seems so keen to seek our 'shared history' here, arguably the easiest place to find it North and South. Is this not a division that should occupy us all a little more? In the same respect, do we also miss the division between the ardent and the indifferent at our peril? Far more carried on carrying on through all these wars than went out to take whatever part, yet we listen to the minority of fighters for whatever cause so much more. It is in those carrying on in spite of, or despite, it all that we are maybe most likely to find any kind of 'shared history' or common ground, but what will happen to those who did not follow any flag when flags come to be half-masted in 2012, 2014, 2016 and 2021?

Notes

1   The judge awarded £10 damages and charged the defendant a further £10 costs and £1 expenses. *Anglo-Celt*, 9 June 1928.

2   *Anglo-Celt*, 9 June 1928.

3   The shootings occurred on 11 December. *Anglo-Celt*, 15 Dec. 1923.

4   Admittedly a description by the barrister arguing for compensation for the Soraghan's child. *Anglo-Celt*, 19 Apr. 1924. The coroner did describe it as 'something contrary to all the instincts of humanity and civilization. Only fiends in human form could be guilty of such a terrible crime…This crime I venture to think and make bold to say is a disgrace to the civilization of our country'. *Anglo-Celt*, 15 Dec. 1923.

5   They died probably because they took a case against the Briody family, the family of Soraghan's first wife. The Briody family felt that Soraghan's farm, possibly land settled on him when he married Miss Briody, should have come to them when she died. Bernard Briody was sentenced to two months in prison the day before the shootings for assault and abusive language against Soraghan and his new wife. *Anglo-Celt*, 15 Dec. 1923, 19 Apr. 1924.

6   The police certainly thought so when Briody and his wife were charged with the murders in 1924, though they were never brought to trial. *Irish Independent*, 25 July 1924; *Anglo-Celt*, 15 Dec. 1923.

7   *Anglo-Celt*, 15 Dec. 1923.

8   *Anglo-Celt*, 1 Aug. 1925.

9   Patrick Kavanagh, 'Epic' in Antoinette Quinn (ed.), *Patrick Kavanagh: selected poems* (London, 1996), 101–2.

10 See Keith Jeffery's discussion of the problems and implications of nomenclature in 'Some problems and lessons of Anglo-Irish War in the twentieth century' in Peter Dennis and Jeffery Grey (eds), *An art in itself: the theory and conduct of small wars and insurgencies* (Canberra, 2006), 34–6; idem., 'British security policy in Ireland, 1919–21' in Peter Collins (ed.), *Nationalism and unionism: conflict in Ireland, 1885–1921* (Belfast, 1994), 163–4.

11 *Freeman's Journal*, 17 Dec. 1923.

12 From An Taoiseach Brian Cowen's speech, 'A decade of centenaries: commemorating shared history' to the Institute for British-Irish Studies conference, University College, Dublin, 20 May 2010.

13 Particularly the response to the Kilmichael chapter in Peter Hart, *The I.R.A. and its enemies: violence and community in Cork, 1916–1923* (Oxford, 1998). See for example Brian P. Murphy and Niall Meehan, *Troubled history: a 10th anniversary critique of Peter Hart's* The I.R.A. and its enemies (Cork, 2008); Meda Ryan, 'The Kilmichael ambush, 1920: exploring the "provocative chapters"', *History* 92 (306), 235–49; John M. Regan, 'The "Bandon Valley massacre" as a historical problem', *History* 97 (325), 70–98; for more spirited commentary see comments and exchanges on http://www.indymedia.ie, http://www.irishdemocrat.co.uk and Youtube. There have been regular exchanges on the letters page of *History Ireland* since the publication in 1998.

14 Micheál Martin quoted in the *Irish Examiner*, 18 Apr. 2011.

15 Hart, *The I.R.A. and its enemies*; Peter Hart, *The I.R.A. at war, 1916–1923* (Oxford, 2003); Timothy Wilson, *Frontiers of violence: conflict and identity in Ulster and Upper Silesia 1918–1922* (Oxford, 2010); Timothy Wilson, '"The most terrible assassination that has yet stained the name of Belfast": the McMahon murders in context', *Irish Historical Studies* 145 (May 2010); Eunan O'Halpin and Daithí Ó Corráin, *The dead of the Irish Revolution* (New Haven, forthcoming 2013); Anne Dolan, 'Killing and Bloody Sunday, November 1920', *Historical Journal* 49 (3) (2006), 789–810.

16 See for example Stathis Kalyvas, *The logic of violence in civil war* (Cambridge, 2006); Joanna Bourke, *An intimate history of killing: face-to-face killing in twentieth century warfare* (London, 1999); Charles Tilly, *The politics of collective violence* (Cambridge, 2003); Christopher R. Browning, *Ordinary men: Reserve Police Battalion 101 and the final solution*

in Poland (London, 1998); Donald Bloxham and Robert Gerwarth (eds), *Political violence in twentieth century Europe* (Cambridge, 2011).

17 For a full discussion of the revisionist debate see Ciaran Brady (ed.), *Interpreting Irish history: the debate on historical revisionism, 1938–1994* (Dublin, 1994).

18 See John M. Regan, 'Southern Irish nationalism as a historical problem' in *Historical Journal* 50 (1), 197–223, and Robert Lynch, *The Northern IRA and the early years of partition, 1920–1922* (Dublin and Portland, 2006); both raise questions about the excessive concentration on the Southern or Twenty-six County interpretation of the 1919–23 period particularly, itself a chronology that reflects events in the South much more closely than in the North.

19 See 'Taking it out on the Protestants' in Hart, *The I.R.A. and its enemies*; 'The Protestant experience of revolution in Southern Ireland' and 'Ethnic conflict and minority responses' in Hart, *The I.R.A. at war*.

20 See for example 'Remembering 1798' in R.F. Foster, *The Irish story: telling tales and making it up in Ireland* (London, 2001), 225–34.

21 Cowen, 'A decade of centenaries'.

22 Cowen, 'A decade of centenaries'.

23 See for example *Irish Times*, 22 July 2011.

24 *Irish Times*, 22 July 2011.

25 For a fuller discussion see Anne Dolan, '"It is not possible for this history to be truthful…"' in Katie Holmes and Stuart Ward (eds), *Exhuming passions: the pressure of the past in Ireland and Australia* (Dublin and Portland, 2011), 19–36.

26 R.F. Foster, 'Something to hate: intimate enmities in Irish history', *Irish Review* 30 (spring/summer 2003), 1–12: 11.

27 See Jay Winter, 'Thinking about silence' in Efrat Ben-Ze'ev, Ruth Ginio and Jay Winter (eds), *Shadows of war: a social history of silence in the twentieth century* (Cambridge, 2010), 6–10.

28 Joseph Dunne to James L. O'Donovan in O'Donovan papers, National Library of Ireland, MS 22,301.

29 David Fitzpatrick, 'Militarism in Ireland, 1900–1922' in Thomas Bartlett and Keith Jeffery (eds), *A military history of Ireland* (Cambridge, 1996), 399.

30 P.S. O'Hegarty, *The victory of Sinn Féin* (Dublin, 1924; new edn 1998), 91.

31 *Irish Times*, 13 Oct. 2011.

32 Monaghan County Museum, Marron collection, 1986:6D6.

33 See David McKittrick, Seamus Kelters, Brian Feeney, Chris Thornton and David McVea, *Lost lives: the stories of the men, women and children who died as a result of the Northern Ireland Troubles* (Edinburgh, 1999).

17

Beyond Amnesia and Piety

Fintan O'Toole

Marion Square is the main public space of the city of Charleston, South Carolina. Within it, a tall, four-sided iron screen contains a sixteen-foot-long bronzed sculpture of an abandoned tallith, a Jewish prayer shawl. Jews also use the tallith as a burial shroud, with one of its four fringes removed as a symbol of death and mourning. The sculpture, erected in 1999, is a subtle and moving memorial to the Holocaust and to survivors of the concentration camps who came to live in the city.

Given the scale of the horror it recalls and the quiet sensitivity of the sculpture, it might be reasonable to assume that it would be among the least controversial acts of commemoration imaginable. Yet it was in fact highly contentious. Many within and outside the Jewish community questioned the appropriateness of erecting a monument to the Holocaust in a city that has no public memorial to the anonymous black slaves who built it. Several survivors themselves suggested that the money would be better spent on schools or health services.

And, in truth, the effect of the monument is deeply strange. For at certain times of the day, it is literally overshadowed by another memorial, a tall, white, granite column with a statue on top, rising eighty feet above the square. The statue, erected in 1896, is of John C. Calhoun, sometime vice-president of the US and a long-time senator for South Carolina. Calhoun was a virulent racist, a defender of slavery as a 'positive good', and a strong opponent of the idea that all human beings are created equal. He maintained that the condition of slavery in the Southern states of America was the highest that Africans could ever hope to attain. In an infamous Senate speech in 1837, he claimed that 'Never before has the black race of Central Africa, from the dawn of history to the present day, attained a condition so civilised and so improved, not only physically, but morally and intellectually.'[1] The erection of such a towering monument to Calhoun was, of course, highly political—part of the process of re-legitimising slavery, the Jim Crow laws and white domination.

The coexistence of these two monuments in a public space where they serve only to mock each other is a reminder that there is nothing especially Irish about contested memory. There is no time and place in which commemoration is innocent. At the very least, it is always in tension with amnesia: why is one person or event to be remembered and so many others forgotten? Why the Holocaust and not slavery? But just as frequently, commemoration is intended to be a moral act, the valorisation of a set of values. Marion Square in Charleston is an especially stark example of the obvious truth that these values can be contested. One of its memorials is a warning against racism. An accompanying plaque evokes 'the denial of human rights' and the 'pitiless will to dominate others'. The other is itself an implicit denial of universal human rights and a celebration of the pitiless will to domination. The starkness of this opposition may be unusual, but only as a matter of degree.

Commemoration, therefore, is not determined by the calendar. It is a matter of choice. It is not essentially about history—it's about culture. It is about ideas of the 'historic' that are always shaped by present-day concerns and power structures. It hovers somewhere between anthropology and politics. On the one side, it relates to a basic instinct of collective mourning. It is a form of ancestor worship for societies that are very unsure as to who their ancestors really are. On the other side, it is a form of political genealogy. Medieval kings (especially in Ireland) employed professional bards to construct elaborate gene-alogies proving their descent from Adam, or at least Abraham, in order to give a sense of depth, permanence and inevitability to their current exercise of power. States, communities and political movements do the same thing—often with the same basic purpose and sometimes with as little reluctance to make outlandish claims. In neither the anthropological nor the political urges to commemorate is history—the sifting of evidence about the past—especially relevant, except as a complicating irritant.

These forms of commemoration are, of course, based in part on acts of forgetting. Amnesia, as the French thinker Ernest Renan famously suggested in 1882, is essential to the foundation of nations. 'Forgetfulness, and I shall even say historical error, form an essential factor in the creation of a nation.' What must be forgotten? The 'deeds of violence that have taken place at the commencement of all political formations [...] Unity is always achieved by brutality.' A nation is also based on a common forgetting of its inevitably mixed ethnic origins. 'But the essence of a nation is that all its individual members should have many things in common; and also that all of them should hold many things in oblivion...It is good for all to know how to forget.'[2]

Which raises the obvious question: what should historians have to do with any of this? They are not ostensibly in the business of promoting values, of creating rituals of mourning, or of validating current power structures. If, as Renan suggests, amnesia is built into the process of the creation and main-tenance of a sense of national identity, historians, whose business is memory, ought to run as far as possible in the opposite direction.

They might well be joined in that race, moreover, by many citizens on both parts of the island of Ireland. In *The jesting of Arlington Stringham* by the English writer Saki (H.H. Munro), the eponymous politician says the people of Crete 'unfortunately make more history than they can consume locally'. The same can be said of Ireland, and over the next decade we will have an astonishing overproduction of official historical memory. We are a hundred years on from the tumultuous set of interrelated events from which the Free State, Northern Ireland and, though this is conveniently forgotten, the United Kingdom in its present form all emerged. Beginning with the Ulster Covenant of 1912 and running all the way through to the end of the Civil War in 1923, we have a fast-running conveyor belt of centenaries. Many people will ask whether they can consume them all without risking intellectual obesity.

For many citizens, the obvious response is not to bother. Many, especially in Northern Ireland, dread all this stuff and its proven capacity to reinforce tribal and sectarian identities. In the so-called Republic, meanwhile, it could be hideously embarrassing to be commemorating the struggle for independence while the state is effectively governed from Frankfurt and Brussels. (It is already notable that the Irish Labour Party, finding itself imposing austerity in government, chose to play down the centenary of its own foundation in 1912.) Even in Britain, the events of those years carry an uncomfortable reminder that Britain itself is a contested construct. How, for example, might memories of Ireland's breakaway from the UK play into plans for a referendum on Scottish independence, itself perhaps timed to coincide with the seven-hundredth anniversary in 2014 of the Battle of Bannockburn?

Refusal to engage with the decade of commemorations is therefore a rational option. But it is not an especially respectable one, and it is almost certainly an overly pessimistic reaction. There are two strong reasons for historians to play a humble but insistent part in the framing of commemoration (humble because historians cannot expect to control the process; insistent because rigour, openness and balance as well as being basic professional standards are also important civic values that require staunch defence).

Firstly, historians are citizens. They may not set out to be part of the processes of value-formation or ritual mourning or the making of political agendas—but they are. Unless they choose to write impenetrably for their peers alone, they are part of the wider social discourse in which collective identities are formed, tested and reshaped. To pretend otherwise is, apart from anything else, bad history—any good historian understands herself as a creature of time inextricably bound up in the specificities of a particular moment. And as citizens, historians have some responsibilities. Historians must recognise that they have no more ownership of the making of images of the past than economists have possession of the real economy. Groups and individuals in civil society will continue, as is their right, to recreate those images for themselves. But they can be helped by historians to deepen their own engagement with the complexity of historical processes. With Northern Ireland still in a fragile state and the Republic in long-term turmoil, there is the opportunity for commemorations to be exploited, as they have so often been in the past, by the most reactionary forces in Irish culture. But there is also the opportunity to challenge crude versions of history, and it would be cowardly to avoid it.

Secondly, commemoration is itself a part of the historical process—and is therefore open to radical change. To say, for example, that acts of commemoration serve the needs of particular groups at particular times sounds pessimistic. It implies that commemoration is mere invention, that its use of the past is always cynical and instrumental. But why should this be so? Commemorations serve needs, but needs change. What various religious, ethnic and political entities needed to encode in commemoration even twenty years ago may not be what they need to encode now. Hugh, in Brian Friel's *Translations*, says that 'words are signals, counters. They are not immortal. And it can happen [...] that a civilisation can be imprisoned in a linguistic contour which no longer matches the landscape of…fact.'[3] Commemoration, too, is encoded in language. Its signals and counters are not immortal. Commemoration may be imprisoned within certain historically determined contours, but if those contours no longer match the landscape of fact, they may be open to change. The 'facts' of Ireland have changed radically over the last decade. Religious identity has been altered by the collapse of the institutional and political authority of the Catholic Church. Notions of pluralism, even if they often remain at the notional level, are the common currency of public discourse. Anglophobia has lost its power among mainstream Irish nationalists, as the extraordinary success of Elizabeth II's state visit to the Republic in 2011 amply demonstrated. Ideas of ethnic identity may retain their hold, but they are being complicated and challenged by the long-term effects of the large-scale immigration of people from Central and Eastern Europe, Africa, Latin America and elsewhere.

The effects of these shifts are not simple—change of this nature is as likely to encourage a nostalgia for old imagined certainties as to spark greater openness. But they do at least create a sense of fluidity in which new forms of collective remembrance may be more adequate to changed circumstances. The process of meeting current needs may not allow commemoration to escape entirely from the business of collective myth-making, but it is surely possible that it can lead to more complex, subtle and generous myths.

Thirdly, the past is itself powerful. People may approach it with a closed mind, seeking only confirmation of what they already 'know', but historical sources impose their own complexities. Historians know this very well: if sources were not slippery and ambiguous and contradictory, their work would have been done a long time ago. But professionals tend to think that things must be different for the untrained amateur. Why should this be so? If anything, popular culture is now entirely supportive of the idea that the past is never quite what you think it is.

The advent of the TV genealogy show and the pursuit of genealogy itself as a popular pastime have dramatised for millions of people an idea of the past not as a closed book but as a tale of the unexpected. Mysteries, secrets, scandals and the return of repressed family memory are now the very stuff of genealogical research, both as an active hobby and as a spectator sport. Most people would now be deeply disappointed to discover that their family tree did not have at least a few twisted and gnarly branches. The free online availability of first-hand documents like the 1901 and 1911 censuses has accustomed huge numbers of people to the idea of documentary history—and to the idea that the documents may heavily qualify what you thought you knew. The challenge is to make an attitude that is now commonly applied by individuals to their own family histories equally applicable to communal and public histories.

There are, then, good grounds for a cautious optimism about the possibility of fruitful engagement by historians in the decade of centenaries. What matters, though, is that they engage *as* historians. This, in turn, has two aspects. The first is professionalism. The duty of historians to be good citizens does not trump their duty to be good scholars. Rigour is not negotiable. It is not the job of historians to tell people what they want to hear. Nor is it even their job to serve ideas of 'peace and reconciliation' at the expense of the search for truth. The decade that is being marked is not only about violence and conflict, but it is undeniably steeped in bloodshed, animosity and disastrous division. History should not wallow in these swamps, but it cannot stay clear of them either.

Politicians, clergy and others are perfectly entitled to try to shape more palatable narratives to suit the times and their own agendas. They will do so anyway. In the Republic, the 1916 Rising was commemorated in a deliberately romantic and emotional manner. In 1965 the RTÉ Authority met to discuss the TV station's plans for covering the centenary of the 1916 Rising. According to John Bowman's intriguing history of RTÉ, *Window and mirror*, there was agreement that the rebellion should be portrayed as 'a nationalist and not a socialist rising'.[4] The committee decided, moreover, that the overall approach to the commemoration should be 'idealistic and emotional' rather than 'interpretive and analytical'. By 1998, on the far side of the Troubles, the Republic's official commemoration of the bicentenary of 1798 was shaped by a government instruction that 'Attention should shift from the military aspects of 1798 and be directed towards the principles of democracy and pluralism which the United Irishmen advocated'.[5] Such shifts are not necessarily contemptible, but they are usually self-defeating. Bigots are not persuaded and good historical procedure is undermined. In any event, they should not be allowed to shape the work of historians who, after all, can also be said to serve society much better by confronting it with the unadorned evidence of the human costs of conflict.

The second aspect of historians behaving *as* historians is the necessity *not* to present a united front. Politicians, civil-society groups and the media may ask: 'What do the historians think about this?' To which the correct answer will always be 'Many different things.' If the desire to be helpful, to contribute to public understanding, involves the pretence that there is a single, settled historical view of any episode being commemorated, it is better to be unhelpful. Historians draw their public authority from open scholarship, not from a collective magisterium. Incestuous point-scoring is of no use to anyone. Honest and robust argument, though, shows the public that history is not a fixed body of knowledge but an endless search for understanding and meaning.

Given these limitations and possibilities, it might be worthwhile to sketch some basic principles that should underlie the approach to the decade of commemoration.

1 Commemoration is not celebration

There is a tone to be adopted in all of this, one that does not set out to denigrate the participants in the upheavals but that does recognise that human tragedy is at the heart of this period. The First World War, which defines the entire period, is many things but it is always a catastrophe. Sacrifice, idealism and even heroism are all aspects of the interlocking conflicts of the decade, and they must be given their due. But so must the futile slaughter of the battlefields, the starvation of the Dublin Lockout, the 'collateral damage' of the Rising, the viciousness of sectarian violence, the brutal treatment of many suffragists and the narrow nature of the two states that eventually emerged. The twenty-eight children who died in the 1916 Rising, for example, cannot be simply washed away in the rhetoric of 'blood sacrifice'.

Does this mean that unionists will not celebrate the foundation of Northern Ireland or that trade unionists will not celebrate the emergence of their movement from the trauma of 1913? Of course not. But there is an over-riding requirement for tact and decency. Commemoration must tread softly because it treads on torn flesh and sunken bones.

2 Inclusiveness is not equal-opportunities tribal myth-making

Given the dominant language of the post-Belfast Agreement era, everyone will be committed to inclusivity. But there are two very different ways of being inclusive. One is the official paradigm of 'two traditions' that must be granted 'parity of esteem'. This leads, in reality, to fair and balanced mutual exclusivity, an exquisitely calibrated doling out of tribal sugarplums. Here's the Battle of the Somme for the Prods and the 1916 Rising for the Teagues; Stormont for the unionists and the first Dáil for the nationalists. And we will all agree to respect each other's pieties so nobody gets offended.

This would be worse than amnesia. We need instead a much more radical inclusivity that starts with the notion that there are not two histories but one history with many strands. All of the events have to be commemorated as part of the same package, not least because they are utterly intertwined. But inclusivity also has to extend to the 'what' as well as the 'how' of commemoration. The decade is not just about the 'national question'. It is also about social milestones like the 1913 Lockout and the suffragist struggle that culminated in votes for women in 1918. Even within nationalism, the mainstream, non-violent tradition has to be given its due. And, of course, everything has to be placed in the overarching context of the original sin of modernity, the First World War. Finally, inclusivity has to extend to so-called ordinary people—people do have a right to engage with history. There is a temptation to cordon off the centenaries into academic conferences and seminars, to keep the explosive material of the past out of the hands of the ignorant plebs who do not know how to handle it. This is misguided in itself—an engagement with history is one of the foundations of citizenship. But it will also fail: refusing to engage with people and then blaming them for being ignorant is an excellent way of making sure they retreat into the comforting certainties of predigested historical myths.

3 Involve artists as well as historians

Commemoration is as much an act of imaginative sympathy as it is of histori-cal reconstruction. Good art thrives on details and is inherently resistant to cliché—both necessary qualities in any attempt to make commemoration at once immediate and complex. And artists tend to challenge, rather than shore up, assumptions.

There is no need in this process to become overly anxious about the business of literal accuracy. Art is not precious or sacred—historians are perfectly right to point out where an imaginative representation differs from the documentary record. But this engagement has to avoid pedantry. Art functions according to its own rules and necessities; the question for historians is whether it ends up creating a seriously distorted view of the past or, more optimistically, whether it succeeds in creating a concrete and immediate distillation of people and events that have otherwise retreated into the great abstraction of death. Good artistic engagement with history personalises the past. Its rubric might be that of the Roman satirist Horace, *Mutato nomine de te/ Fabula narratur*: just change the name and the story is told about you. This name-changing is all the more potent when the name is one that might previously have been spat out with venom.

4 Broaden the canvas

One of the real achievements of Irish historians in recent decades has been the insistence on understanding the Ireland of 1912–23 in the context both of the United Kingdom and of Europe. It is important that this widening of perspective carries through to the process of commemoration; indeed, if there is to be a single act of tailoring commemoration to the needs of the present moment, this is surely the most justifiable.

The resonance of the European context is as obvious as it is powerful. Germans, at least, tend nowadays to talk of the 'second Thirty Years War', seeing 1914–45 as a single conflict to which the foundation of the European Union was the ultimate response. The crisis in the EU is thus a valid context for reflections on the much deeper crisis that brought it about. That the EU is at a moment of deep uncertainty about its purpose, values and identity is an unpleasant reality at so many levels, but it could have a rather benign bearing on the context for commemoration. It could help to shift the conversation from an internal replaying of the rights and wrongs of Irish history to a more useful and more urgent debate about the relationship of the terrible first half of the twentieth century in Europe to the questions that confront the continent now.

For somewhat different reasons, it is important that the decade of centenaries is not one in which the British state participates only as a benignly disinterested (and therefore, perhaps, smugly patronising) observer. How many British people are aware at all that 2020 and 2022 will mark the centenaries of the foundation of their own state? How many British historians even think of the fact that there are not two political entities that emerged from the decade—Northern Ireland in 1920 and the Irish Free State in 1922—but three: the United Kingdom as currently constituted? The British state and British intellectuals have as much of a stake in the decade of commemorations as do their Irish counterparts.

5 Commemoration is about the future as well as the past

Historians rightly cringe at questions like 'What would the men of 1916 think of us now?' But reflections on the meaning of the past for communal visions of the future do not have to be so crude, especially since events have conspired to put back into play so many of the things that seemed largely settled as a result of the fateful decade of conflict. Irish sovereignty is again a largely aspirational notion; a form of home rule has returned, albeit with Germany rather than Britain as the hegemonic power. The idea of 'the Republic' is up for grabs in a way that it has not been since Irish independence.

There is little to be gained beyond a certain masochistic pleasure by flagellating ourselves with the whips of the early twentieth-century idealism that we have failed to honour. But there is a wide space for genuine reflection on what those ideals actually were, and on the successes and failures of the institutions that were supposed to embody them. This is not a process of sanctification—it must include the possibility that current failures may be rooted not in a failure to follow the original vision but in the short-sightedness of that vision itself or in the hypocrisies of some of those who espoused it. But it is nonetheless sobering to read, for example, a line from the Democratic Programme of the first Dáil of 1919: 'It shall be the first duty of the Government of the Republic to make provision for the physical, mental and spiritual well-being of the children.' If a statement like that were to become a promise for the future rather than a piety from the past, the act of commemoration might address the living as well as the dead.

Notes

1   Junius P. Rodriguez (ed.), *Slavery in the United States: a social, political and historical encyclopedia*, vol. 1 (Santa Barbara, 2007), 600.
2   Ernest Renan and William G. Hutchinson, *The poetry of the Celtic races and other studies* (Port Washington, 1896; new edn New York and London, 1970), 66–75.
3   Brian Friel, *Translations* (London, 1981), 43.
4   John Bowman, *Window and mirror: RTÉ Television: 1961–2011* (Dublin, 2011), 82–4.
5   Quoted in Roy Foster, *The Irish story: telling tales and making it up in Ireland* (London, 2001), 225.

18

Lest We Forget: Commemoration Fever in France and Ireland

Pierre Joannon

The French, no less than the Irish, are obsessed by history. In 1940 Elizabeth Bowen wrote in one of her reports from Ireland to the British Ministry of Information: 'I could wish that the English kept history in mind more, that the Irish kept it in mind less.'[1] Likewise, the French are not known to be suffering from memory loss—quite the contrary. Consequently, there is nothing that the French or the Irish love quite so much as a good commemoration.

However, the exercise has its limits. Like the abuse of drink, the abuse of commemoration is fraught with danger. Intoxication with hard liquor and with ceremonies of remembrance can lead to a state of prostration and stupor crowned more often than not by a painful hangover. With the prospect of commemorating all the crucial events that took place during the decade of the Great War, the Irish are already dreading the pain of the mornings after nights of unbridled excess. For their part, the French have started to ask themselves if this frenzy of remembrance is not becoming an insidious disease, to be diagnosed and cured before it is too late. This recent change of heart is all the more remarkable in that, as Roy Foster recently pointed out, it is France that 'set the fashion' and France 'where the notion of the present validating itself through remembering and citing the past is a long intellectual tradition.'[2] It should therefore be of interest to the Irish that the mother of all commemorations is suddenly pondering on the fortune and misfortune of its offspring.

In France, as in most Western democracies, when a problem arises in the public sphere, a commission is appointed to make recommendations. After a reasonable or unreasonable length of time, a superb report is produced, and is received and welcomed with a polite interest at best or cautious silence at worse. It is then put online or sent to gather dust on the shelves of the state's stationery office. During the presidency of Nicolas Sarkozy, two commissions tried to shed light on the dilemma of public commemoration: the 'Commission sur l'avenir et la modernisation des commémorations publiques', appointed by Secretary of State Alain Marleix on 13 December 2007 under the chairmanship of retired historian André Kaspi, and the 'Mission d'information sur les questions mémorielles', appointed by the French National Assembly on 25 March 2008 under the chairmanship of the president of the Assembly, Bernard Accoyer.[3]

Both commissions have covered roughly the same ground, each from a different angle. Their aim is summarised by the title of the Accoyer report: *Rassembler la Nation autour d'une mémoire partagée*—'Gathering the nation together around a shared memory'. Between the two of them, these reports are more than five hundred pages long. Needless to say, their arguments and conclusions cannot be summed up within the limitation imposed by a short chapter. I will only try to extrapolate a few ideas relevant to the present debate on the forthcoming Irish commemorations of the events that occurred between 1912 and 1923.

Central to the reflection on the subject is the interpenetration of the two divergent and yet complementary notions of memory and history. The most comprehensive analysis of the entangled relationship between these two aspects of our intricate connection to the past is the seminal work of French philosopher Paul Ricoeur, *Memory, history and forgetting*, published in 2000. Often quoted is the warning by this great thinker on the matter:

> I continue to be troubled by the unsettling spectacle offered by an excess of memory here, and an excess of forgetting elsewhere, to say nothing of the influence of commemorations and abuses of memory—and of forgetting. The idea of a policy of the just allotment of memory is in this respect one of my avowed civic themes.[4]

This concept of a 'fair memory' is closely akin to the probity expected from the scrupulous historian. It is not easy to reconcile it with the functions of commemoration, which can differ from one country to the next. Most of the time, commemoration is an exercise in popular psychotherapy conceived to enable people of various origins and different political creeds to live together in peace and harmony by sharing a common vision of the past. It can have other motives as well. In Ireland, remembrance practices such as re-enactments, reconstruction of historical artefacts, heritage parks, memorial gardens and interpretative centres are also aimed at attracting tourists, exploiting historical sites and connecting with the diaspora. It occurs to me that this thriving commemoration industry is less driven by historians than by civil servants, notably in the Republic those of the Office of Public Works, undoubtedly one of the most imaginative and effective departments of the state.

The policy of commemoration is by nature partial, fragmentary and selective. The trustworthiness of the 'fair memory' as well as the indispensable concern for historical integrity can only suffer from the mixture of reference to, and oblivion about, the past which is at the heart of any commemoration, even if, as Martin Mansergh has pointed out, 'There is nothing intrinsically wrong in drawing out the most constructive elements of the past, without ignoring the negatives.'[5] The problem is that the negatives are either concealed or, in some instances, given excessive prominence, most unsatisfactorily in either case. The bicentennial commemoration of the French Revolution was keen to insist on the Declaration of the Rights of Man and on the unifying theme of liberty, equality and fraternity. Precautions were taken to ignore the massacres of September 1792 and the republican campaign of extermination of the *Vendéens*. In contrast, we have seen in recent years a certain number of public initiatives aimed at acknowledging the responsibility of the state in the fate of victims of its past and more recent policies: French Jews deported to concentration camps during the Second World War; Africans forcibly removed from their homeland and transported as slaves to Martinique, Guadeloupe and La Réunion; French settlers repatriated after Algerian independence; indigenous auxiliary troops abandoned into the hands of their slaughterers or reluctantly accommodated on French soil; Armenians massacred by the Turks. These repentance pledges were commendable insofar as they were establishing beyond doubt that the nation was able and willing to face its darkest past as well as its shining hours of glory. However, these acts of contrition failed to achieve the anticipated result of reconciling and integrating the aggrieved minorities. Vociferous lobbies felt encouraged to cultivate a sense of acute victimisation, endless recriminations and permanent demands for more penance and more compensation. The mainstream population felt wrongfully accused and put upon by this legislative recognition. Faith and pride in the fatherland was suddenly overshadowed by the shame of discovering the unpardonable sins of a wicked motherland.

These outbursts of self-contempt were met with strong criticism. A quotation of Albert Camus, chosen as the epigraph of the Accoyer report, set the tone of what was to follow: 'It is good that a nation should have enough tradition and honour to find the courage to denounce its own errors. But it must not forget the reasons for having self-esteem.' The main objection stemmed from the fact that these exposures of past misdeeds were enshrined in laws voted in by the French Parliament. Nobody questioned the intentions of the legislators, and a simple resolution would have seemed appropriate in the circumstances. What was considered as most disturbing was the fact that, by its essence, the law prescribes a norm that implies a certain immutability and permanence, whereas history is by definition subject to fluctuation and revision. The former is carved in stone, the latter is simply words on paper. Echoing Oscar Wilde when he said that 'the one duty we owe to history is to rewrite it', we might observe that with the law it is the contrary that is true: the only duty we owe to the legal norm is to respect, obey and comply with it.

The *lois mémorielles*, or memory laws as we call them, run many risks. The first one is the risk of unconstitutionality: in a democracy worthy of the name, Parliament has no right to decide what is the truth and to give an official interpretation of historical events. The second risk is to compromise the freedom of opinion and the freedom of speech. This is not a theoretical danger. The well-known historian of the Ottoman Empire Bernard Lewis was condemned by the 'Tribunal de grande instance' of Paris on 21 June 1995 for having refused to qualify as genocide the 1915 Turkish massacres of Armenians. Olivier Pétré-Grenouilleau, a French historian of the slave trade, was brought to court for having contested the fact that slavery was a genocide, and for having demonstrated that there was an African and an Arab dimension to the event. Although the charge was eventually withdrawn, a nasty slander campaign showed that the law could have very unpleasant consequences. There is also a serious risk to the teaching and researching of history. These laws challenge the very foundation of history as a course of study free to determine its aims and methodology. The community of historians in France was quick to spot the danger. The association Liberté pour l'Histoire, launched in 2005 by a thousand historians led by such renowned scholars as René Rémond, Pierre Nora, Mona Ozouf, Paul Veyne and Françoise de Chandernagor, lost no time in waging its well-argued war against the memory laws encroaching on the freedom of objective historical research.[6] A leader of the British House of Commons once said 'History is too serious to be left to historians.' Perhaps, but one might add that it is too difficult to master to be left to ill-equipped politicians and judges. Another risk is to render fragile the consensus that cements the will of the people to live together by institutionalising the internecine warfare between various segments of the population. Last but not least, there is a strong risk of diplomatic tension arising from the fact that these laws tend to become global insofar as what they denounce is not imputable to the state and did not even take place on the national territory. A cooling of French diplomatic relations with Turkey was the consequence of the memory laws qualifying as genocide the 1915 massacres of Armenians and the associated penalties for denying this status.

Having thus erected a barrier of criticisms against the handful of French memory laws, the members of the Accoyer commission did not dare to ask for their abrogation as it would be considered too offensive to the various minorities whose victimhood they recognise. But they expressed the wish that, in future, Parliament would resist the temptation of foraging in the past and passing similar memory laws that should never have been enacted in the first instance. This odd intellectual pirouette proves that 'constructive ambiguity' is not a mode of thought and action (or inaction) limited to the Northern Ireland peace process. It is sometimes put to good use on the banks of the Seine, for better or worse.

If I have devoted some space to this peculiar French problem, it is because of the impossibility of talking about our attitude to commemoration without mentioning the corner into which we have painted ourselves. By doing so, it was also my intention to beg our Irish friends to stay away from this perilous path. Irish TDs seem to me too pragmatic to emulate our parliamentarians, but if ever they were tempted to manipulate history and invoke their sense of duty to embark in this illegitimate process, it might be useful to give them the advice that Graham Greene puts in the mouth of the English journalist addressing *The quiet American*: 'Don't play with the matches.'

Everybody agrees that public commemorations at national level are too numerous in France. We have twelve such days of remembrance, twice as many as in 1999. The result is disaffection. Part of the loss of interest is the feeling of overdose. 'Too many commemorations', insists André Kaspi, 'kills commemoration.' But there is another factor, more recent and more perverse, denounced by Pierre Nora. It is 'the crisis of historical consciousness' attributable to a set of factors highlighted in both the Accoyer and the Kaspi reports: the progress of relativism and individualism, the impact of deconstructivism on modern historiography, the cult of immediacy imposed by the Internet and social media, and a mixture of lack of curiosity for, and sheer ignorance about, things past. I do not think that the French who have been so imbued with their national history are the only ones to suffer from this recent syndrome of historical amnesia. I would be prepared to bet that after 2023 the Irish will be so sick of commemorations of all kind that they will be ready to agree with Shelley who wrote in the final chorus of *Hellas*: 'The world is weary of the past/ O might it die or rest at last.'

The remedy suggested by the authors of the Kaspi report is to limit to three the number of national commemorations: 11 November to remember all those who died for France at any given time and not only the *poilus* (soldiers) who fought in the Great War, the last survivor of whom passed away in May 2011 (this recommendation was voted on last February by the French Parliament); 8 May to celebrate the victory over Nazism; and 14 July to pay respect to the values inherited from the French Revolution. All the other commemorations would not be suppressed but would be organised at regional or local level, and their periodicity would be reappraised.

To alleviate the exhaustion that menaces the French, the Irish and probably many others, we should invent where they do not exist—and improve where they do—other forms of linkage to the past. The teaching of history is one of the essential aspects of the subject as it commands the sensibility to, and knowledge of, what happened to our forebears. Programmes should be updated and expanded within the curriculum. And the sober requirements of the 'fair memory' dear to Paul Ricoeur and respect for the integrity of historical methodology should be adhered to faithfully. As a matter of principle, the need for objectivity and balance is so obvious that I do not have to expand the argument any further.[7]

New means of communication should be put to good use, even if by nature they may not be as scrupulous as one would desire and expect. Newspapers, the Internet, blogs, television and cinema have an immense role to play. Neil Jordan's film *Michael Collins* has done more to enhance the figure of the Big Fellow than all the commemorations at Béal na mBláth since the creation of the Free State. In France, the series of films made by the late Pierre Schoendoerffer on the French wars in Indochina and Algeria are more eloquent, informative and thought-provoking than huge history tomes on the subject. *La 317ème section*, filmed without grandiloquence and effects, is by far superior to all the American films on the Vietnam War put together.

Museums are another tool. Among the most recent initiatives taken in France is the Musée de la Grande Guerre du pays de Meaux, officially inaugurated on the 11 November 2011. It displays no less than fifty thousand artefacts and documents that add considerably to our perception and understanding of the brutal transition from the nineteenth to the twentieth centuries. Could similar projects be undertaken in Ireland? I believe so. Take for example the National Museum of Ireland's exhibition on *Soldiers and chiefs: the Irish at war, at home and abroad since 1550*. It explores how soldiering and war have affected the lives of Irish people and helped to create modern Ireland. In view of its resounding success, it has deservedly been made permanent. Looking beyond the borders of the nation state, this exhibition connects Ireland to Europe and the world in a transnational narrative, which is what contemporary history should be all about.[8] If I may venture another suggestion, would it not be of interest to the country to transform the beautiful Parliament House of College Green, if ever it is vacated by the Bank of Ireland, into a museum of the Irish constitutional tradition from Grattan to the present day. Matching the GPO—legitimate shrine of the physical-force tradition—it would highlight and reconcile the two formative trends that were the building blocks of contemporary Ireland.

The Accoyer report also suggests that we should work towards what the historian, statesman and member of the European Parliament Bronislaw Geremek has called the 'reunification of European memories'. Whether we like it or not, whether we are conscious of it or not, we cannot nowadays define ourselves only as French or Irish. We now share a hyphenated identity that makes it all the more indispensable to look beyond the limits of our respective borders. The writing of our histories, as well as our policies of remembering and commemorating, must take into account the European dimension and the European influences that have shaped the fate of our respective countries.

In this context, France and Germany have taken a bold and exemplary step. On 23 January 2003 the Youth Parliament assembled in Berlin for the fortieth anniversary of the Elysée Treaty that gave birth to the 'Franco-German couple' suggested the creation of a common school textbook. The idea was enthusiastically endorsed by the French president, Jacques Chirac, and the German chancellor, Gerhard Schröder. It was put on the agenda of decentralised cooperation between the two countries, and eventually approved by the two governments in October 2003. The desire to favour the emergence of a historical awareness common to young people in Germany and France within the process of European unification was so strong that obstacles, and there were plenty, were swiftly overcome. A scientific commission made up of ten French and ten German experts was appointed to outline the project. A contract was signed with two publishing houses, Editions Nathan in Paris and Ernst Klett Verlag in Stuttgart, which were given the task of implementing the prerequisites of the scientific commission. Each chapter of the textbook was jointly written by two historians, one French, one German. In 2006 a common Franco-German textbook for the equivalent of Leaving Certificate and A-Level students was published under the title *Histoire/Geschichte*. Far from being an official manual, it was offered in both countries as a complement to the national curriculum at the discretion of the teachers. Its contents were limited to five chapters: memoirs of the Second World War; technical, economic, social and cultural relations since the war; Europe between the US and the USSR from 1949 to the fall of the Berlin Wall in 1989; Europe in the world from 1989 to the present day; the Germans and French since the Second World War. Such was the success of this initiative that two other volumes intended for younger pupils were published in quick succession: a textbook on Europe and the world from the Congress of Vienna to 1945, published in 2008, and one on Europe and the world from antiquity to 1815, published in 2009.

Needless to say, this extraordinary venture has implications for others. It should be an inspiration to our western neighbours. The transformation of Ireland in the last thirty years, the membership of Britain and Ireland of the European Union, the Northern Ireland peace process, and the new relationship between the three interested parties exemplified by the Good Friday Agreement of 1998 seem to me to pave the way for a similar approach, allowing historians on both sides of the border and on both shores of the Irish Sea to collaborate more closely in order to favour the emergence in the archipelago of a common historical awareness within the process of European unification. If Germany and France were able to do it, why should Ireland— North and South—and Great Britain not be able to carry out an equivalent modernisation of their historical consciousness in spite of the obvious difficulties that it would entail?

The recognition of the complexity of the task should not deter us from advancing in that direction, if only because it is the only cure for the commemoration hangover that we are heading for. The alternative, as suggested by Roy Foster, is total abstinence: 'Should we', he said, 'go so far as to follow the suggestion that the next commemoration might take the form of raising a monument to Amnesia, and forgetting where we put it? Not entirely: as a historian, I have to be rather shocked by the idea. But as an Irishman I am rather attracted to it.'[9] As a Frenchman, I am too, in a way. But everything considered, I strongly believe that we should not become historical teetotallers. If Guinness is good for you, there is no reason to suppose that history, taken in moderation, should not be just as beneficial.

Notes

1   Eibhear Walshe (ed.), *Elizabeth Bowen's selected Irish writings* (Cork, 2011), 54.
2   R.F. Foster, *The Irish story: telling tales and making it up in Ireland* (London, 2001), 28.
3   Assemblée Nationale, *Rapport d'information no 1262* (Paris, 2008).
4   Paul Ricoeur, *Memory, history, forgetting* (2000; translated from the French, Chicago, 2004), xv.
5   Martin Mansergh, 'The value of historical commemoration' in *The legacy of history* (Cork, 2003), 18.
6   Pierre Nora and Françoise Chandernagor, *Liberté pour l'Histoire* (Paris, 2008).
7   John M. Regan, 'Dr Jekyll and Mr Hyde: the two histories' in *History Ireland*, Jan./Feb. 2012, 10–13.
8   Enda Delaney, 'Directions in historiography. Our island story? Towards a transnational history of late modern Ireland' in *Irish Historical Studies* 148 (2011), 599–621.
9   Foster, *The Irish story*, 35–6.

Conclusion

John Horne

Ireland will not be alone in marking the events that transformed the world a century ago during the decade of the First World War. From a divided Middle East to a reunited Germany, from Poland and the Czech/Slovak Republics— which first won their modern independence in 1918—to a Hungary that still mourns the territory it lost in 1919, the legacy of the 'Greater War' of 1912–23 is written into the geopolitical landscape, just as it is with the partition of Ireland. The legacy is even stronger in the cultural sphere. Rituals that are now commonplace were invented to reflect the enormity of the war's losses, such as the two minutes' silence and the honouring of an 'unknown soldier' representing all the national dead. Nor is it only a European story. The war's impact on Africa and Asia helped set decolonisation in train, while the Paris Peace Conference, brokered by the US, ended a world centred on Europe.

With a legacy such as this, what exactly is singled out will depend on the perspective of each country and on how its more recent history is related to the war. In Ireland, we can no longer see the Great War as an alien imposition— Britain's imperialist war—and thus as merely the 'backdrop' to the Irish story, since that story is one manifestation (and a particularly important one) of the war itself. Several chapters in the 'Histories' section of this volume suggest why this was so by considering Ireland in relation to Britain, Australia, Europe and the wider world. The war's impact on Ireland was nonetheless highly distinctive, and few other European countries when addressing the centenaries will grapple with recent national events quite as closely linked to it as the conflict in Northern Ireland.[1] Moreover, because the centenary decade marked the birth of contemporary Ireland, commemoration in both parts of the country will go beyond war and partition to include Irish feminism and the achievement of women's suffrage, the Lockout of 1913 and the emergence of the labour and trade-union movements, not to mention the responses of Irish artists and writers to the social as well as political upheavals of the decade.

If the national framework thus remains central, commemorating the events of the Greater War also requires attention to the local and global levels, without which the national dimension becomes isolated and artificial. Much of the Irish rediscovery of the Great War comes from an interest in family history, itself an international phenomenon.[2] And the local and personal indicate better than almost anything else just how complex were the actions, identities and allegiances during the turmoil of 1912 to 1923. The 'peace dividend' in Northern Ireland and its collateral effect in the Republic have allowed us to appreciate this reinvigorating complexity of our history, as the chapters in the 'Memories' section of this book show. Tom Burke and Ian Adamson, for example, reveal the importance of civic associations in recovering or preserving respectively the 'memory' of Dublin's military connection to the Great War and the unionist heritage of military service. But they also show how these are closely intertwined with family memories. Interest in the decade ahead will include individuals who want to trace the story of their grandparents' and great-grandparents' generation, and also to find out more about the role of their own localities in the history of the period. At the same time, it is no less important to understand how events in Ireland were part of broader patterns that reshaped much of Europe (with the emergence of new nation states in the eastern half of the continent) and also brought major change to the United Kingdom as a consequence of Irish independence.

All this means that the centenaries come at an extraordinary moment in our relationship to the founding decade of contemporary Ireland, and it would be a pity not to make the best and fullest use of them. This book has centred on the relationship between 'history' and 'commemoration'—the 'pitfalls and potential', as Edward Madigan puts it in the introduction. The polemics occasioned by the 1798 bicentenary are there to remind us of the pitfalls.[3] Without endorsing any judgement as to whether or not historians toed the line of official blandness, edited out the awkward bits or were generally swayed by the needs of the present, the tension is obvious. If history is about reconstructing and interpreting the past for its own sake, commemoration is about drawing meaning and value from the past for the purposes of the present. That difference is what makes the relationship between them so awkward.

None of the contributors to this volume reject the claims of commemoration as a legitimate function of society. Very many of them, however, question what its relationship with professional history should be. Yet this is not just a binary relationship between government and academic historians. As Fintan O'Toole reminds us, everyone is involved. The mass media and cultural institutions (such as libraries, art galleries and museums) along with public opinion in all its forms—what we might call the 'public sphere'—will be producers and consumers of centenary activities. It is here that the relationship between history and commemoration will be worked out in three political systems (the Republic, Northern Ireland and Great Britain) that were reshaped by the events in question. How this is done will help determine our success or otherwise in realising the potential of the centenaries for a fuller understanding of past and present, and for achieving what (Pierre Joannon reminds us) the French philosopher Paul Ricoeur called 'fair memory'. Here, too, we are not alone; the same issues will be played out in other countries.

This makes it worth thinking a little further, by way of conclusion, about the tension between history and commemoration. One option might be to establish a clear division between the two: cold-eyed, critical history in one corner and moral values and political aspirations in the other—an intellectual separation of powers. It has its attractions. But neither history nor commemoration works quite like this. Since the Enlightenment, at least, we have lived in historical time as opposed to time defined in religious or other terms. We measure our lives by the flow of history, whose receding past influences the present and shapes the future. But the flow of history also makes the present different from the past, often radically so. Professional history as we know it today was born of this perception in the nineteenth century. The saying of its founder, Leopold von Ranke, that historians reconstruct things 'as they really were' is not (as it is so often taken to be) the naive aspiration to an impossible objectivity but rather the statement of a deep truth—that the past is fundamentally different from the present and must be understood in its own terms rather than in response to current needs.[4]

Yet with historical time being so important to the present, histories of various kinds have become a basic unit of account, not least for the nation states that emerged over the same period, while anniversaries, jubilees and centenaries have provided secular commemorative calendars to rival or replace the older religious kind. This has not been simply a matter of arbitrary invention and mythology, though both have played their part. In societies founded on professional expertise and scientific knowledge, academic history has been vital in constructing historical time and identifying the markers of the past. Ranke and the influential German school not only pioneered the apparatus of modern historical scholarship—archives, peer-reviewed publications, journals for exchanging research findings, and so on—they also helped create German historical awareness throughout the period of unification. We have only to look back to the role played in the fiftieth anniversary of the Rising in 1966 by two founding figures of the academic history of Ireland, Theo Moody of Trinity College, Dublin, and Owen Dudley Edwards of University College, Dublin, to find something of the same process.[5] It is this social function of history, for the public sphere as well as for the state, that makes it inevitable that professional history as such—though not necessarily all academic historians of the period—should be involved in the forthcoming centenaries.

How this might best occur perhaps depends on mutual recognition by all concerned of the difference between history and commemoration *as activities*, a recognition that could help structure the link between them. If the tension is inevitable, it should also be creative. Pierre Joannon points to the opposite example of the French 'memory laws', whereby legislators seek to impose particular views of the past on the present. While there is no suggestion of this happening in Ireland, the example speaks to the more general trend by which politicians and officials will of necessity select aspects of the past and assign them values, especially in the more solemn rituals. But is there any reason why this activity, which is not the business of historians, should not borrow something of the cold eye of history in order to avoid bland pieties and to achieve 'fair memory'?

This will undoubtedly be most difficult for the big official ceremonies with a clear political function, such as those to commemorate the Easter Rising and the Battle of the Somme in both parts of the country in 2016. It is hard to commemorate (with its echo of the sacred) and to demystify at the same time, but perhaps not impossible. Is there any reason, for example, why the civilian victims of the Rising should not be explicitly incorporated into the ceremony at the GPO as an acknowledgment of the messy realities behind the heroism and as a salutary reminder that the path of violence (and this applies to both sides) always exacts a terrible price? Or, in the continued and understandable use of the 16th (Irish) Division and the 36th (Ulster) Division to foster a commemorative 'parity of esteem' between nationalists and unionists and between North and South, is there room to acknowledge that it was Germans, not fellow Irishmen, whom they killed and were killed by—and Turks and Bulgarians in the case of the 10th (Irish) Division? Ireland was present and active in Europe's first great twentieth-century bloodletting, but Irish voices have not often been heard speaking from this perspective to the theme of European reconciliation. In the commemorative events to which both Ireland and the United Kingdom will be invited in 2014–18, there will be opportunities to do just that.

But much of what happens over the centenary decade will not be rituals of this kind. The terminology is important here. 'Marking' the different centenary events, which implies that they were historically significant, is perhaps not the same as 'commemorating' them, which is a collective act of remembrance that confers them with a higher, implicitly consensual meaning. The notion of marking is more open-ended, and allows officialdom to endorse the critical work of history and to incorporate it into the heart of the larger commemorative venture. This could entail a range of state-sponsored actions to broaden the impact of historical scholarship—centenary bursaries for research students, publication subsidies, and opportunities for historians to engage with public figures as they draw meaning from history for the present. It implies government support for activities that result in ideas, arguments and conclusions that are not known in advance or vetted for their compliance with the official tenor of the big commemorative events. A good recent example is the public lecture sponsored by the Irish Department of Foreign Affairs and delivered in Dublin by the First Minister of Northern Ireland, Peter Robinson, in which he reflected on the significance of Edward Carson for a more inclusive form of unionism in Northern Ireland in the future. The event included a discussion of Carson by two leading historians, Paul Bew from Queen's University, Belfast, and Michael Laffan, emeritus professor at University College, Dublin, plus a public debate.[6] There is room for much more of this kind of engagement, in which historians and public figures reflect in their different ways on the meanings of the past. 'Forum', 'debate,' 'discussion'—these are keywords that should recur on the invitations and announcements across the centenary decade. On this basis, there is every reason for historians to assume their public role, and to engage in the wider conversations across these islands and further afield.

Of the activities that governments might sponsor, none is more vital than making the relevant archives accessible, not just for historians but for everyone. The opening of more than seventeen hundred witness statements taken from veterans of the Irish Volunteer movement in 1913 to 1921 by the Bureau of Military History in the late 1940s, and even more their digitisation, is a model of how to democratise the historical record.[7] As Fearghal McGarry points out in his chapter in this volume, these testimonies provide powerful material for (among other things) demystifying and restoring historical complexity to the Easter Rising. They show, for example, how uncertain and ill-defined was the idea of a republic (as opposed to anti-British feeling) for many of those who 'came out' in Easter Week. The Republic was anything but the cogent vision that the Proclamation and legend made it out to be.

Dismantling myths and restoring complexity is fundamental to the historian's practice of 'reconstructing' the past. Equally important is explaining the power that myths had at the time and may have kept since. But such work relies on access to all the relevant material once the thirty-year closure period is over. Only exceptional reasons (usually of a personal, not a political, nature) justify withholding the record for any longer. Yet a large number of series relating to the events of 1912–23 remain closed in the national archives of the Republic of Ireland (Dublin) and the United Kingdom (Kew, London), as well as in the Public Record Office of Northern Ireland and the National Archives of Scotland. Reasons for this state of affairs include inadequate cataloguing and misplaced concerns about 'security' or embarrassing neighbouring jurisdictions. There could be no better expression by the four administrations involved of their responsibility to the cold eye of history than jointly establishing the scale of the historical record for the centenary decade, opening it fully, and, where feasible, making it available through a shared web portal.

The events both marking and commemorating the key moments of the centenary decade are addressed ultimately to the public. Just as historical time belongs to all, so does the knowledge of history and the right to draw on it for the needs of everyday life—whether that be learning history at school or university, the sense of 'identity' conferred by collective memory on groups and institutions, the use of the past in order to criticise the present and think about the future, or the sheer interest and enjoyment of 'heritage' for everyone, including children.

Historians make their own connections with the public sphere independently of the state. A keen dialogue is already evident with other professionals and with those interested in the history of the period. That would seem to explain the success of the 'Marking Anniversaries' lectures organised by the Ulster Museum in March 2012—in which Paul Bew gave an early version of the chapter published in this book—or of the all-Ireland conference held in June 2012 on the topic of public history and the decade of war and revolution, which filled the Royal Hospital, Kilmainham in Dublin.[8] How far events such as these can be made available to a wider audience in both Northern Ireland and the Republic is an important issue. For what is at stake is the capacity to constitute multiple, overlapping audiences for 'public history', audiences that are more likely to hear and talk about the unfamiliar than would be the case with events for predetermined audiences in familiar settings.

The same point is even more acute when it comes to cultural institutions and the media, which have the potential not just to mark the events of the centenaries with all the professionalism at their command but to integrate the interlocking spaces of these islands in order to throw into more coherent relief their shared histories. Whether the Linen Hall Library's temporary exhibition *Ulster will fight* (on the 1912 Solemn League and Covenant) or the National Museum of Ireland's permanent exhibition *The Easter Rising: understanding 1916* should travel south and north of the border respectively are not merely questions for the institutions involved.[9] The same is true of the connections between British and Irish museums, especially given the lack of public awareness in Britain of the Irish experience of the Great War, to which Catriona Pennell draws attention in her chapter in this book. It should be noted, however, that the Imperial War Museums, which are the United Kingdom's lead cultural institution for the 2014–18 commemorations, are seeking active Irish collaboration in the Great War digital archive that they are establishing, which is a welcome sign of change.

The point is that the politicians, academic historians, professionals in cultural institutions and activists in local and civic organisations converge in the public sphere. The density and richness of activities in this domain will check overly homogeneous and pious 'commemoration', and challenge historians to connect with a wider audience even than usual. The multiplication of initiatives in this arena seems more likely than official events to favour an exchange of views between the two parts of Ireland and between both of them and Britain on the decade that transformed the political and cultural character of all three. But in all this, it is the public that will set the demand for books, debates, exhibitions, television and radio programmes, that will guard against commemorative excess (notwithstanding the official events that will inevitably take place), and will decide the broader appetite for cold-eyed history (which the historians will continue to write anyway). The most difficult phase will come with the centenary of the bitterest divisions—partition, the Civil War in the Free State, and the emergence of a two-tier society in Northern Ireland. It is then that commemoration, history and the public's ability to distinguish between the two—and to use each of them to ponder the future of a divided past—will face their ultimate test. But by then, there will be almost a decade of experience to draw on.

Notes

1   Serbia and the other countries of the former Yugoslavia fall into this category, however, as does Turkey in view of the unresolved and continuing tensions over the genocide of the Ottoman Armenians.

2   Jay Winter, 'The setting: the Great War in the memory boom of the twentieth century' in Jay Winter, *Remembering war: the Great War between memory and history in the twentieth century* (New Haven and London, 2006), 17–51.

3   R.B. Foster, 'Remembering 1798' in *The Irish story: telling tales and making it up in Ireland* (London, 2001), 211–34.

4   John Tosh, *The pursuit of history: aims, methods and new directions in the study of modern history* (London, 1984; new edn 2002), 7–8.

5   Mary E. Daly and Margaret O'Callaghan (eds), *1916 in 1966: commemorating the Easter Rising* (Dublin, 2007).

6   Peter Robinson, 'The Edward Carson Lecture: reflections on Irish unionism', Iveagh House, Dublin, 29 Mar. 2012.

7   www.bureauofmilitaryhistory.ie, inaugurated 7 Aug. 2012.

8   'The burden of our history', Ulster Museum, Mar. 2012 (lecture by Paul Bew, 8 Mar. 2012); 'Reflecting on a decade of war and revolution in Ireland: 1912–1923: historians and public history', Royal Hospital Kilmainham, Dublin, 23 June 2012, organised by

the Irish Universities' Historians' Group with the support of Universities Ireland and the participation of the National Archives of Ireland, the Public Record Office of Northern Ireland and the Centre for Cross Border Studies (Armagh). For podcasts of key speeches see www.universitiesireland.ie/2012/05/conference.

9　*Ulster will fight* exhibition at the Linen Hall, Belfast, 4 Sept.–31 Dec. 2012; 'The Easter Rising: understanding 1916', www.museum.ie/en/exhibition/the-easter-rising.aspx (accessed 21 Jan. 2013).

Index